IMAGES
of America

# SPRUCE PINE

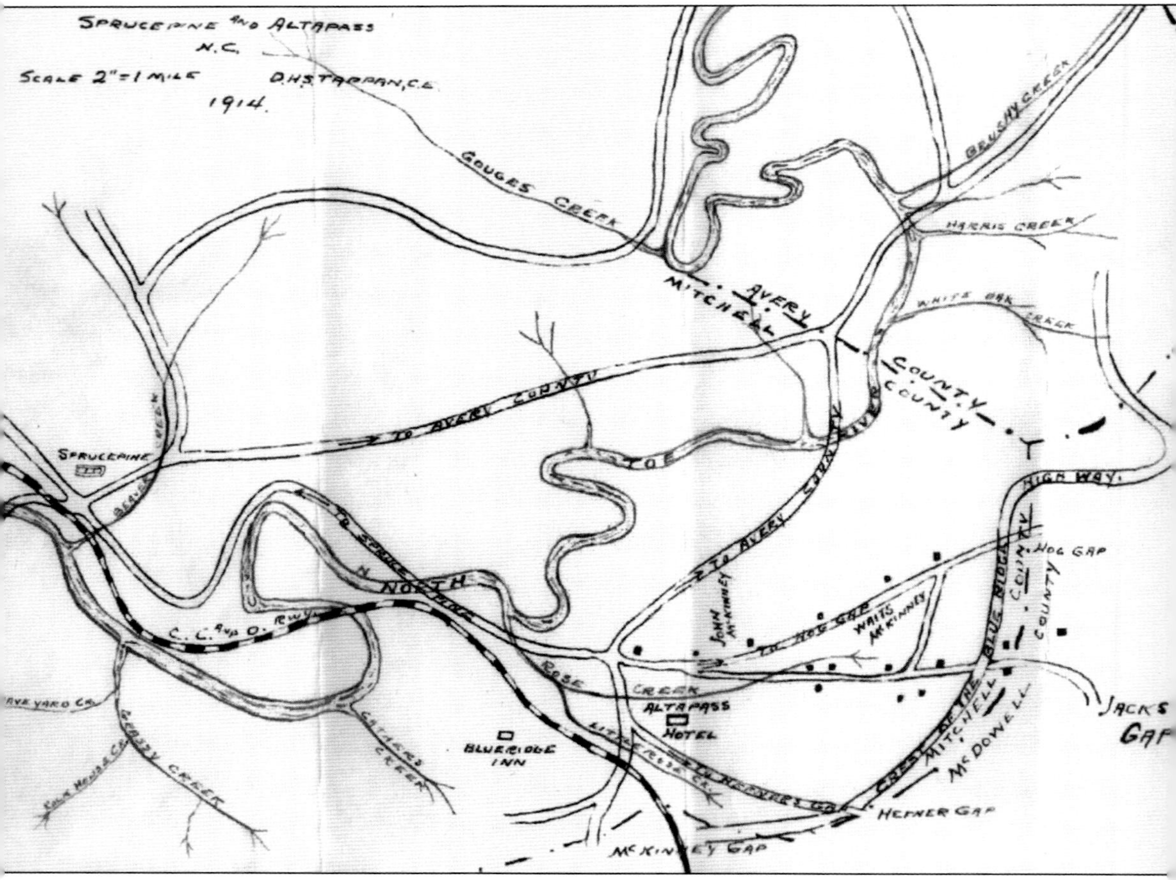


As this map of Spruce Pine in 1914 shows with the layout of roads in the Spruce Pine and adjacent Altapass areas of Mitchell County, the communities were interconnected. At the lower right, the Crest of the Blue Ridge Highway (a precursor to today's Blue Ridge Parkway) skims along the edge of the Blue Ridge escarpment on its way into newly formed Avery County, which was created in 1911. (Courtesy of Hal Harrison.)

**On the Cover:** Eight thousand residents of Mitchell, Avery, and Yancey Counties gathered in Spruce Pine on June 10, 1925, to talk about improving the region's economy. More information on this event can be found on pages 26 and 27. (Courtesy of Fred Pitman.)

IMAGES
*of America*

# SPRUCE PINE

David Biddix and Chris Hollifield
foreword by Gloria Houston

ARCADIA
PUBLISHING

ISBN 978-0-7385-6769-3

Published by Arcadia Publishing
Charleston, South Carolina

Printed in the United States of America

Library of Congress Control Number: 2009924491

For all general information contact Arcadia Publishing at:
Telephone 843-853-2070
Fax 843-853-0044
E-mail sales@arcadiapublishing.com
For customer service and orders:
Toll-Free 1-888-313-2665

Visit us on the Internet at www.arcadiapublishing.com

*To Corey, Amanda, James, Olivia, Ethan, and Rebekah,*
*and all the other children of the Mineral City,*
*so that they might know from whence they came.*

# CONTENTS

# Acknowledgments

A special thank-you goes to former Spruce Pine mayor David Blevins for his knowledge of events and people, and his commitment to the preservation of Spruce Pine's history and heritage. We had an extensive interview with him in order to gather information for this book.

The authors would like to thank the following individuals and organizations for their contributions to Images of America: *Spruce Pine*: Andy Ashurst and *Mitchell News-Journal*; Appalachian Collection, Sherrod Library, East Tennessee State University; Robert and Donna Bailey; Dr. Daniel Barron and AMY Regional Library; Marsha Biddix; Blue Ridge Parkway, National Park Service; Blue Ridge Regional Hospital; Elvira Bryant; Lolita Buchanan; Terry Buchanan; O. D. and Mary Calhoun; Geraldine Canipe; Judy Carson; Central Baptist Church; Tess Burleson Coulter; Mary Lee Cuthbertson; Elizabeth Davenport; First Baptist Church; Phillip Frye; Gerald R. Ford Library and Nancy Mirshah; Alex Glover; Max and Violet Gouge; Rachel Greene; Sheila Grindstaff; Rhonda Gunter; Michael C. Hardy; Phil and Mildred Harris; Hal Harrison; Dana Hollifield; Gloria Houston; Lucille Hovis; Evelyn Hughes; Scott Kardel, Palomar Observatory, California Institute of Technology; Kerry Jenkins; Wayne Ledford; Bruce Leverette; Mayland Community College; Mitchell County Historical Society; Forrest McCall; Eddie McGee; Angela McKinney; Guss McKinney; North Carolina Collection, Wilson Library, the University of North Carolina at Chapel Hill; North Carolina Department of Cultural Resources; Deborah Owings; Roger and Sherry Pendley; Gina Phillips; Fred Pitman; Leo Riddle; Richard and Peggy Riddle; Donn St. John; St. Lucien's Church and Betty Brannigan; Alan Schabilion; Martha Snipes; Bill and Brenda Sparks; Buster and Irene Sparks; Charlie Mae Sproles; Felica Spurling; Luther Stroup; Dempsey Sullins; Doris Thompson; Toe River Model Railroad Club; Trinity Episcopal Church and Steve Botney; University of North Carolina Sports Information; Wayne Ward; Willa Ann Ward; John and Scottie Wellborn; Bill and Emma Lee Wilson; Scott Woody; Brannon and Bryson Young; and Jack Young.

# FOREWORD

*I love those dear hearts and gentle people*
*who live in my home town*

—"Dear Hearts and Gentle People"
Lyrics by Sammy Fain and music by Bob Hillard, *c.* 1949

Those were the words from the contemporary and very popular song I sang on a Friday night as I stood on a kitchen chair, being too short to reach the microphone on the stage of the Carolina Theatre on Lower Street in Spruce Pine, North Carolina. My dad, J. Myron Houston, was the coproducer with O. D. Calhoun of the Carolina Barn Dance, one of the local live variety shows broadcast on small radio stations throughout the middle south in that period. "Dear Hearts and Gentle People," one of the most recorded songs of 1949, had recently appeared in the *Hit Parade* magazine at the newsstand next door to the theater. My mom, Ruth, always careful in selecting the songs I was allowed to sing in my role as fill-in singer when too few performers signed up on Daddy's clipboard to fill the time allotted to the program, deemed the song appropriate for my age.

At that time, and for most of my life, I have considered Spruce Pine to be my hometown, although I recently spent the first night of my life in Mitchell County at the Pinebridge Inn. How is this possible? I have never lived there. I grew up only a few miles out of town in a neighboring county, but the small town with two main streets was, is, and always will be my hometown.

Most of my life has been spent in larger, more cosmopolitan cities, but as an author and lecturer, my publicity materials always list Spruce Pine as my hometown. In part, that is a personal choice. However, the valley of the North Toe River, from its headwaters in northern Avery County to its joining with the South Toe near the Yancey County line, is more closely related, culturally and geographically, to the little town in Mitchell County. The Eastern Continental Divide separates that valley from the rest of Avery County. Several times, I have suggested that the valley secede and join Mitchell County, where it rightfully belongs. I was quite puzzled as a teenager at the demand that I cross the divide twice each day in order to attend high school. The high school in Spruce Pine was much closer. In my mind, the county lines made as little sense as they do to many today. Also, the notion of walking across the long bridge from downtown to the high school held greater appeal than riding a cramped school bus for almost two hours each day.

As I was growing up, we bought most of what we needed, which was not supplied by my parents' own general store, in Spruce Pine. We went to the movies there, and we received much of our news in the newsreels we watched in the town. Many of my relatives lived there, as did most of my parents' friends, so we visited socially as well. For most of my childhood, our mailing address listed the town.

Most of my published writing is set in the North Toe Valley. Those settings have brought numerous visitors to the region. When I have visited schools nationally, most readers can tell me the name of my hometown. It is Spruce Pine, North Carolina, in their minds and mine. Most of those readers had no idea where I actually lived as an adult.

Therefore, little did I know that, when I sang that song on that Friday night, its lyrics would remain true, at least in my heart, for the rest of my life.

As I looked at the photographs located by those who wrote this book, I was surprised to see images that were a vivid part of my own memories. How large the Topliff Hotel looked when it dominated Upper Street in some of my earliest memories. How sweet the taste of ice cream cones on a Sunday afternoon, when, with my cousin Truda, we drove into town with her mother, Wilma, to stand on tiptoe at the counter inside the small white stucco building located nearby some years later.

The combined odors of disinfectant and popcorn butter marked visits to the Carolina Theatre where, held safely in my Daddy's arms, I grasped a warm box of popcorn as we waited for our eyes to grow accustomed to the darkness before we walked down the aisle to locate our seats.

One of my earliest—and warmest memories—of an exciting visit to Spruce Pine was the day before Christmas when I was three years old. On that day, Daddy and I drove to Dr. Williams's clinic, located in the current town hall building. I waited in the car while the nurse wheeled my mom out to the car. Daddy took my new baby brother from my mom's arms and placed him in mine, allowing me to hold him for a moment with his strong hand still supporting the weight of the baby for safety. In that moment, I became a proud big sister. That day was truly one of the happiest moments of my life. I often remember that day as I drive by the town hall, and each time the memory makes me smile.

Being allowed to walk alone up and down the Lower Street on late Friday afternoons, as Daddy worked with Cal Calhoun on the program for the radio broadcast of the Carolina Barn Dance later that evening, was a thrilling prospect, especially when the trains were passing. I stopped and sat on the sidewalk to watch the cars moving swiftly past, sometimes waving to passengers who sat near the windows, wishing that I could go on the adventures that surely waited at the end of their trips. I remembered looking up at the sculpted tin ceilings in the drugstore with the little wire chairs where I sat to drink orangeade, freshly squeezed behind the marble counter. I stopped to visit my pretty cousin who worked in the dime store with its fragrance of Blue Waltz perfume, which seemed outrageously expensive at less than one dollar per bottle.

Later, as a teenager, and with the Houston herd (my brother Jerry's group of seven cousins all sharing a birth year), I remember going to the drive-in, which was located in at least two different places. Having a dinner or a snack was the reason we gave our parents, but seeing others in the age group and, of course, being seen, was the ultimate purpose. The drive-in was a frequent stop when I visited my parents as a young adult, and years later, visits with my daughters to the same drive-in for a foot-long hot dog remain one of their best memories of visits to a small town, in contrast to the larger cities where they lived.

Going with my parents to buy groceries at Spruce Pine Store and Hickey's Superette, and later with my daughters and our many house guests to the chain stores when I visited my vacation place nearby, provided food not only for my appetite, but many memories of showing off my hometown.

Getting acquainted with many from the town whom I had not met through my parents when I had my first job (other than working for my parents) as a waitress at Beam's Steak House provided an even wider circle of friends and acquaintances. It seemed that most folks who lived in town found their way out of town for lunch or dinner.

Trying on prom dresses at Belk's store, when it was located in the gray stone building on Upper Street, was a highlight of my teenage years. Attending various services, weddings, and other celebrations at the Methodist and Baptist churches near downtown were special memories recalled with these photographs. And having my very first book signing—ever—in the corner of the News Center, which also served as a small restaurant on Upper Street, was far more exciting than my first book signing at an international conference. At least two Spruce Pine residents attended that day!

Almost every photograph included in this book brought back some memory for me, even those that were made years prior to my birth. This town holds such a special place in my life, as do its residents, that no matter that I have never lived in the town for even one day, I consider myself to be a "Spruce Pine-ian," a "Spruce Pine-ite," or whatever it is that those who live in and love this little town call themselves. Yes, I too feel that I belong to that fortunate group.

—Gloria Houston

# INTRODUCTION

The old pine tree stood at a crossroads. Travelers on the Marion-to-Bakersville and Burnsville-to-Cranberry Roads passed by it, pausing occasionally for rest and refreshment. The Native Americans had used these routes for trade and transportation long before the arrival of the white man, but their time was drawing to a close. Despite the Proclamation of 1763, a few hardy settlers had moved into the Toe River Valley. In 1765, an inn was constructed at the crossroads near the tree, serving as a stop for weary travelers. In 1780, many of the men who lived in the region mustered and marched past the tree on their way to Kings Mountain and a decisive victory over the British.

Some settlers had adventures, like Kim McHone, who managed to get lost in a laurel thicket on Chalk Mountain, and his misfortune gave the area its first name: Kim Thickets. Others like Isaac English and his wife, Alice, found themselves embroiled in the turmoil of the Civil War. Despite being in the South, many of these settlers supported the Union cause. The English family helped four Union officers who escaped Confederate internment get back to safety. It was an encounter that would later change their lives and the destiny of the region.

In 1856, a post office was established in the valley, but it was named Rose's Creek after a stream in the Altapass section of what was at that time Yancey County instead of Kim Thickets. But the crossroads proved to be attractive to development, and a small community sprang up, causing the post office to move to the inn and prompting Alice English to christen it Spruce Pine after the old tree. As war clouds gathered, divisions in the region resulted in the formation of Mitchell County in 1861, and the war restricted growth of the community while battles raged hundreds of miles away.

After the war, Isaac English purchased the inn and became postmaster. He also crossed paths with one of the Union officers he helped years earlier: James Gere. After exchanging letters, Gere came for a visit, and while at the inn, English showed him samples of rocks and mica that he had collected. Gere was intrigued and offered to go into business with English to mine and market these minerals.

About this same time, the South and Western Railroad began to push into Spruce Pine from Tennessee. The goal was to descend the Blue Ridge to the markets of the southeast. In 1903, the rails arrived in Spruce Pine, and the roads began to move across a new bridge (near the present downtown bridge) to the rail bed on the other side. The town moved too, as businesses pulled up roots and left the English Inn for new locations beside the railroad. An entrepreneur who had just finished medical school came to town to set up practice, and he, along with other investors, believed that Spruce Pine would become a crossroads for commerce in the valley. Dr. Charles Peterson became the de facto father of Spruce Pine and an institution for more than 50 years. As the town expanded, a decision to approach the North Carolina State Legislature for formal status as an incorporated town was made, and on February 5, 1907, Spruce Pine was formally incorporated by legislative action. A second incorporation was passed by the legislature on March 6, 1913.

The arrival of the railroad and the development of the mining industry brought explosive growth, and Spruce Pine truly became the crossroads and hub of activity for the entire Toe River Valley. The train brought in supplies and shipped out raw materials from the burgeoning minerals and timber industries. From the 1930s throughout the 1960s, Spruce Pine became a destination, with crowds flocking to town each weekend to enjoy three movie theaters, two pool halls, a bowling alley, traditional music, shopping, and dining out. The depot served as a starting point for trips via passenger rail service throughout the United States. Bus service ran between Asheville and Spruce Pine, and the Topliff Hotel, like the English Inn before, served travelers with comfortable accommodations. The area's first newspaper and radio station were also in Spruce Pine.

The 1970s, 1980s, and 1990s brought change as traditional industries like furniture and textiles began to decline, and consolidation in the mining and railroad industries changed business practices. A new bypass, combined with new shopping opportunities, began to draw traffic away from downtown. Once again, Spruce Pine began to change. Tourism became a focus, and the Pinebridge Complex was one of several attractions offered to visitors, along with new shops and businesses. Traditional merchants, with a few exceptions, left the downtown area, and chain stores began to replace locally owned retailers.

Today the town that the railroad and the mining industry built has many of the same familiar structures, but change once again is in the air. Spruce Pine looks to the future by embracing its past yet seeks to discover new opportunities for growth and development. The old tree is gone, but the town once again stands at the crossroads, looking to adapt to the challenges of the 21st century. This book seeks to document the true story of the Mineral City and its people, their struggles, tragedies, and triumphs.

# One

# The Spruce Pine at the Forks of the Road

## A Community Begins

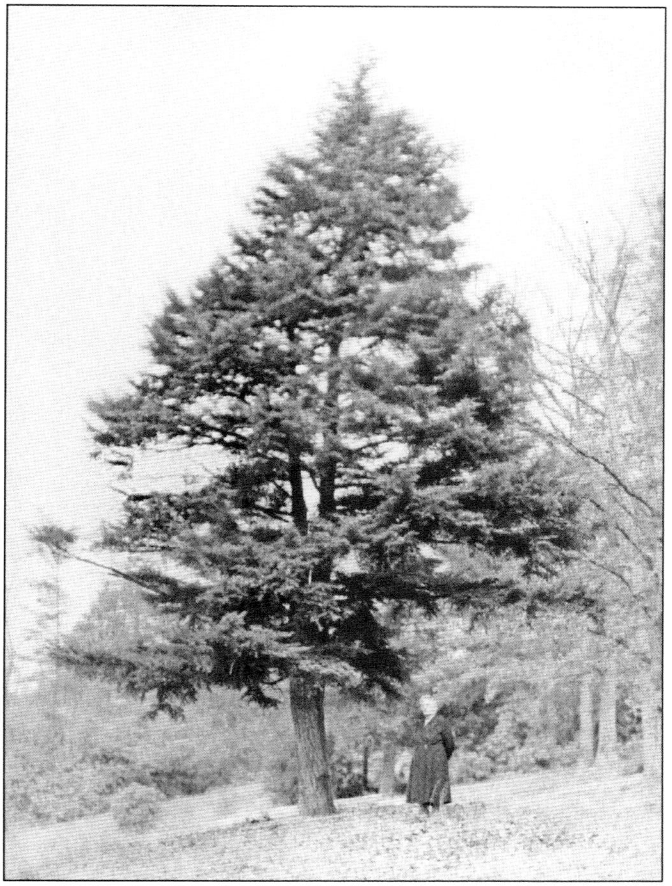

This tree gave Spruce Pine its name on April 26, 1859. Legend has it that the name was changed that day when Alice English looked out a window at the English Inn, whose new post office needed a name, and saw the tree. Photographer Jim Jones captured daughter Ora English Burleson standing by the famous landmark that is now gone. (Courtesy of Daniel Barron.)

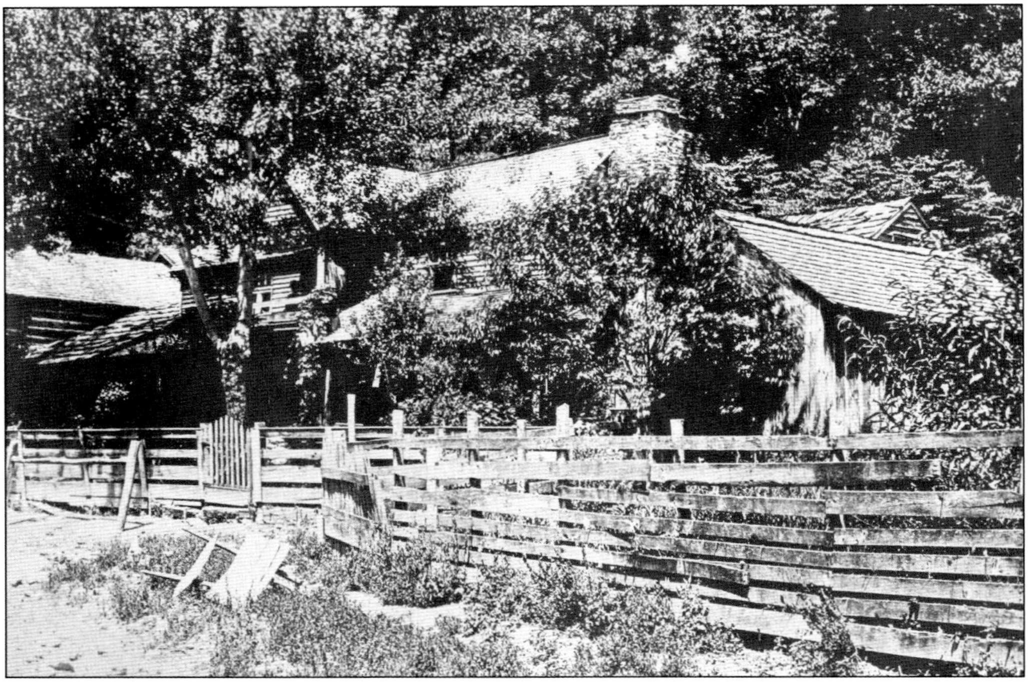

The English Inn is where Spruce Pine traces its origins. It was originally constructed in 1765–1767 and was purchased by Isaac English in 1866 from his brother-in-law. This image, taken in 1879, shows the front of the inn as it appeared at the crossing point of the Marion-and-Bakersville and Burnsville-and-Cranberry Roads. (Courtesy of Bill and Brenda Sparks.)

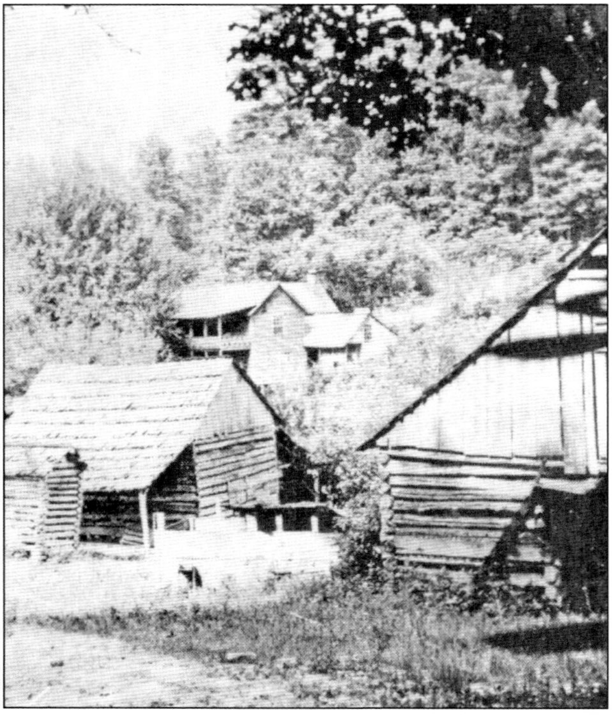

This view of the English Inn, taken around 1912, shows the corncrib and stable on the property. Mica processing was underway in a section of the inn, and its days as a stop for travelers were nearing an end as the railroad arrived, drawing the new town across the nearby Toe River. The English Inn is reputedly the largest log structure in North Carolina. (Courtesy of Chris Hollifield.)

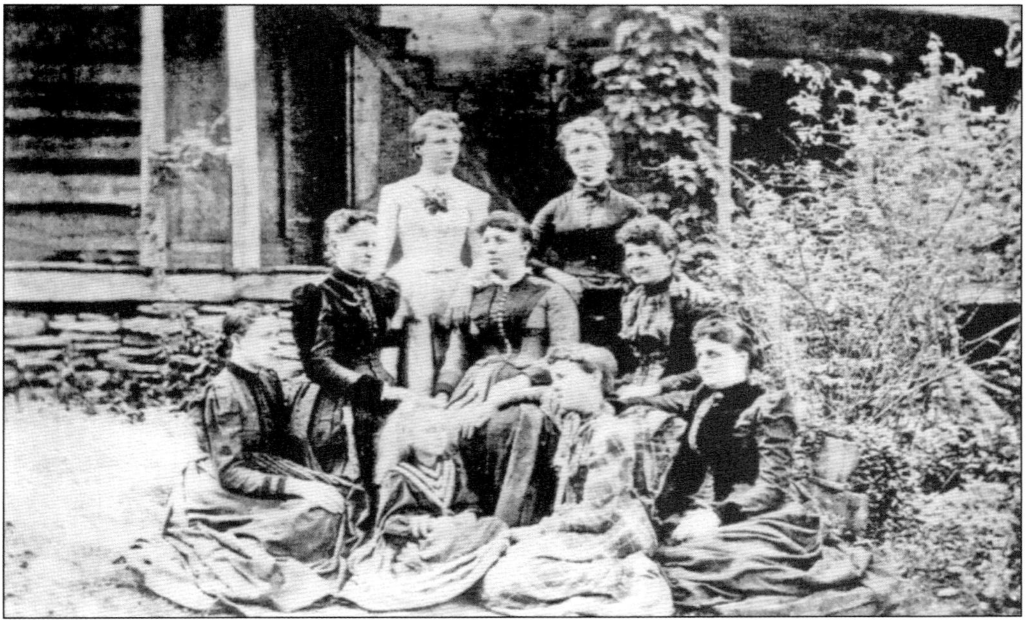

Isaac English's daughters posed in front of the English Inn for a portrait around 1889. Mary is in the middle, with the others, clockwise from the top left, Ora, Minnie, Josephine "Dotie", Sarah "Sadie," Cordelia "Cordie," Mabel, Emma, and Illia. (Courtesy of Chris Hollifield.)

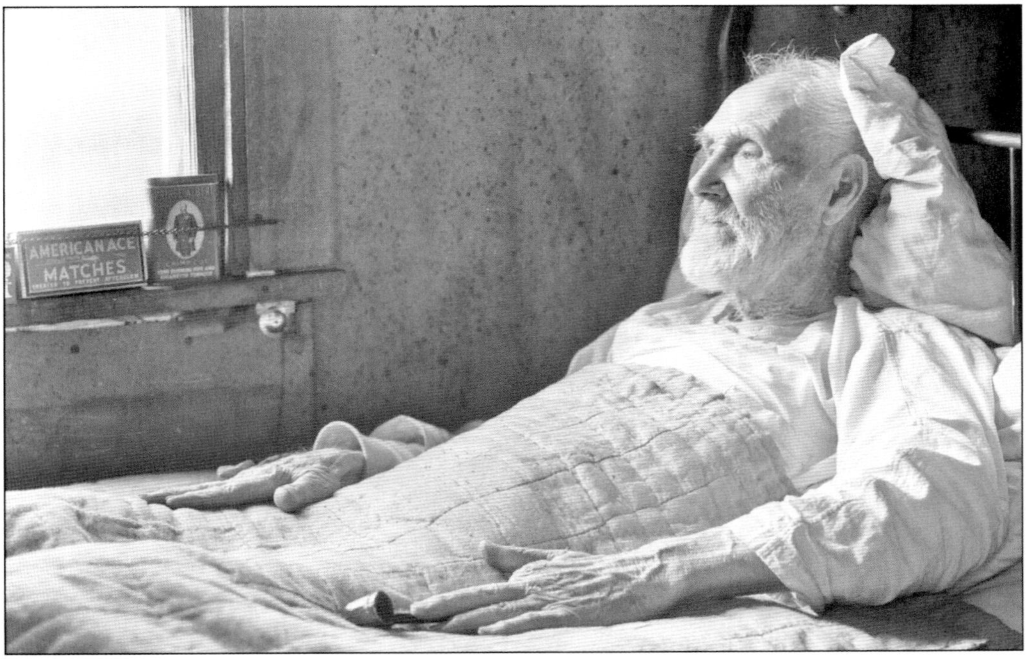


Spruce Pine was also known as Kim Thickets, named after Kimbel McHone, an early settler in the region. He became lost in a laurel thicket on Chalk Mountain, hence the name. Pictured here is his son Zack, who was featured in Muriel Earley Shepard's *Cabins in the Laurel*, recounting stories about the Civil War. (Courtesy of the North Carolina Collection, the University of North Carolina at Chapel Hill.)

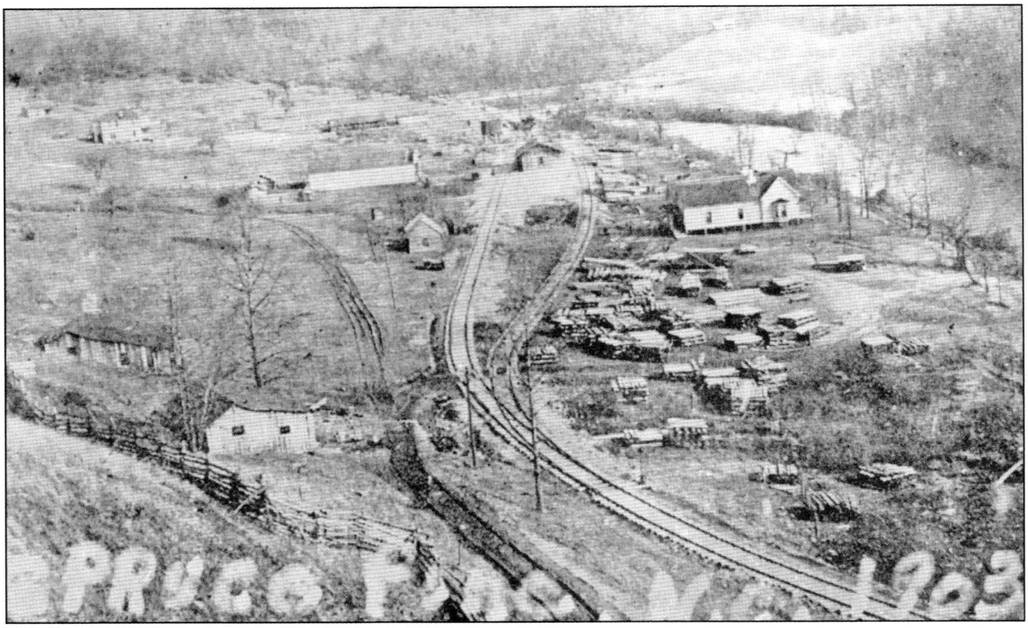


The South and Western Railroad, the forerunner of the Clinchfield Railroad, arrived in 1903 to an area across the Toe River near the English Inn. A depot was constructed, and a town began to spring up as construction crews started the arduous task of getting the rail line down the Blue Ridge escarpment at Altapass. These photographs show the early town, with the depot in the center, the stationmaster's house on the right, the L. A. Berry store to the left of the depot with a wood yard office down from the store, and the Taylor Phillips Hotel at the far left. A livery stable and water tower for trains are up from the depot, with a blacksmith shop and the Fred Sullins house at the bottom of the photographs. (Above, courtesy of Chris Hollifield; below, courtesy of Hal Harrison.)

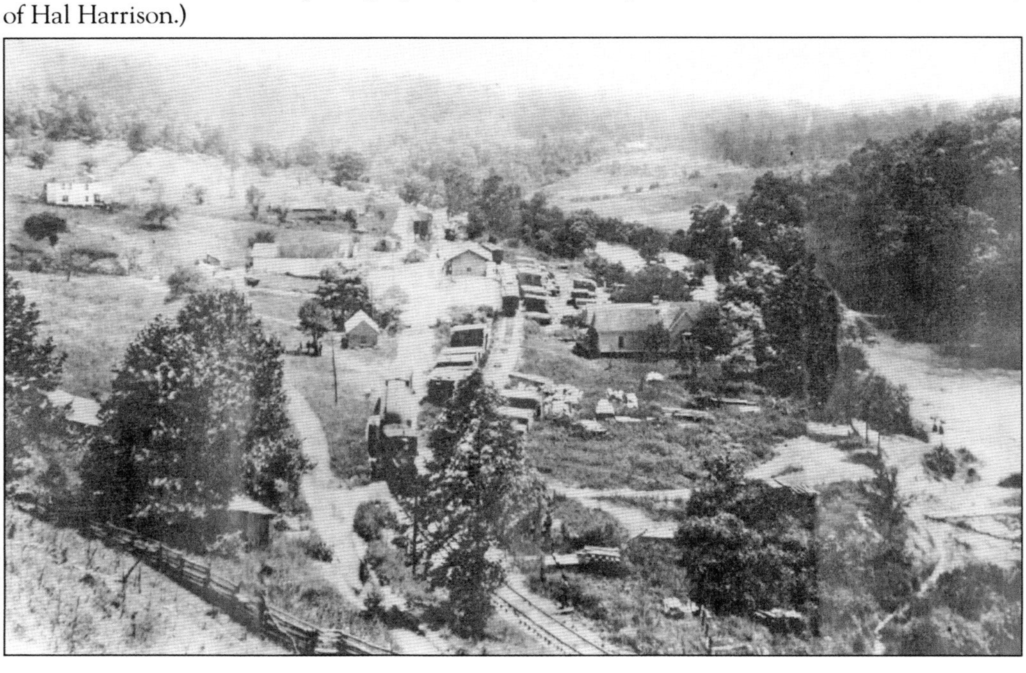

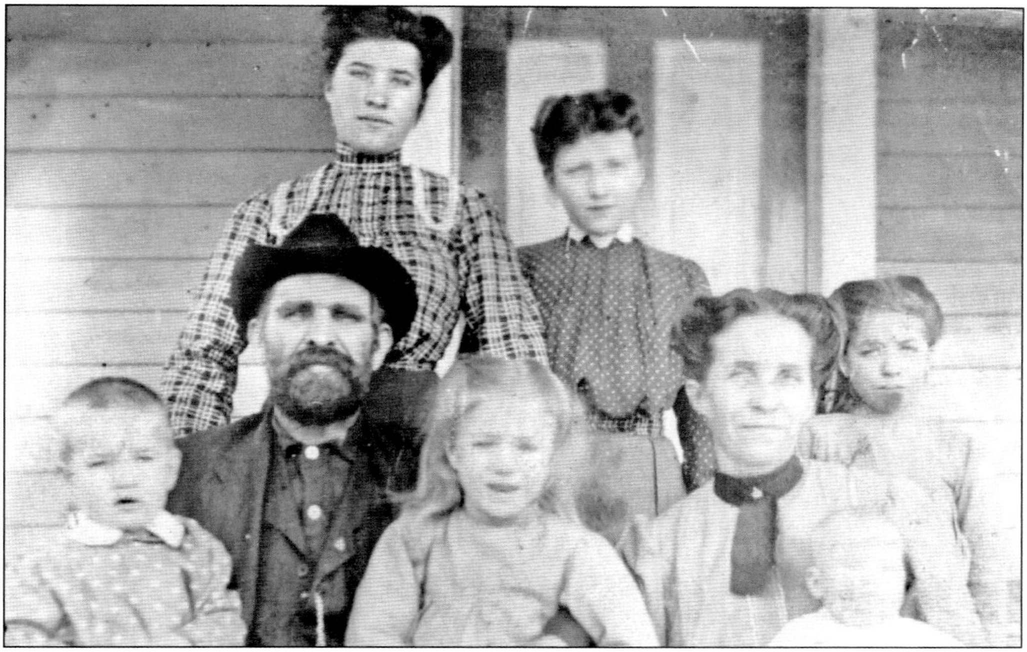

Some of the earliest settlers in Spruce Pine were the Harrison family. Reuben Benjamin Harrison is pictured here seated with his wife, Juda, and children (from left to right) Roscoe, Lizzie, Cary, Corrie, Bessie, and Maude. Benjamin was Spruce Pine's first mayor. W. Mc. Wilson, L. A. Berry, and T. A. English were town commissioners, and Weldon Buchanan was appointed town marshal. Spruce Pine was chartered by the North Carolina State Legislature on February 5, 1907. (Courtesy of Hal Harrison.)

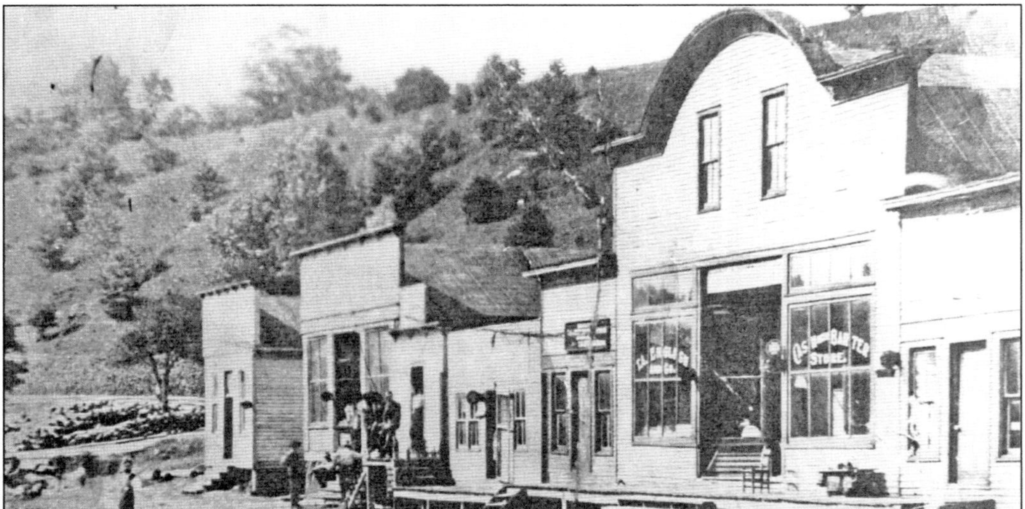

Resembling a Wild West town of the 1800s, downtown Spruce Pine sits on lands acquired by John Cox, Dr. Charles Peterson, and Tom Byrd from the Holston Holding Company. They paid $17,000 for 160 acres that the company originally purchased from L. A. Berry for $2,200 when it began construction of the railroad through Spruce Pine. The land was originally owned by the Blalock family. (Courtesy of Chris Hollifield.)

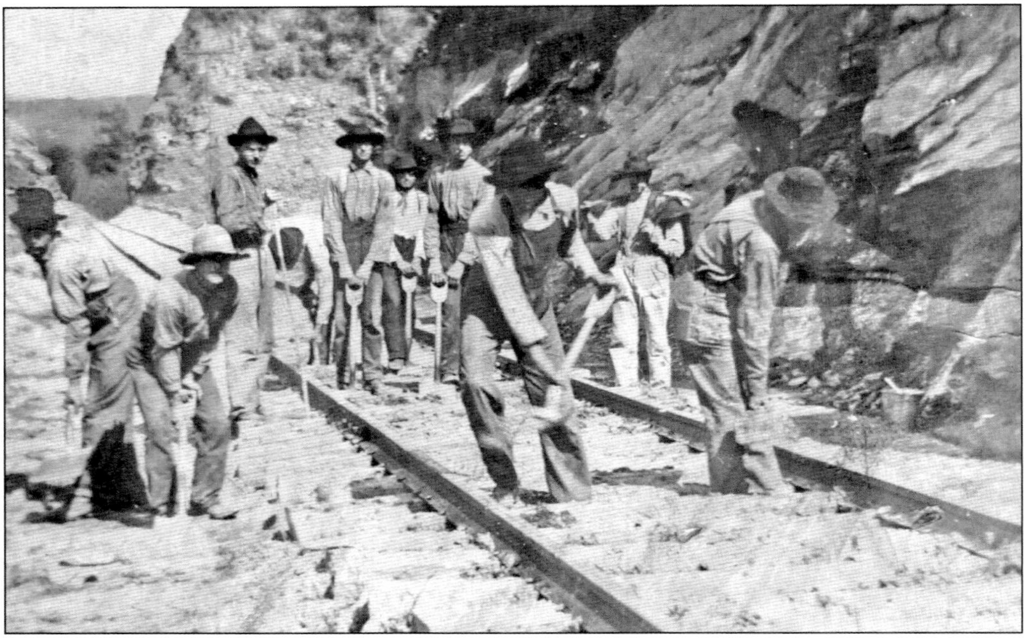

Building the South and Western Railway (later the Clinchfield) involved tremendous amounts of manual labor and astronomical costs, estimated in some locations of more than $1 million per mile of track. The railroad brought jobs for able-bodied men willing to do the work. This photograph is of a crew between Penland and Spruce Pine in the early 1900s. (Courtesy of Eddie McGee.)

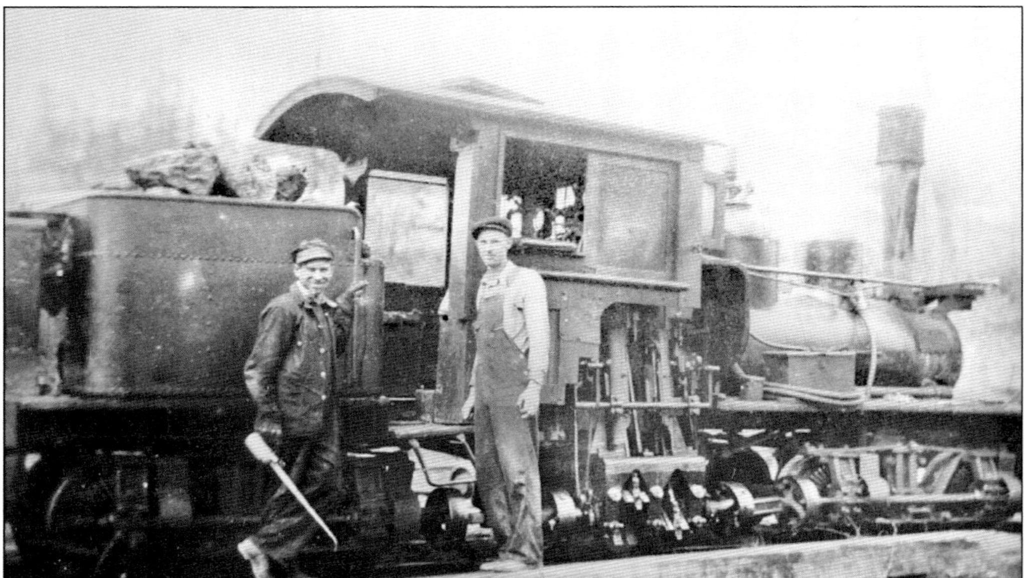

The railroad sprouted several spur lines that fed wood cut from forests and ore from mines to burgeoning mining, furniture, and acid wood industries. These lines operated in Mitchell, Avery, and Yancey Counties into the 1970s, when the last spur line, the Yancey Railroad, was destroyed by a major flood. This photograph is of the Tennessee Eastman No. 56 train in 1932 at Altapass. (Courtesy of John Wellborn.)

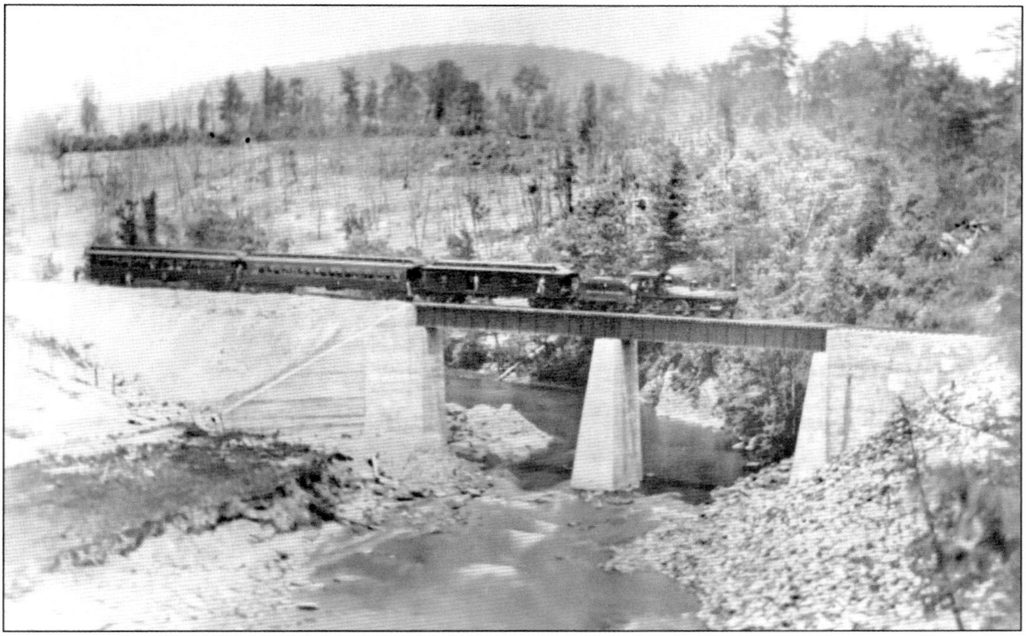

The newly constructed railway down the Blue Ridge to Marion traveled down the famous Loops at Altapass to its destination, the markets and ports of South Carolina. This train, crossing the Toe River Bridge south of Spruce Pine, may have been the first passenger train to Marion. (Courtesy of the Toe River Model Railroad Club.)

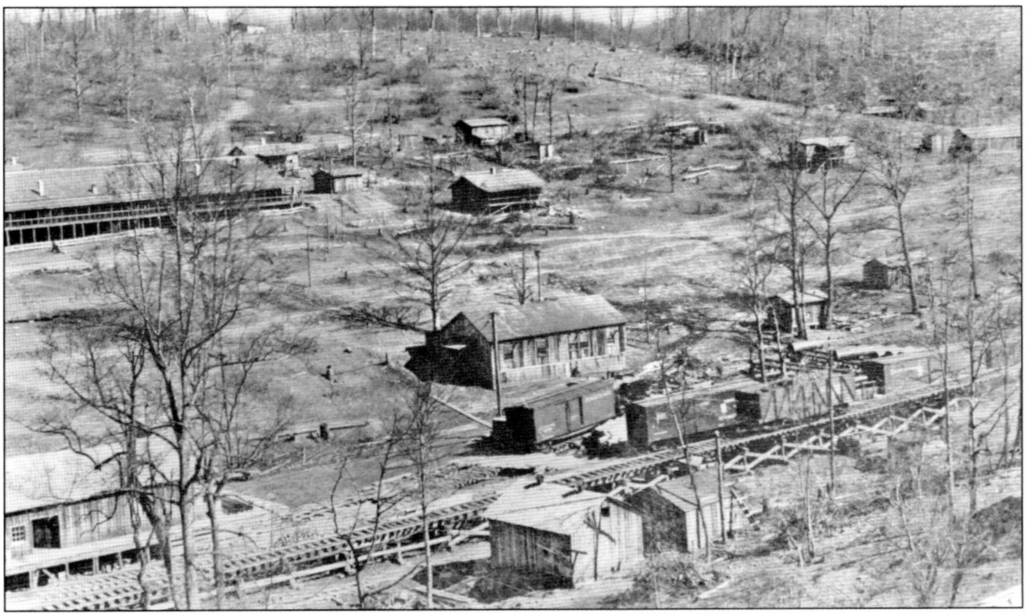

As the railroad descended the Blue Ridge, the Altapass community began to blossom, growing rapidly with the construction of the Altapass Hotel and the Holston Orchard by the Holston Company. When the hotel burned on May 18, 1926, the community's dreams of being the largest town in the region vanished. This photograph is of the Altapass station at the community's peak. (Courtesy of the Toe River Model Railroad Club.)

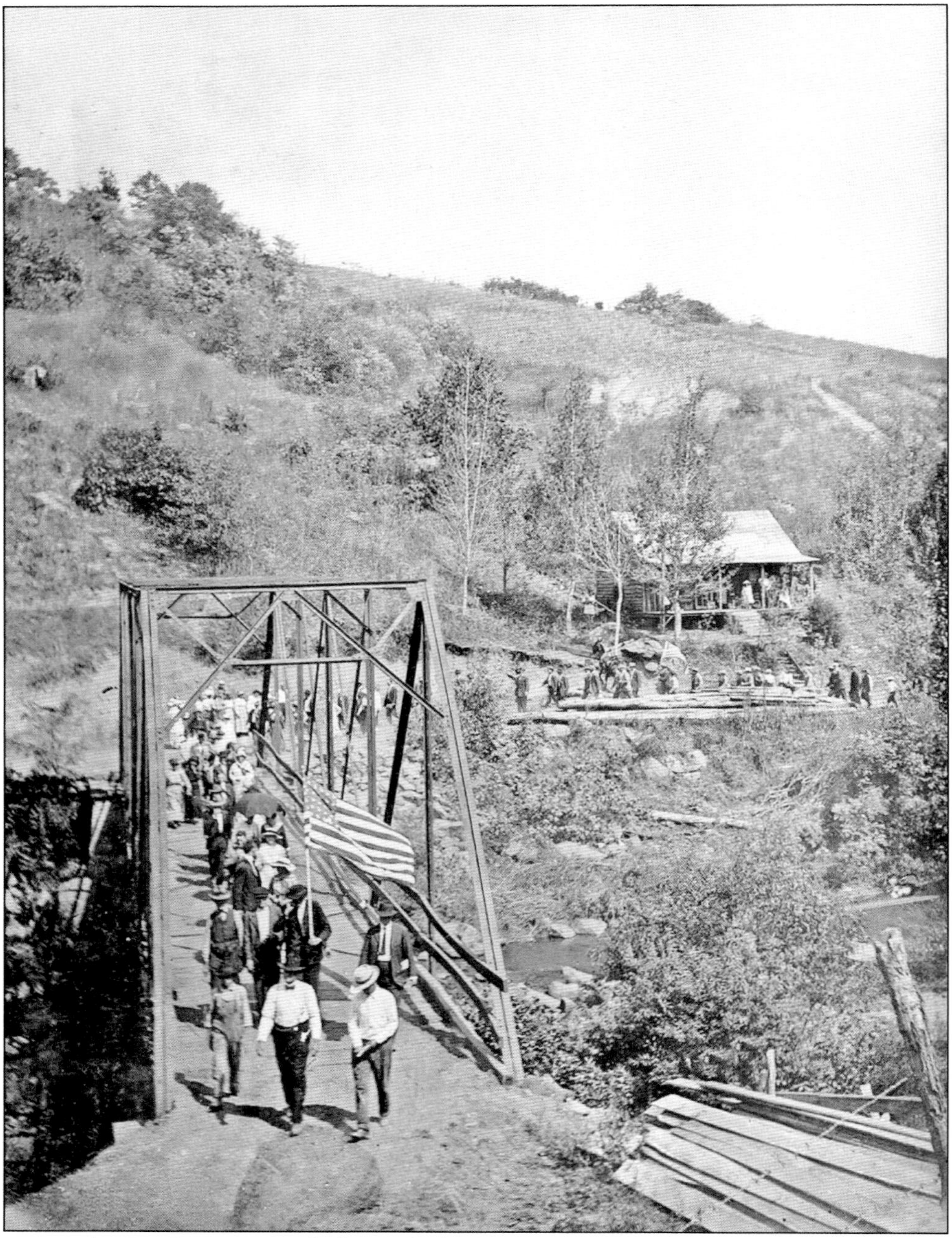

Crossing the Toe River was a challenge for both the railroad and regular road traffic. Before a bridge was constructed, shallow-bottom boats were used. In winter, crossings were made over the ice when the river froze solid in cold weather. A bridge for the Marion-to-Bakersville Road was constructed across the Toe River near the present-day Carolina Theatre on Lower Street. This patriotic parade shows Spruce Pine's earliest residents crossing the bridge, heading toward the English Inn. The bridge has a jaded history. Legend has it that a herd of cattle fell through it into the Toe River while crossing. It was destroyed by the flood of 1916. The original concrete pilings for the bridge are still visible from downtown Spruce Pine. (Courtesy of Michael C. Hardy.)

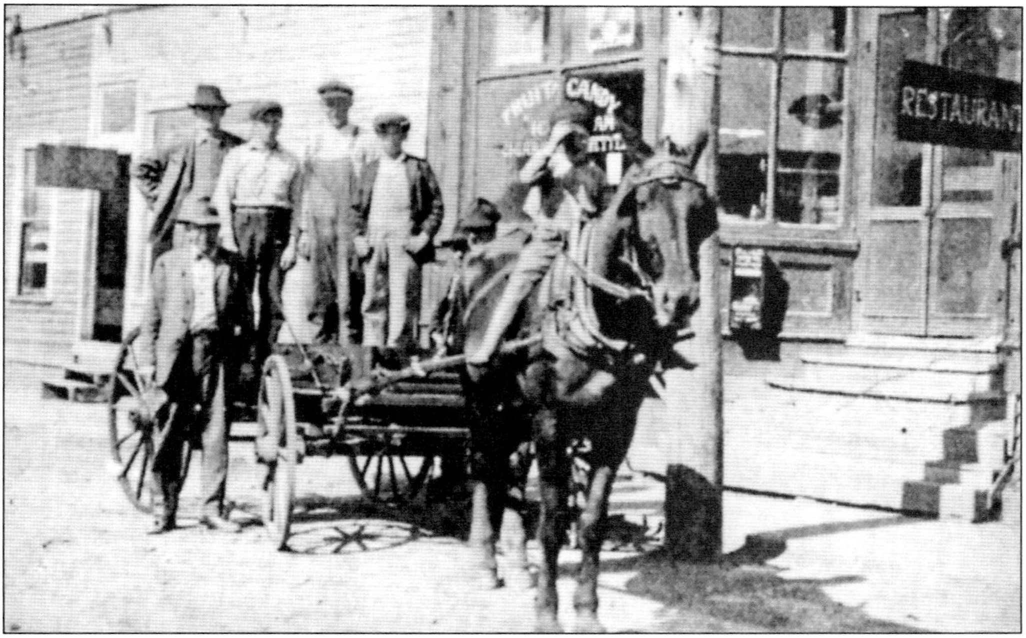


L. A. Berry opened the first store on Lower Street in 1903, moving his business from near the English Inn to a building across from the railroad depot. T. A. English took over, operating it until the Harris Mining Company opened the Spruce Pine Store. In this photograph, Spruce Pine Store manager Sam Cannon stands by the store's delivery wagon, and Waits "Deputy" Sullins is astride the horse. (Courtesy of Chris Hollifield.)

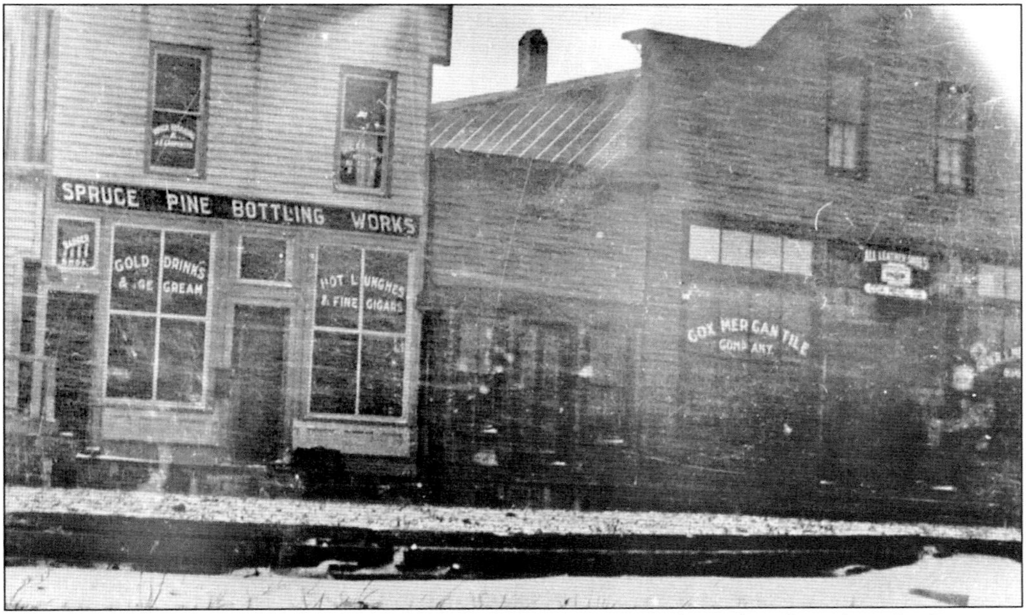


This view of Lower Street was taken in the 1900s from across the railroad tracks, which ran on both sides of the depot. Dr. Charles Peterson's office is on the second floor of the building on the left. Cox Mercantile is in the building on the right, which was home to the L. A. Berry and also the T. A. English stores. (Courtesy of the Ray Howell Collection.)

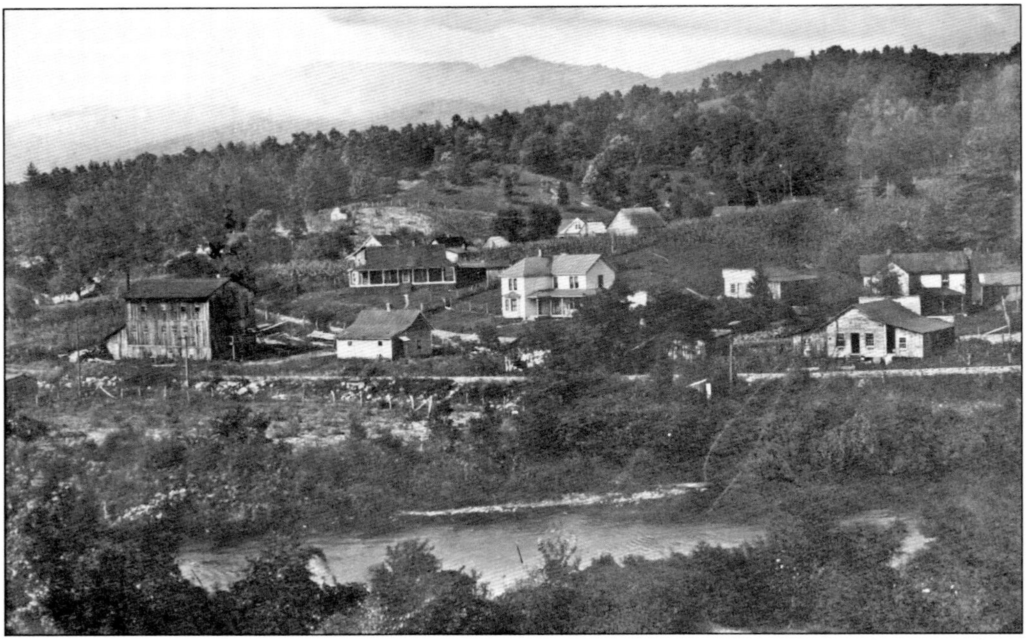

This 1909 shot of west Spruce Pine shows the Bakersville road with houses in the area where Webb Funeral Home now stands. The Toe River and railroad are in the foreground. (Courtesy of Elvira Bryant.)

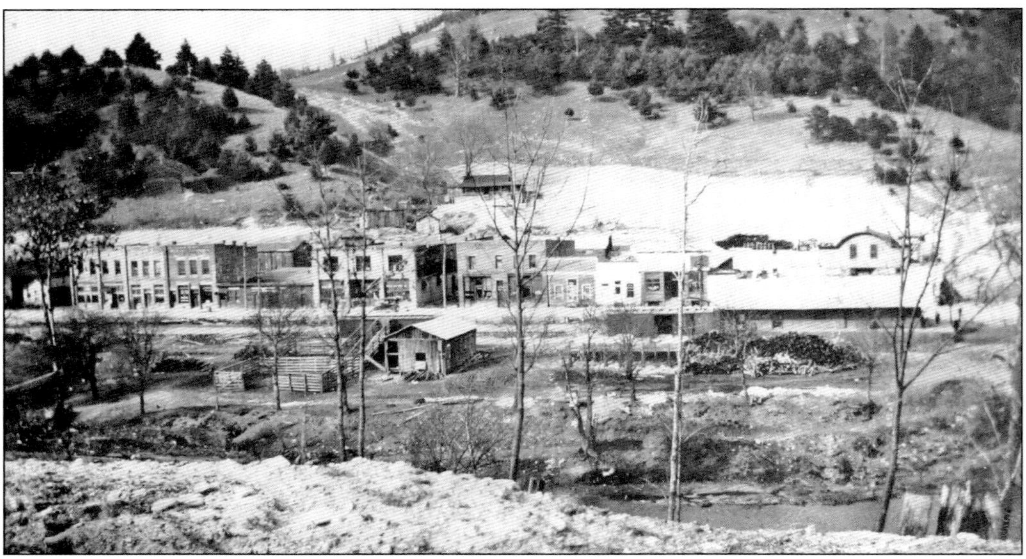

This photograph of Spruce Pine in the 1910s shows both the old and new. At the right is the original town, with the T.A. English Store on the right. The new town is at the left, with Spruce Pine's first brick building (the Spruce Pine Pharmacy) in the center of the photograph. It is still standing. (Courtesy of Doris Thompson.)

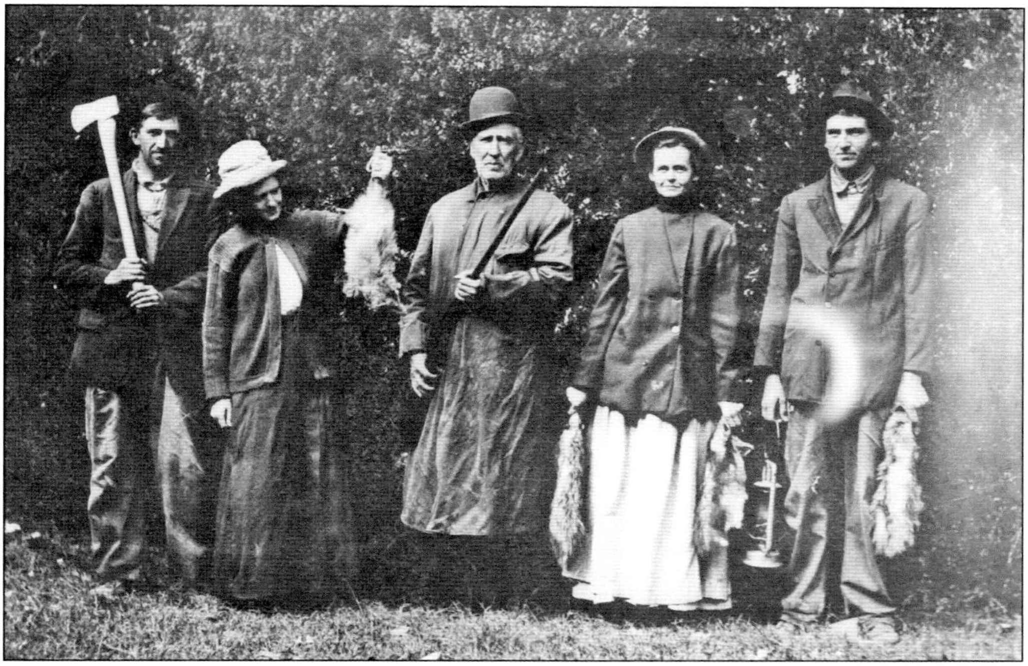

The George Greenlee family poses after a successful hunting expedition. The Greenlee family was one of the first to settle in the region. They named the area Grassy Creek from the lush meadows where their livestock grazed. (Courtesy of Elvira Bryant.)

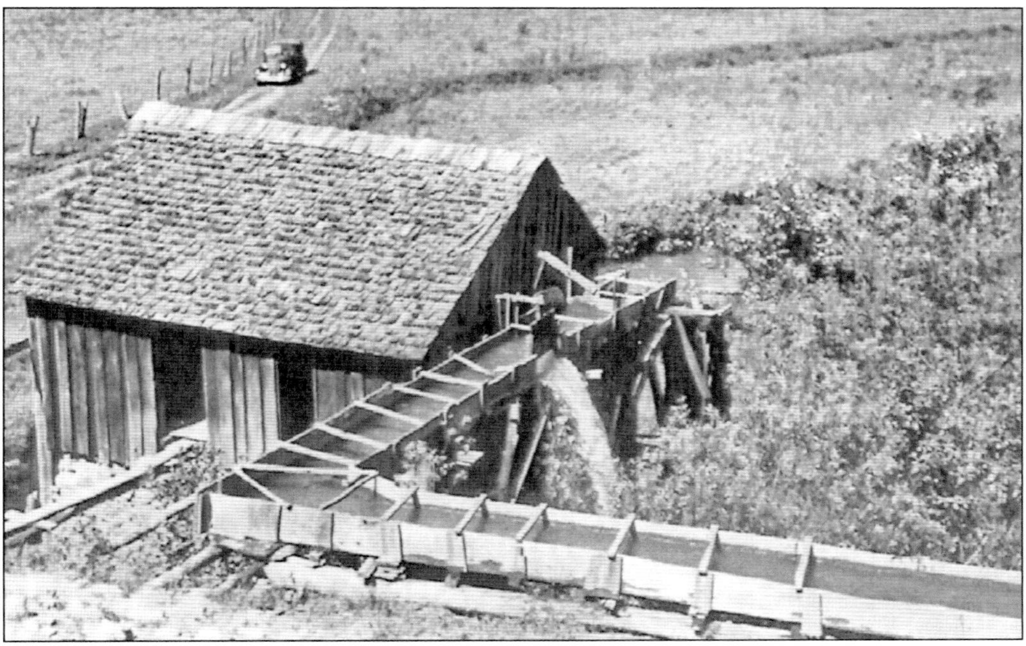

The Greenlee family settled near Spruce Pine along Grassy Creek, south of town. They operated this gristmill for years. Located near the present-day Spruce Pine Chevrolet car dealership, the beginnings of North Carolina Highway 226 can be seen in the background. (Courtesy of Chris Hollifield.)

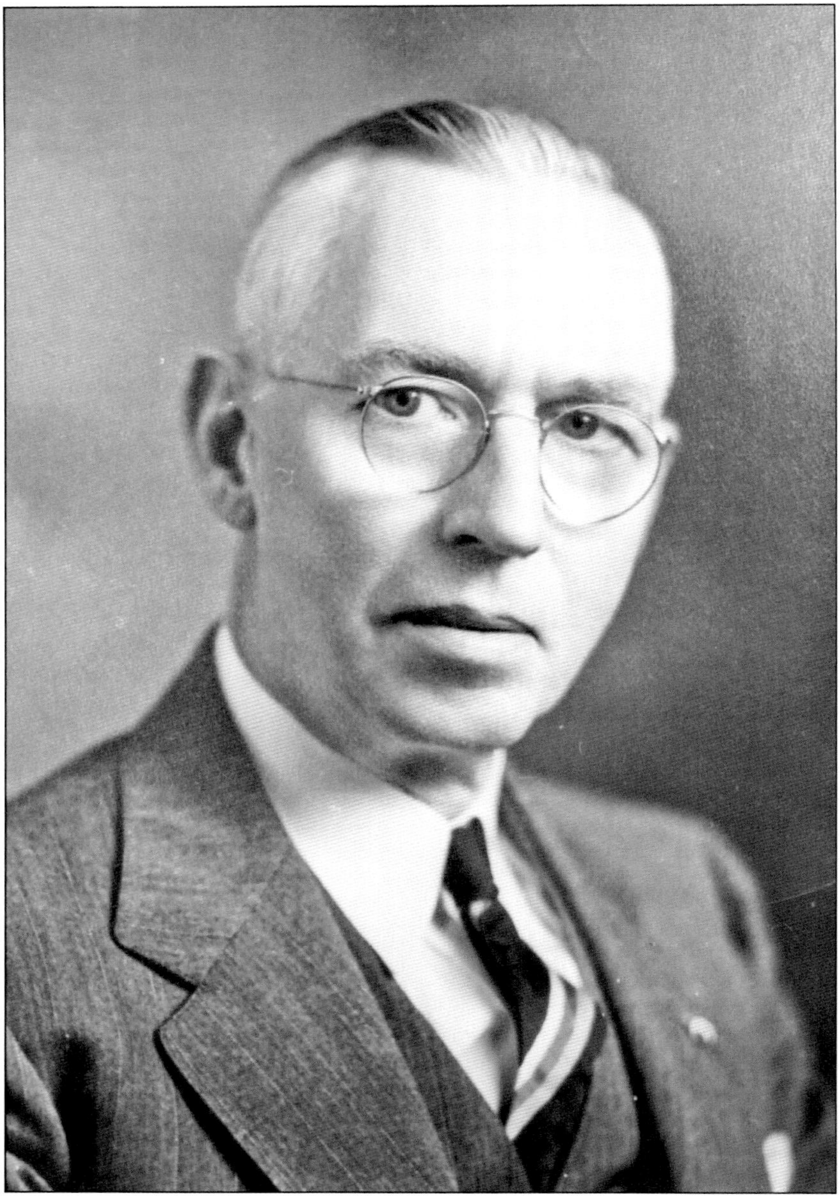

Dr. Charles Peterson could be considered the father of Spruce Pine. He arrived in town in 1907 after leaving the Relief community in Mitchell County to complete his studies at North Carolina Medical College in Charlotte and Davidson. He was practicing medicine when he was only 23 years old, continuing for 52 years until his death in 1960. He delivered 4,000 children during his career. Peterson helped purchase the land where downtown is located and laid out streets and lots, signing the deeds to most of them. He built the town's first brick building and pharmacy, and he led efforts to construct a hospital in Spruce Pine, serving as its first chief of staff in 1954. He also served as the mayor of Spruce Pine, a state representative (1923, 1935, and 1945), and a state senator (1941 and 1949) for Mitchell County, where he worked to abolish the electric chair as a form of capital punishment. Affectionately known as "Dr. Charles," Peterson was a vital part of the lives of most Spruce Pine residents from birth to death. (Courtesy of Wayne Ward.)

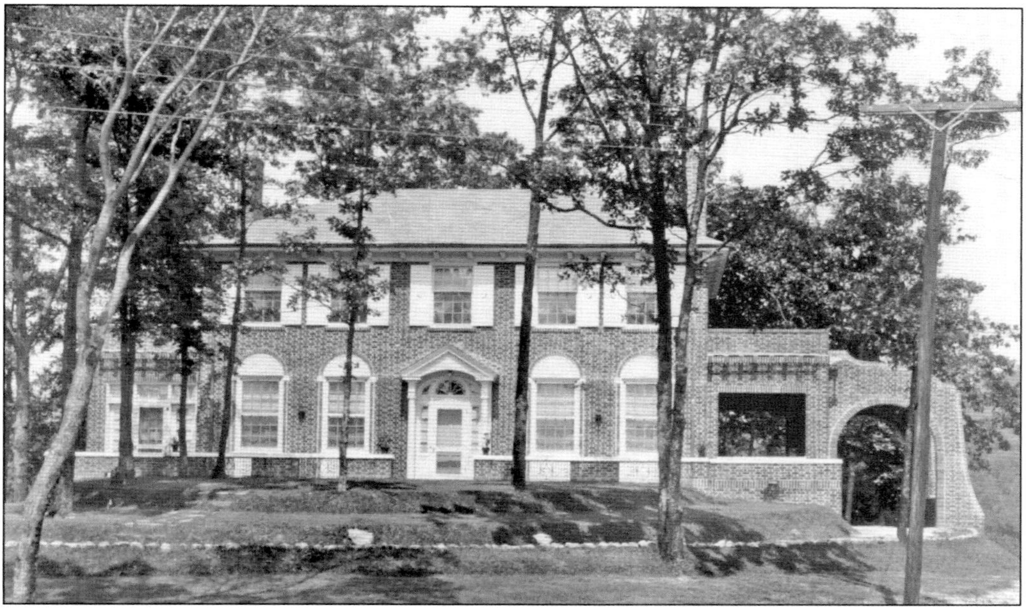

Dr. Charles Peterson built this house on a knoll overlooking Spruce Pine in 1928. Architect D. R. Beeson of Johnson City, Tennessee, designed the Colonial Revival–style home. At the time, the structure was the most impressive and substantial home in town. It still stands on a lot behind the Spruce Pine Library at the corner of Diamond Street and Hazel Avenue. (Courtesy of Bill and Emma Lee Wilson.)

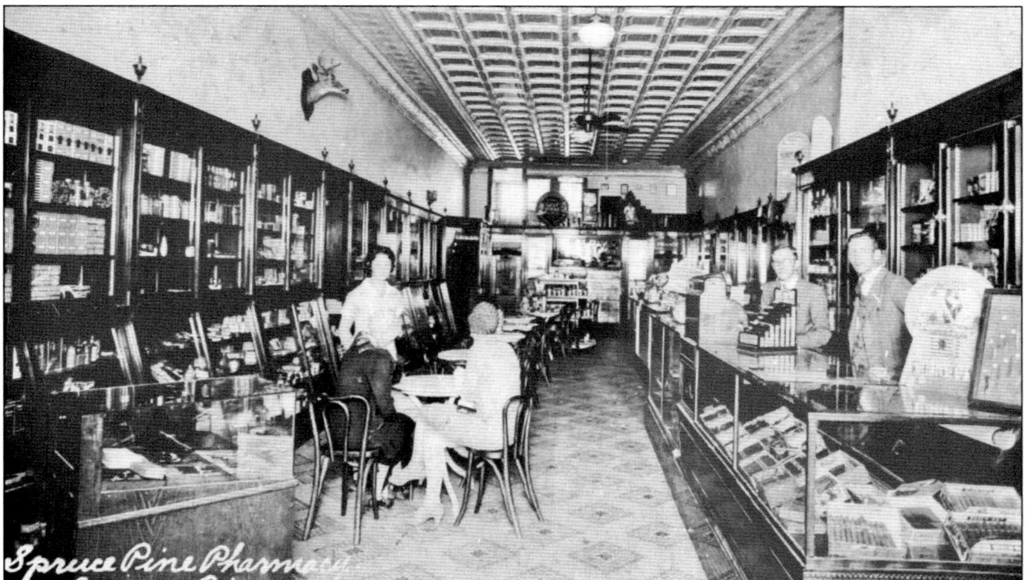


The Spruce Pine Pharmacy was opened by Dr. Charles Peterson in the town's first brick structure in 1916. In 1930, it moved into a new building next to its original location, and Peterson's medical practice was opened upstairs. It moved again in the 1990s, taking the famous wood cabinetry to a new building. The 1916 building was damaged and the 1930 location destroyed by an arsonist on August 5, 2007. (Courtesy of Wayne Ward.)

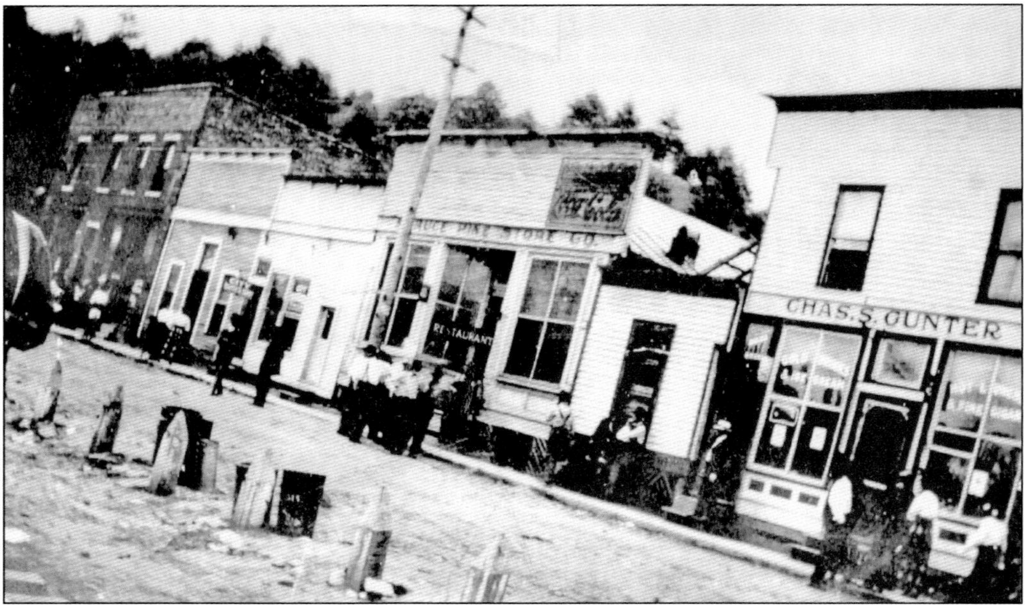


This images shows downtown Spruce Pine in 1916. The burgeoning town has begun to grow, with its first brick building (the Peterson building) at the far left. This structure still stands on Lower Street at the corner of Link Street. Charles Gunter's store is at the right near the former Belk building. Gunter had mining interests and later constructed the Gunter building on Upper Street. (Courtesy of Willa Ann Ward.)

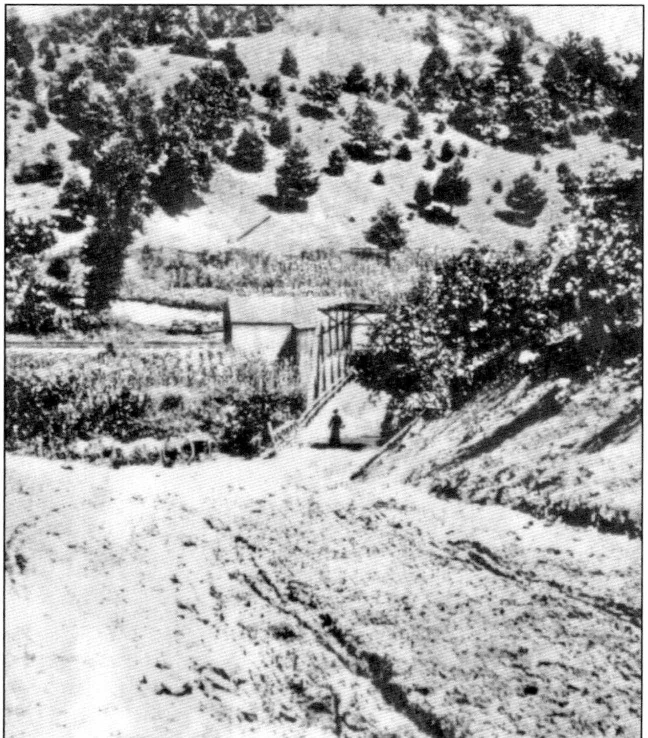

Most roadways were little more than dirt paths, even main thoroughfares like the Marion-to-Bakersville road. This view of the road as it approaches the Toe River Bridge was taken about 1912. (Courtesy of Chris Hollifield.)

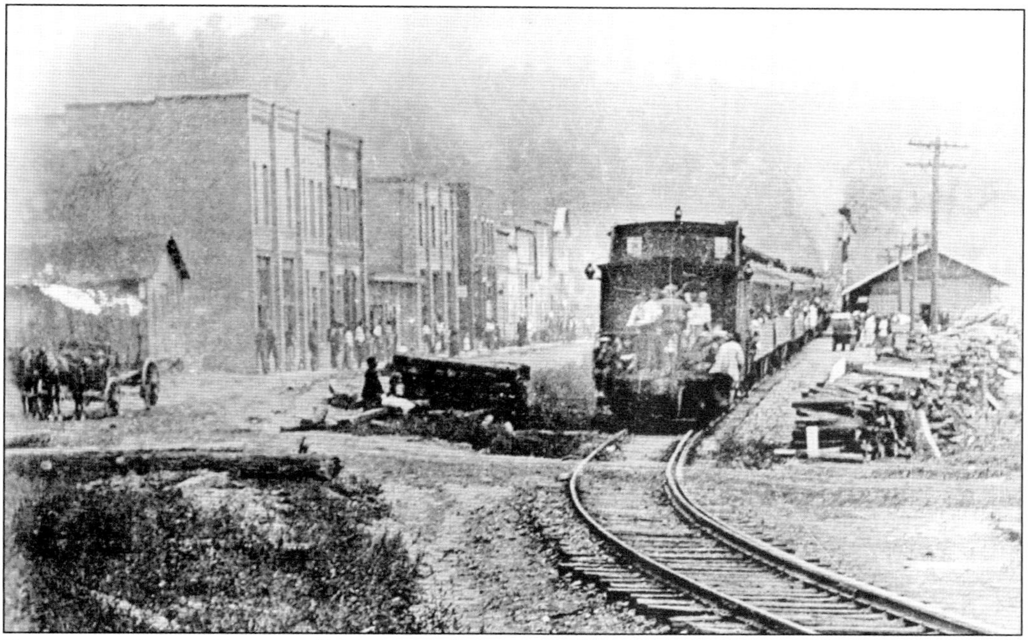

Downtown Spruce Pine rapidly expanded as mica, feldspar, and clay mining began in earnest and the railroad made it down the Blue Ridge at Altapass, continuing on to Spartanburg, South Carolina. The population quadrupled between 1918 and 1928, and the construction of buildings tripled the size of the downtown area. Surprisingly, there was only one road where an automobile could be driven. The presence of the railroad depot helped make the town the focal point of trade in the Toe River Valley, as minerals and lumber were shipped out and goods were brought in to the region. These views, taken from opposite ends of town around 1920, show a bustling community where the Clinchfield train stopped twice a day. (Both, courtesy of Chris Hollifield.)

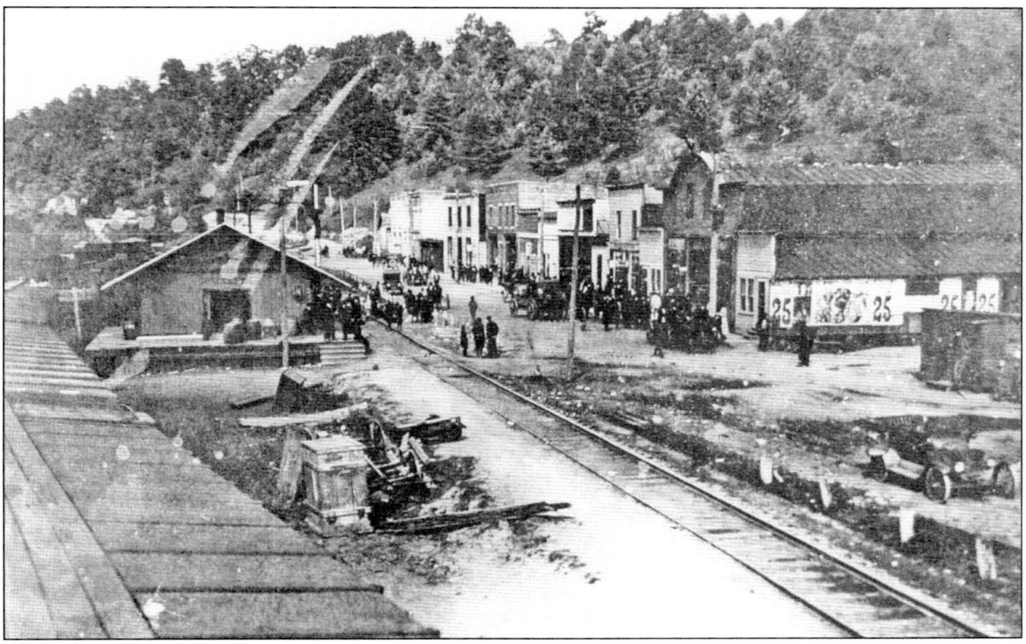

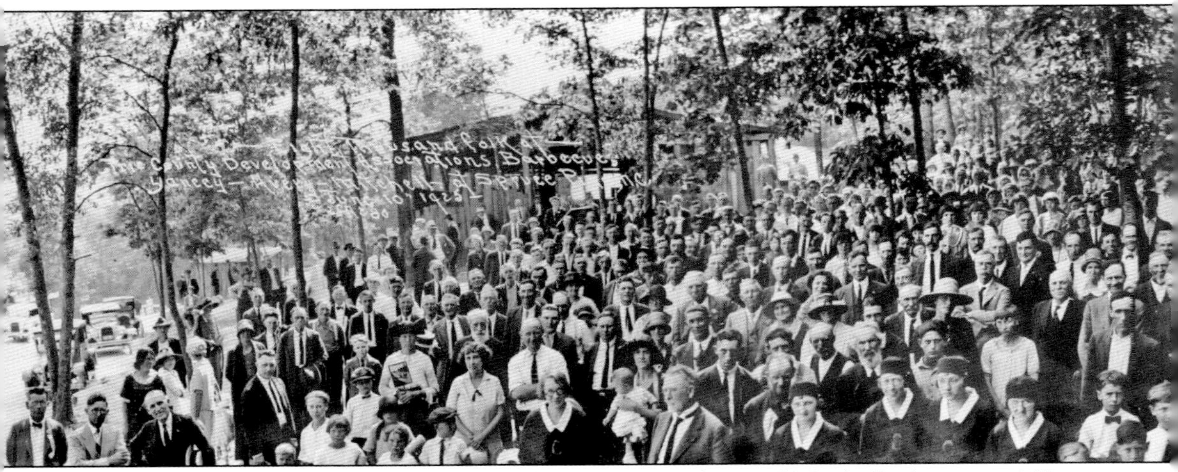

June 10, 1925, was a momentous day when 8,000 residents of Mitchell, Avery, and Yancey Counties gathered at the fairgrounds in Spruce Pine for a barbecue and meeting of the Tri-County Development Association. This group was dedicated to improving roads and developing economic opportunities for the three counties. Politicians and other dignitaries were at this meeting;

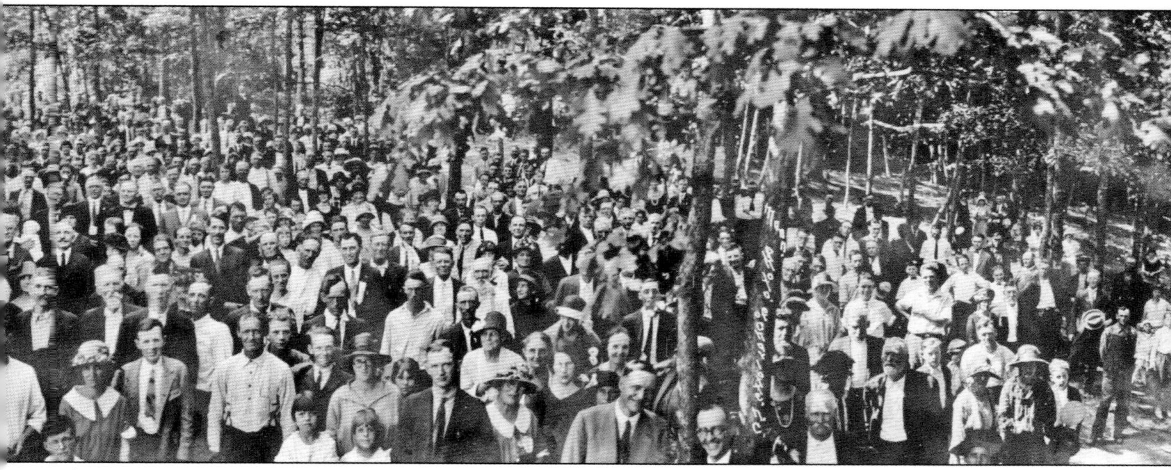

former Tennessee governor Alfred A. Taylor is pictured just to the left of the centerfold. Prominent members of the Bailey family, who were landowners and founded the Deer Park estate, are just to the right of center. Shortly after this gathering, additional mines were opened in the region, bringing jobs and other improvements for citizens. (Courtesy of Fred Pitman.)

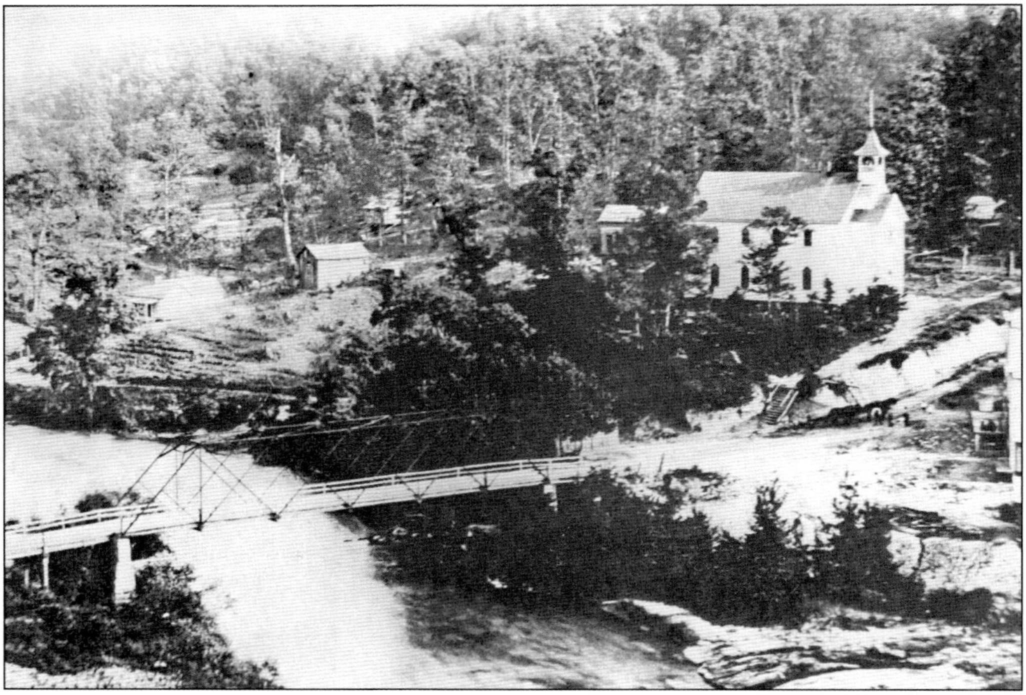

The First Baptist Church sat just across the Toe River from downtown at the south side of the bridge. This portion of the Marion Road was improved for automobiles and trucks to travel between the railroad depot and the Burleson mica plant at the top of the hill above the church. (Courtesy of Elvira Bryant.)

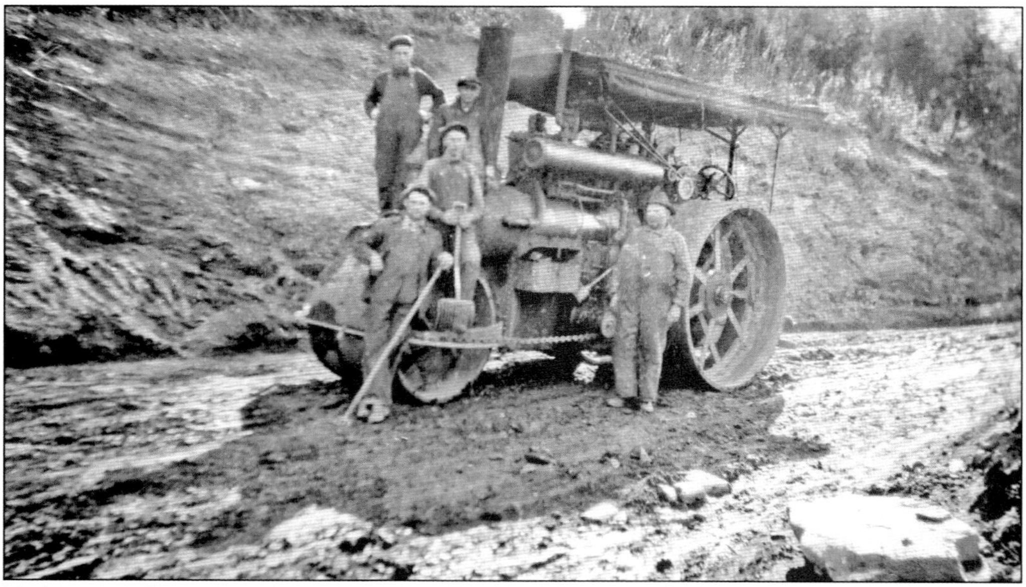

Highways in the mountains were often treacherous with few cars and many families using animals for transportation. North Carolina began a systematic improvement of roads in the 1920s. Here an unidentified crew works on the road between Bakersville and Spruce Pine. (Courtesy of Wayne Ward.)

# *Two*

# THE MINERAL CITY
## A REGIONAL CROSSROADS

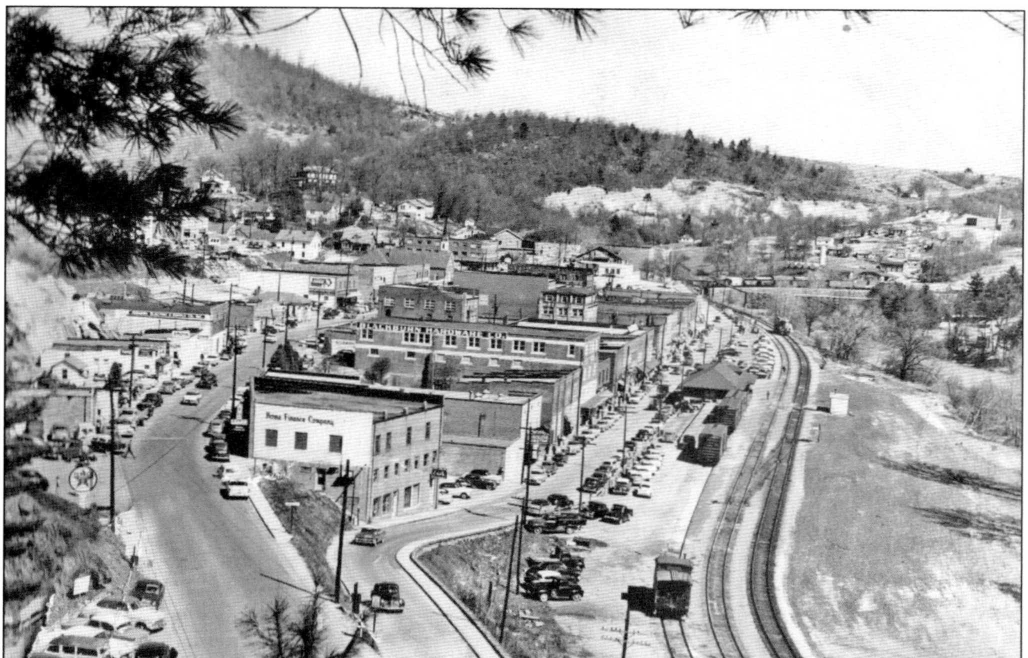

This image shows Spruce Pine's heyday in the mid-1950s. This view from the hill opposite the old bridge shows a bustling downtown area. The mining industry was booming, and Spruce Pine's population was increasing. New schools, a new hospital, a golf course, WTOE Radio, and improvements to parks and other recreational activities were just a few of the changes taking place at this time. (Courtesy of Spruce Pine Public Library.)

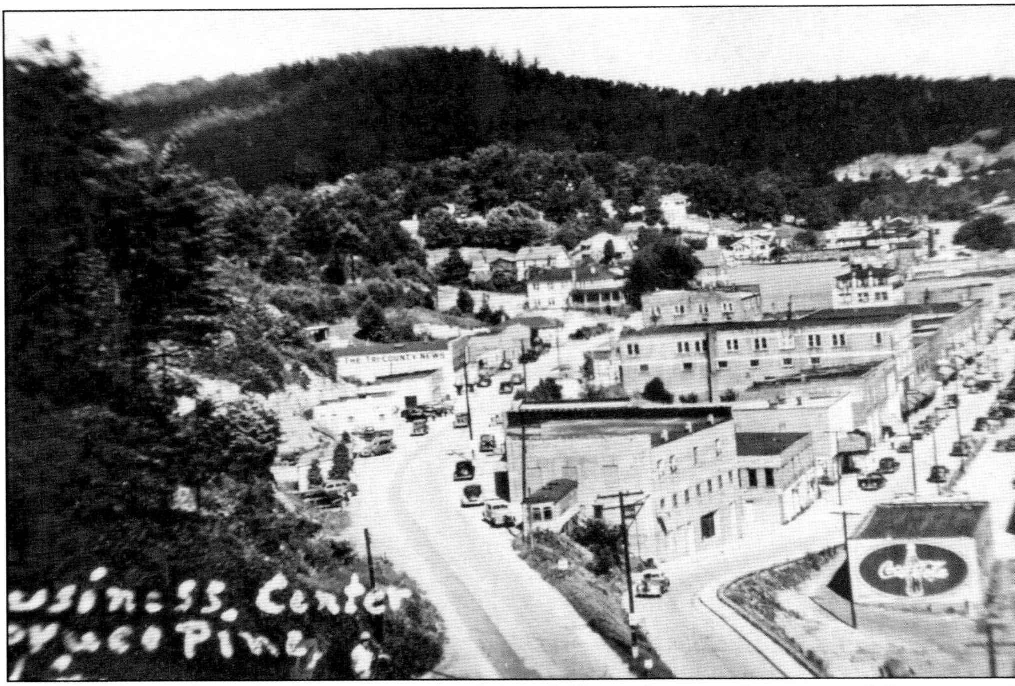

In this image of Spruce Pine in the 1940s, the Topliff Hotel is near the center of the picture. It would soon be destroyed by fire. At the lower right is the Coca-Cola warehouse that served the region, and to its left is an old diner made from a streetcar. It was demolished in 1949 as part of a town beautification campaign. (Courtesy of Guss McKinney.)

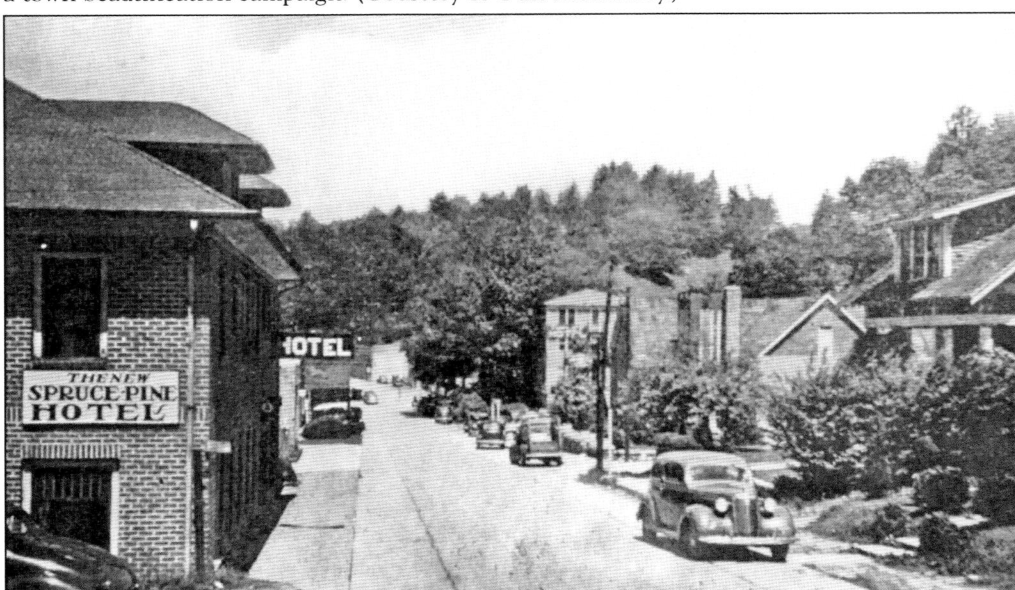


The new Spruce Pine and Topliff Hotels dominate this photograph of Upper Street in the 1930s, with the First Presbyterian Church on the right. In 10 years time, this scene would change dramatically after the Topliff burned down and a variety of businesses were built along the street. (Courtesy of Elvira Bryant.)

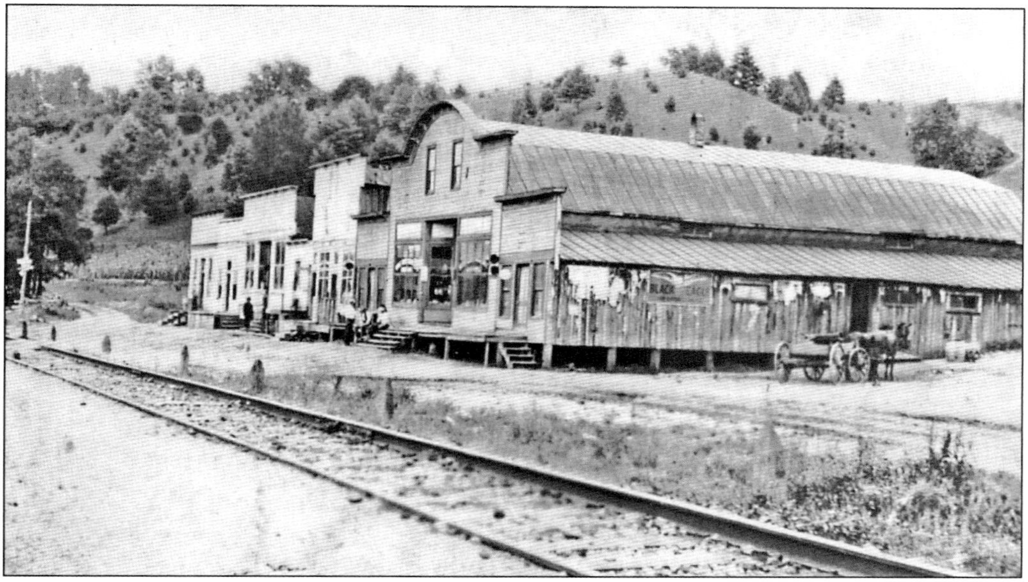

The large building at the right initially housed the L. A. Berry Store and later the T. A. English and Cox Mercantile stores. The Harris Mining Company razed the building and constructed a modern brick structure on the site, moving its Spruce Pine Store into it in 1923. It was a general merchandise operation in the style of company stores of the time, and it operated until 1955, when Belk Broome moved into the building. This structure still stands today. These photographs show the same location in town approximately 35 years apart. (Above, courtesy of Chris Hollifield; below, courtesy of Wayne Ward.)

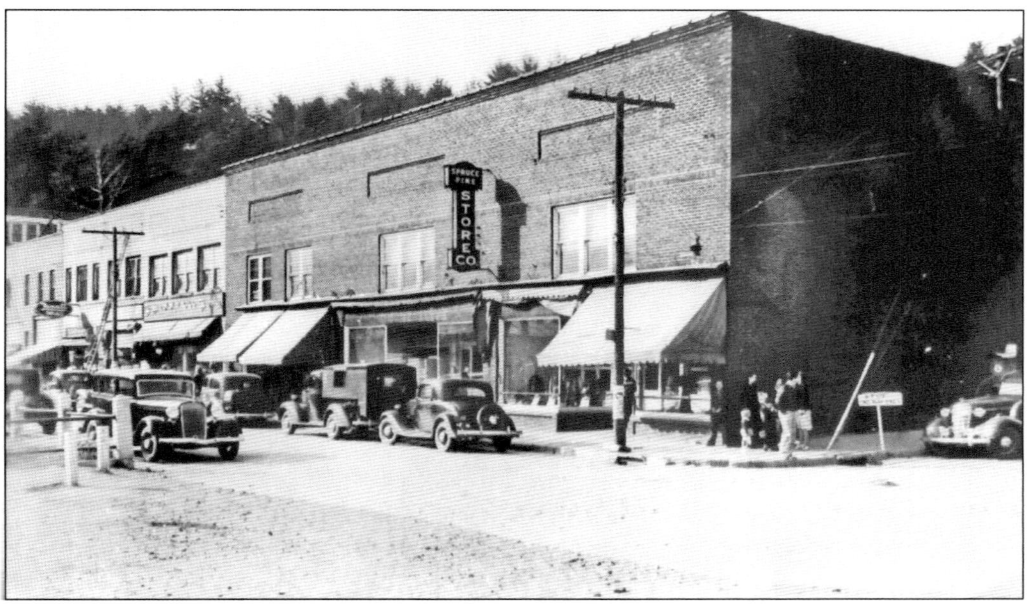

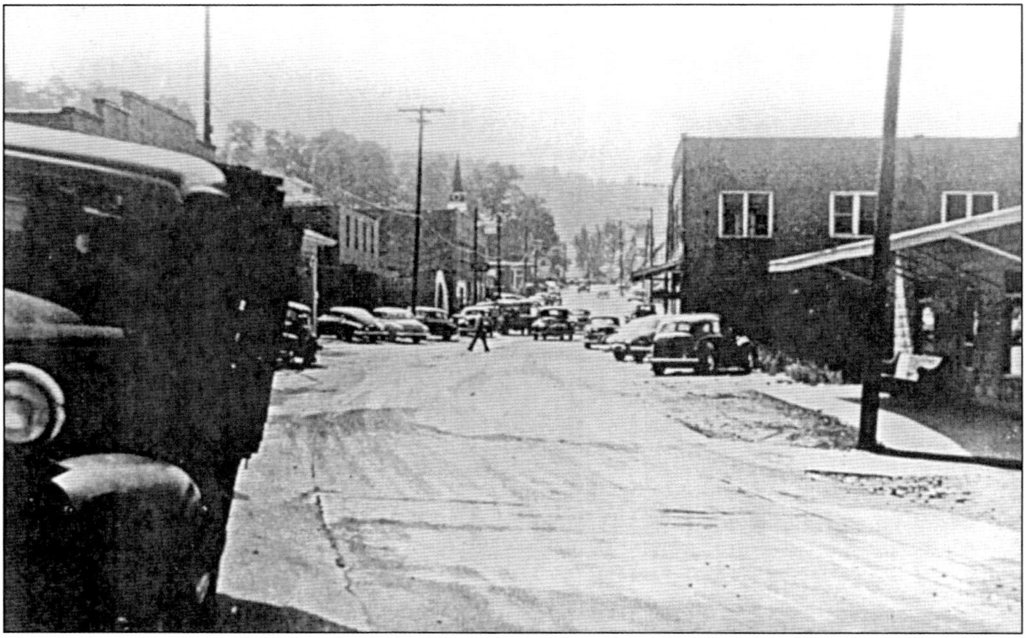

This view of Upper Street in 1950 shows the newly constructed Ray Howell Hardware and Aldridge and Greene Ford buildings in the location of the old Topliff Hotel in the upper left. Floyd Smith's restaurant is at center right. (Courtesy of Guss McKinney.)

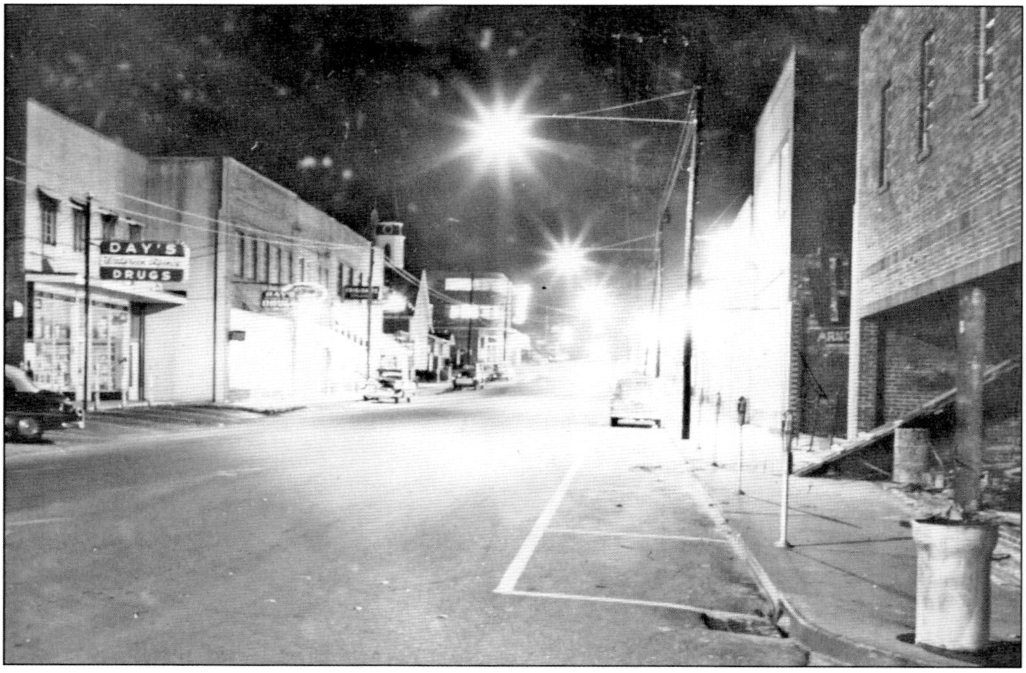


This image shows Upper Street at night around 1953. The newly constructed Day's Drugstore, opened by L. G. Day in 1951, is center left, with the Ellis building being constructed at the right. The News Center was in the Ellis building for years. It is now the location of the Home of the Perfect Christmas Tree Store. (Courtesy of Spruce Pine Public Library.)

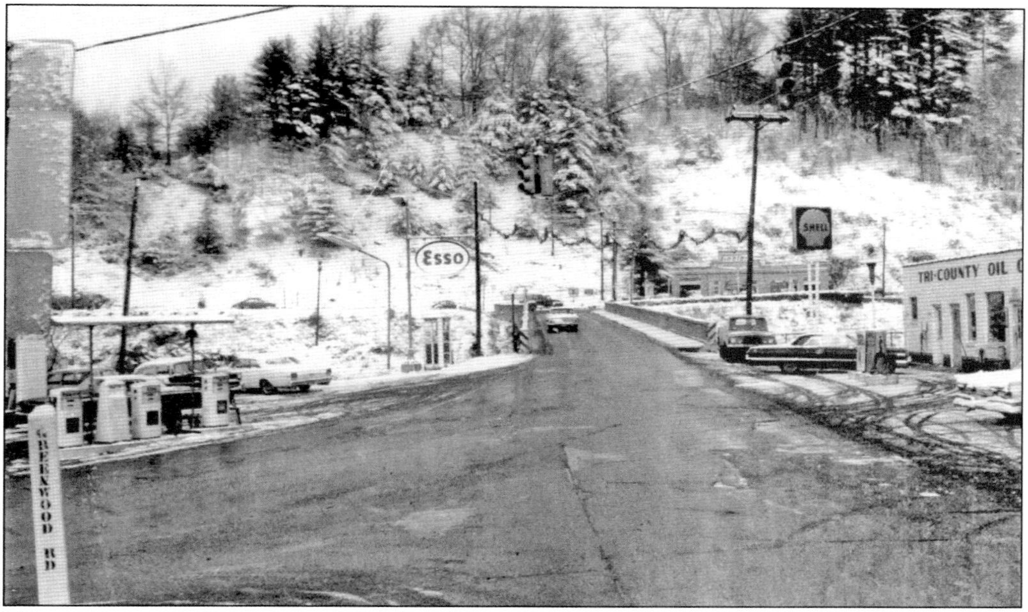


The intersection of Greenwood Road and Summit Avenue highlights the infamous bottleneck bridge crossing the Toe River and carrying the traffic of U.S. Highway 19-E and N.C. Highway 226. The Tri-County Oil Company is located to the right. Traffic jams were an everyday occurrence here before the construction of the Spruce Pine Bypass in 1977 and a new bridge across the Toe River in 1986. (Courtesy of Chris Hollifield.)

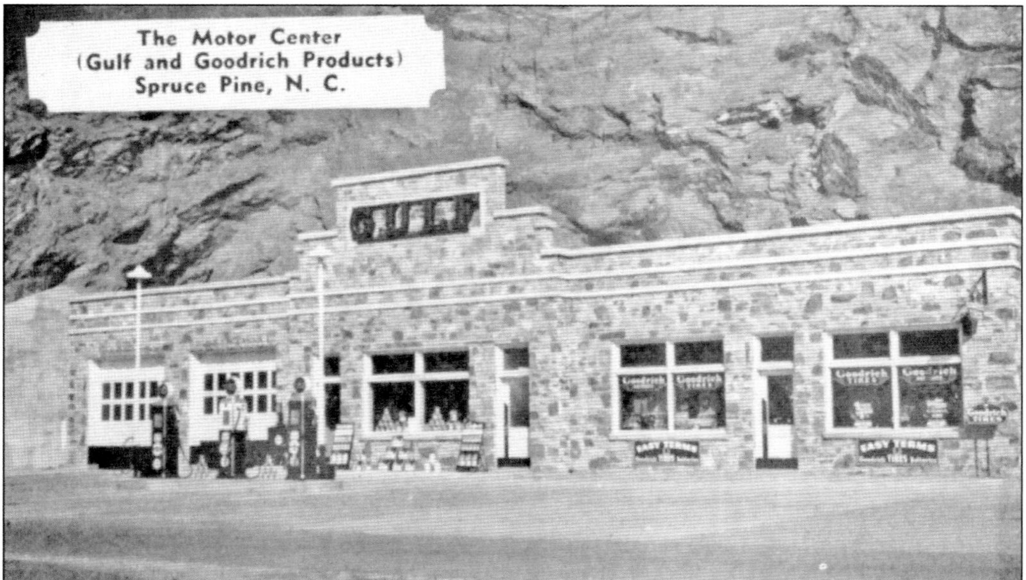


Located near the Toe River Bridge, the Motor Center was operated by several individuals. It is most well known for rock slides that periodically closed the station for repairs, including one that hit just before it opened for business. It was finally the victim of a major rock slide that destroyed the building in the late 1990s. The site is now home to the town clock. (Courtesy of David Blevins.)

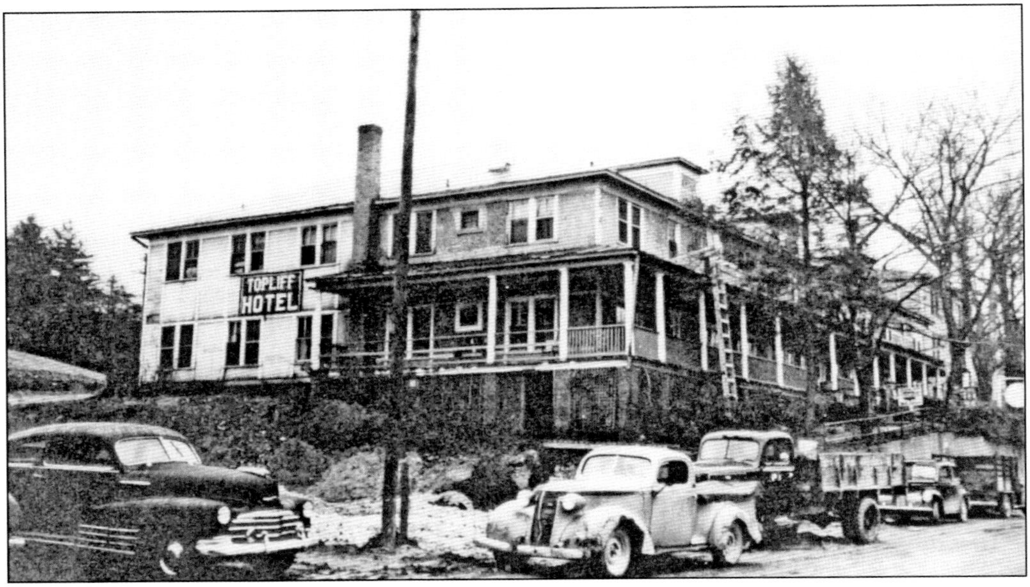


The Topliff Hotel was the center of town life from the 1900s to the 1940s. Serving businessmen, tourists, and other visitors, the hotel was a popular destination. It was operated by Charles H. and Dora M. Topliff, who retired to Spruce Pine in the 1920s, buying the business from Taylor Phillips and constructing additions in 1922 and 1925. The hotel had a grand ballroom (pictured below) where civic events, dances, and other social activities took place. Doctors David L. Phillips and Melvin Webb had offices in the building, and several individuals, including Brad Ragan, called the Topliff home. It was destroyed by fire on August 6, 1948, and was not replaced. (Above, courtesy of Buster Sparks; below, courtesy of Emma Lee Wilson.)

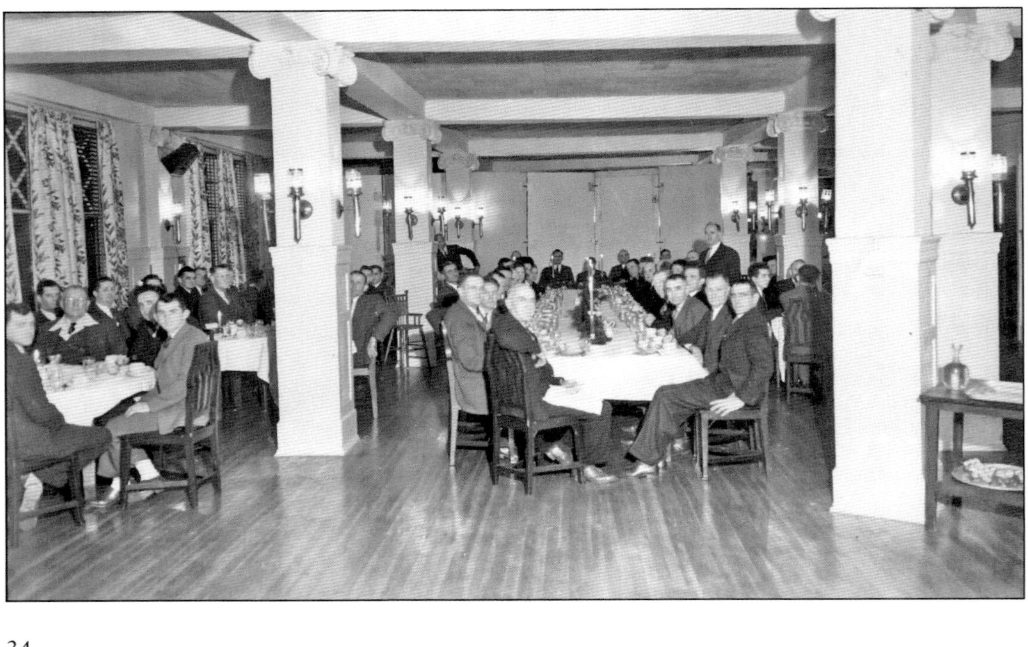

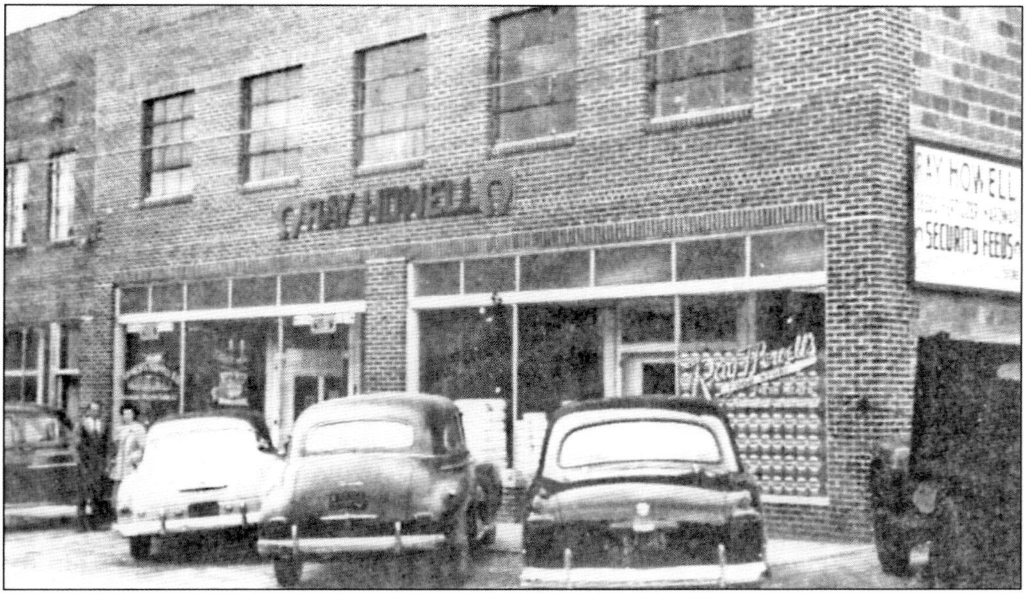


Ray Howell opened his food and general store on Upper Street in a building erected after the Topliff Hotel fire. He operated the business until the 1970s, when he sold it and began a successful real estate firm. He is pictured with his wife, Georgia, in front of the store. (Courtesy of the *Mitchell News-Journal.*)

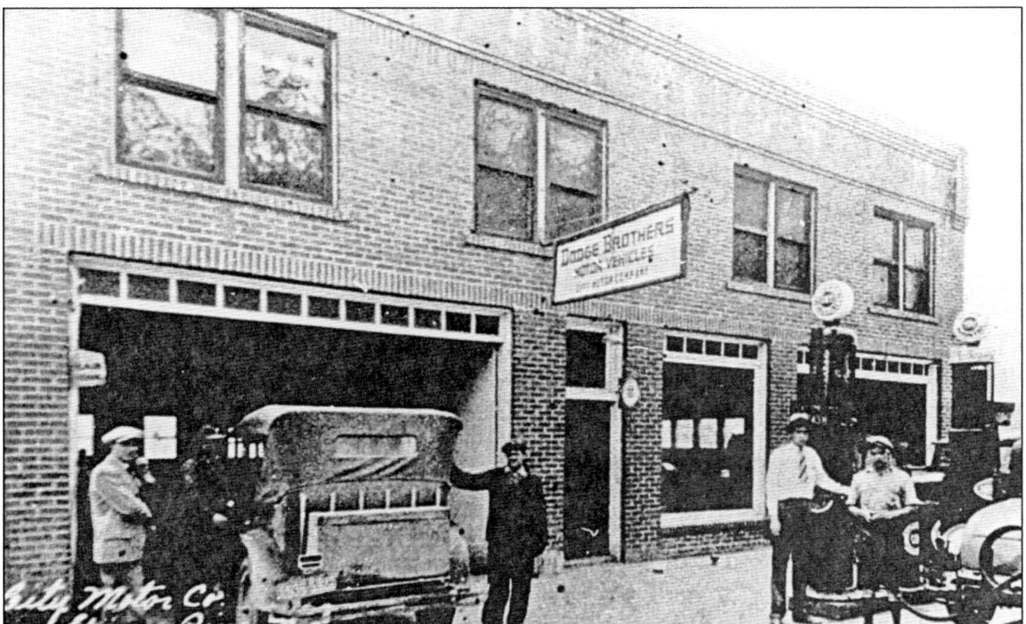


The City Motor Company was the Dodge dealership on Upper Street. It was located in a building next to present-day People's Furniture. W. G. Pippin and George Day started the company in 1930–1931. It was later home to a pool hall, and it served as the first home of Mayland Community College's automotive mechanics program before it was destroyed by fire in the 1970s. (Courtesy of Guss McKinney.)

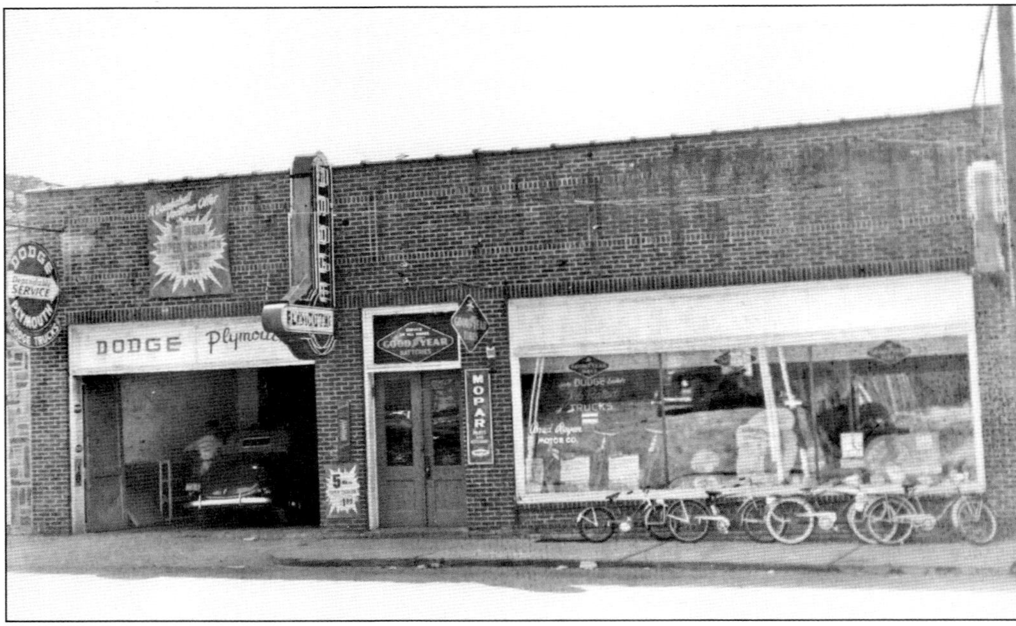


Brad Ragan was a traveling tire salesman when he bought a struggling car and tire dealership on Upper Street. He combined it with operations in Mooresville and Salisbury, North Carolina to form the Carolina Tire Company. His operations grew worldwide and were based in Spruce Pine until his death in an airplane crash in 1979. (Courtesy of Mildred Harris.)

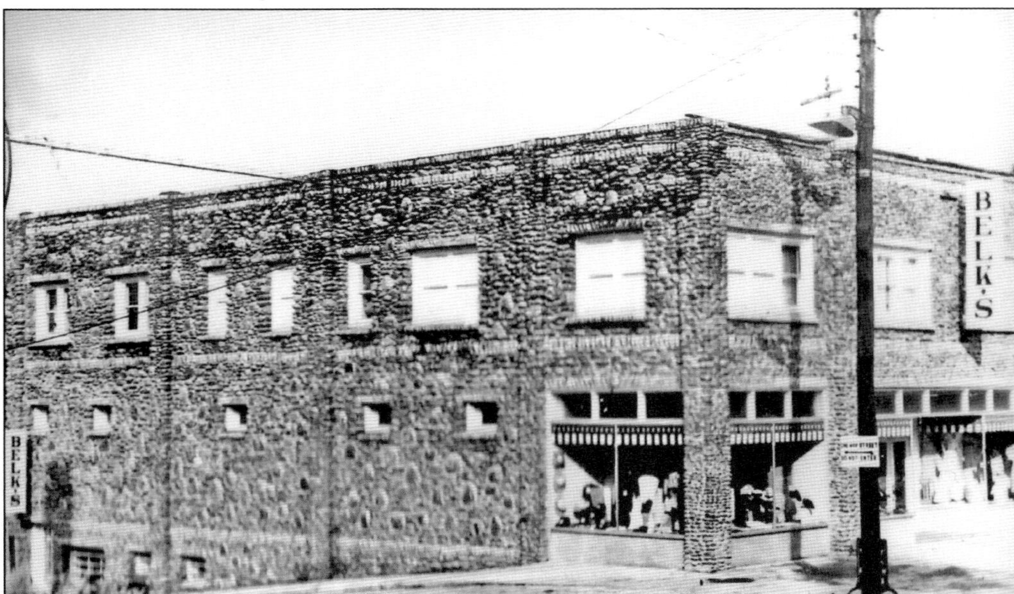


Charles Gunter constructed this building at the corner of Topaz Street and Oak Avenue in 1941. Belk Broome was the first occupant. It moved into the building following a disastrous fire on Lower Street in which three businesses were destroyed, including Belk. It remained there until 1955, moving to the Spruce Pine Store location on Lower Street and staying in business until 1992. (Courtesy of North Carolina Department of Cultural Resources.)

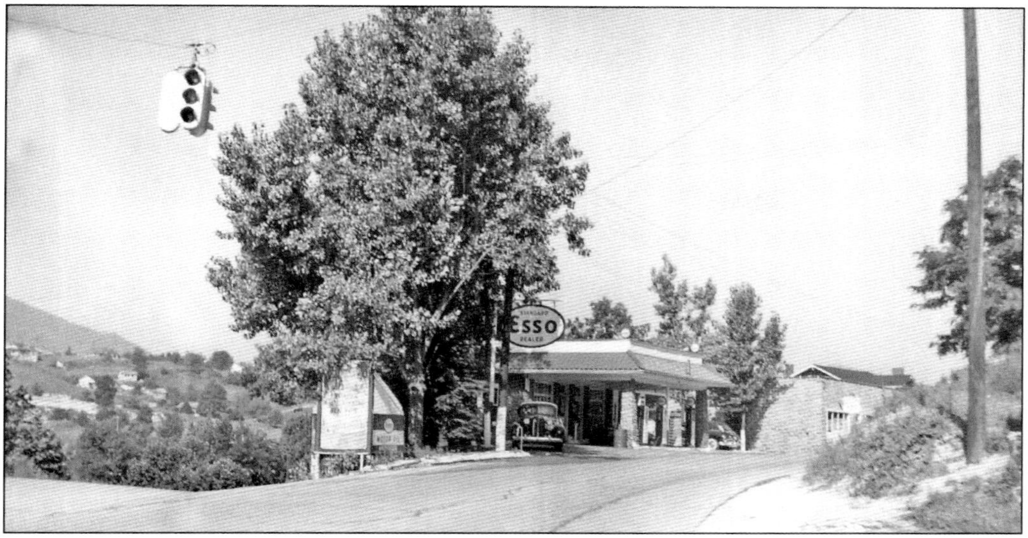


Hugh Price was the proprietor of the Esso service station at the intersection of Locust and Oak Avenues in the 1940s. It was later operated by Buddy Hand. This building was torn down and replaced by a more modern station operated by Ernest Canipe. (Courtesy of Daniel Barron.)

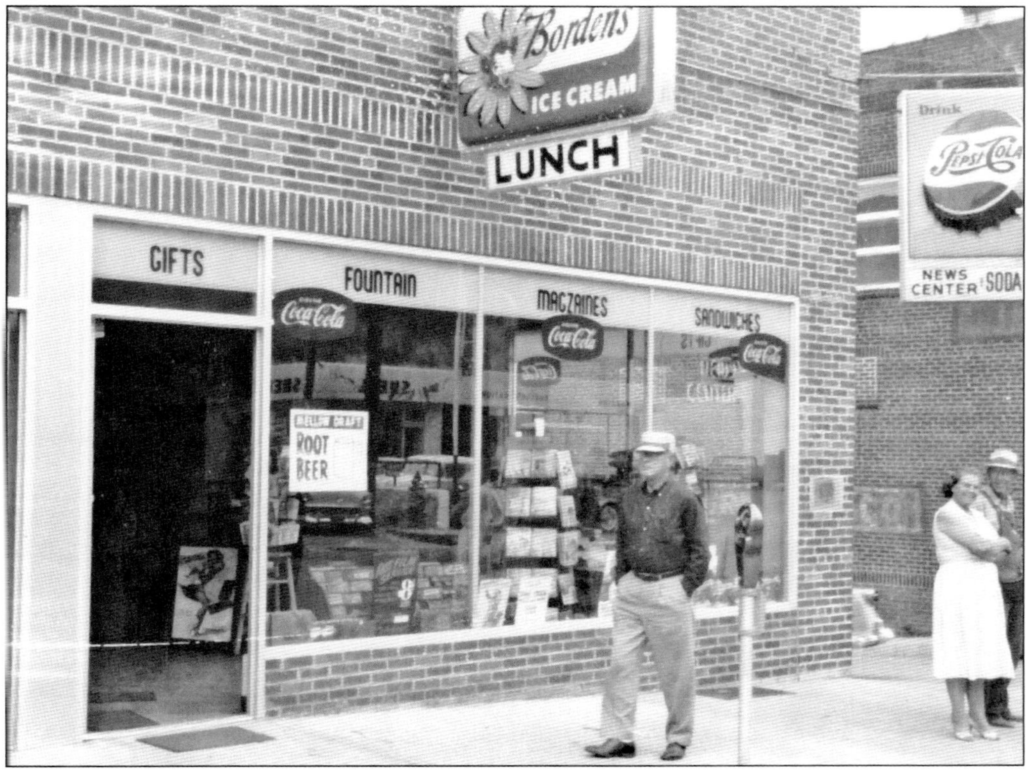


The News Center was a Spruce Pine institution for years. Starting on Lower Street, it moved into the Ellis building on Upper Street in 1954. It featured paperback books, newspapers, magazines, and sundries. Later a lunch counter was opened in the rear that evolved into the CedarCrest Restaurant, a Lower Street staple in the 1980s and 1990s. (Courtesy of Spruce Pine Public Library.)

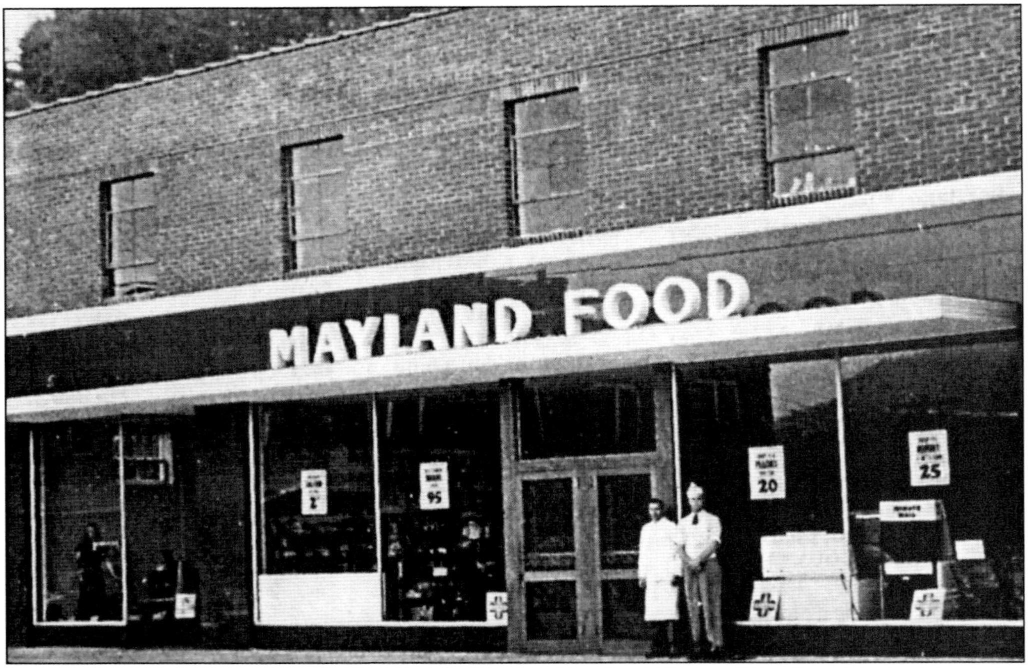


Charles Phillips was the founder of the Mayland Food Market, which opened in the late 1940s across from People's Furniture on Upper Street. The Wilma Eloise store was located next to it. Phillips came to Spruce Pine from Hickory, and his son Tommy ran the business after his death. Frank Hoilman is pictured with Phillips in this 1951 image. (Courtesy of Chris Hollifield.)

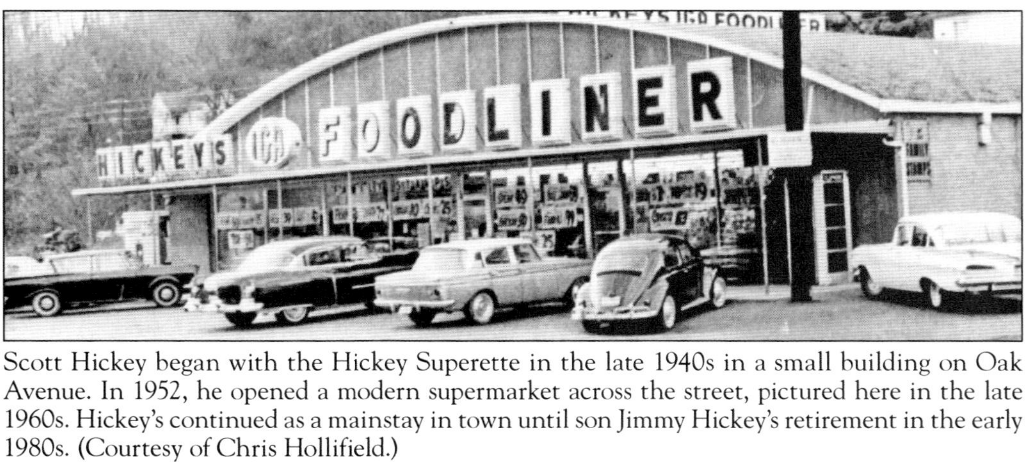


Scott Hickey began with the Hickey Superette in the late 1940s in a small building on Oak Avenue. In 1952, he opened a modern supermarket across the street, pictured here in the late 1960s. Hickey's continued as a mainstay in town until son Jimmy Hickey's retirement in the early 1980s. (Courtesy of Chris Hollifield.)

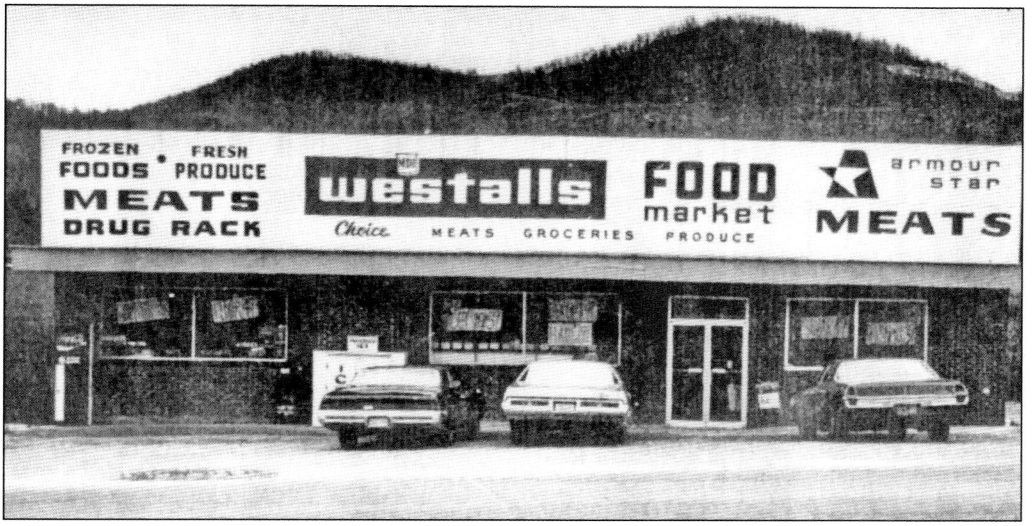


Tom and Violet Westall opened their supermarket on the Burnsville Highway near Harris High School in 1960 and operated it until 1978. They began with a hot dog stand in 1934, followed by a soda shop in 1936, a restaurant from 1940 to 1945, and M&W Market from 1945 to 1960, all on Lower Street. (Courtesy of Chris Hollifield.)

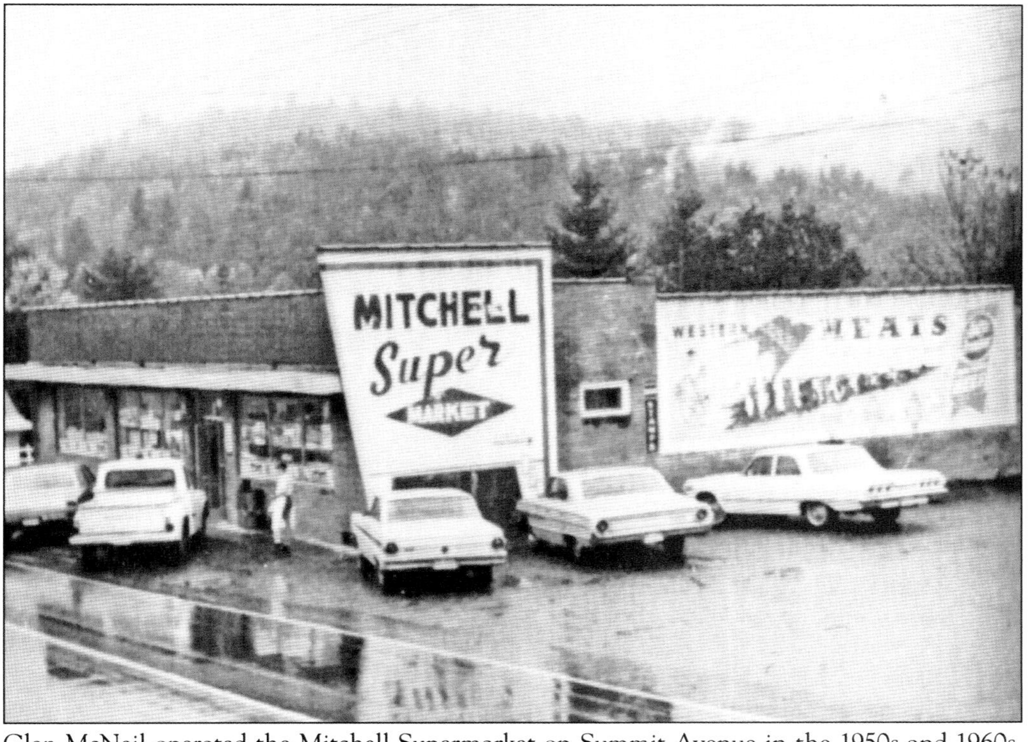


Glen McNeil operated the Mitchell Supermarket on Summit Avenue in the 1950s and 1960s. Along with Westall's and Hickey's, it ushered in the era of supermarket shopping and the decline of community grocery stores in Spruce Pine. They were soon replaced by chain supermarkets in modern shopping centers. (Courtesy of Chris Hollifield.)

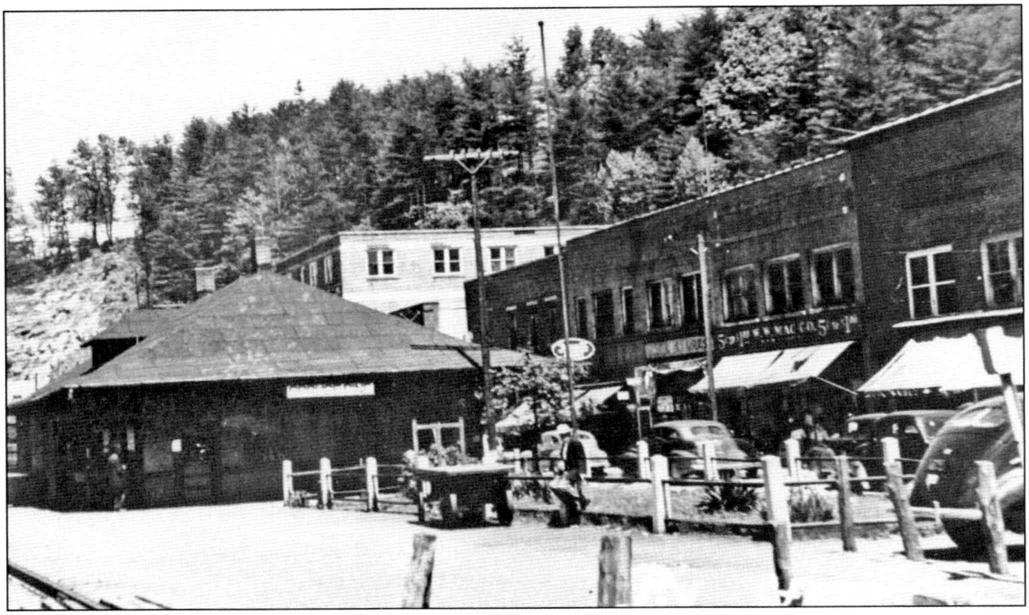

This classic view of Lower Street in the 1940s shows the Spruce Pine Depot as it appeared to train passengers approaching from Altapass. With poor roads and few cars, taking the train into town from Altapass or Penland for supplies or a visit on Saturdays was popular, and merchants extended their hours to accommodate the crowds. This depot opened in 1924. (Courtesy of the Ray Howell Collection.)

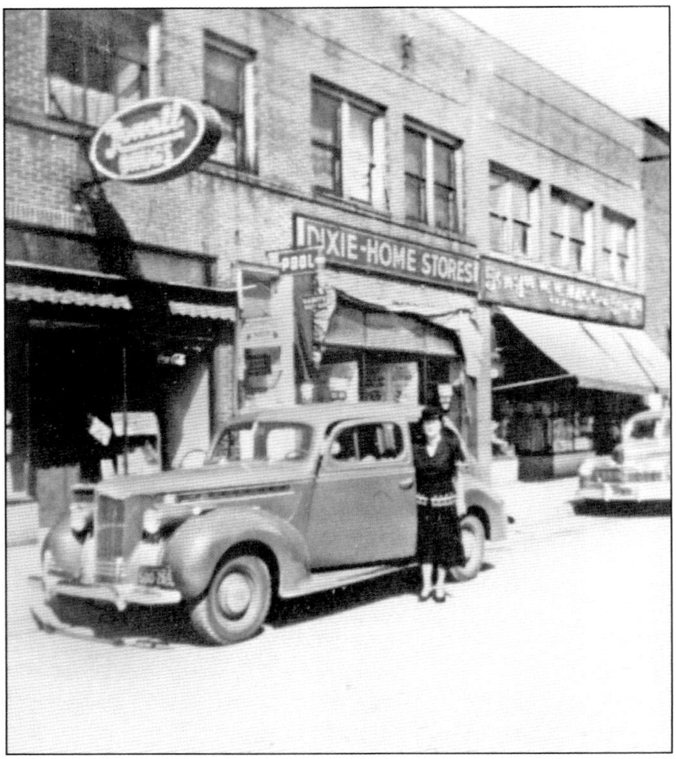


The Dixie Home Store on Lower Street occupied a spot between the Spruce Pine Pharmacy and the Co. Mac Dime Store. Based in Greenville, South Carolina, the store offered groceries and other products to shoppers, and in 1955, it merged with the Winn-Lovett Stores to form the Winn Dixie supermarket chain. (Courtesy of John Wellborn.)

# *Three*

# CHALK AND SLATE
## A MINER MAKES HIS MARK

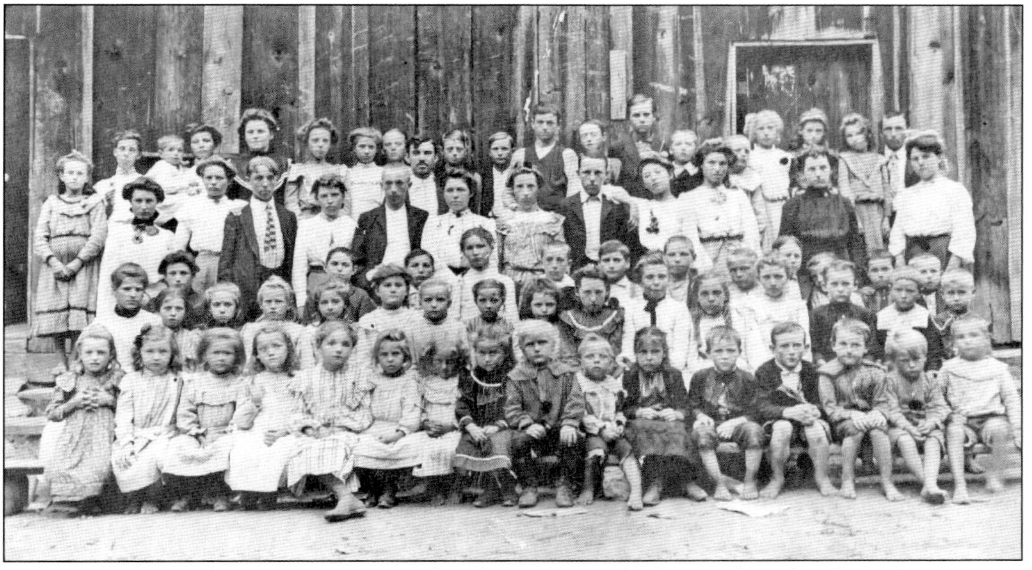

This image shows the Mount Vernon School in 1906. In the late 19th and early 20th centuries, education took place in small one-room schoolhouses in many Mitchell County communities. One of the earliest schools in Spruce Pine was the Mount Vernon School, which was located in the Beaver Creek area. Pictured from left to right are (first row) Annie Washburn, ? Proffitt, Zula Fisher, unidentified, ? Proffitt, Marjorie Davenport, unidentified, Edith Grumley, Bela Berry, Richard Wiseman, Mrs. Joe Patrick, unidentified, Lawrence Autrey, Rom Duncan, and two unidentified; (second row) unidentified, Jamima Biggerstaff, Myrtle Davenport, ? Washburn, Helen Fisher, Stella Fisher, Nell Swann, Essie Biggerstaff, Lizzie Pendley, Edith Rowe, Mae Patrick, Virdie Patrick, Annie Harrison, Dowe Woody, Spence Autrey, and unidentified; (third row) Julie Rose, Walter Buchanan, unidentified, Sadie Duncan, Avery Rose, unidentified, Ed Buchanan, Bill Wiseman, two unidentified, Lonnie Gunter, and Lynn Davenport; (fourth row) Ora Duncan, unidentified, Eva Washburn, Ben Biggerstaff, Bertie Pendley, Arthur Rose, Grace Blalock, Clara Rose, Lane Rowe, Kate Blalock, Minnie Buchanan, Edith Rowe, and Maude Wiseman; (fifth row) Eva Patrick, Irma Fisher, Bill Fisher, Mable Wiseman, Aby Biggerstaff, Carrie Harrison, Sadie Wiseman, Charlie Slagle, Arthur Washburn, Dudley Berry, Dallas Duncan, Isaac Duncan, Willis Gunter, Lindsey Pendley, Robert Wiseman, Bess Berry, unidentified, Essie Buchanan, and Paul Rose. (Courtesy of Chris Hollifield.)

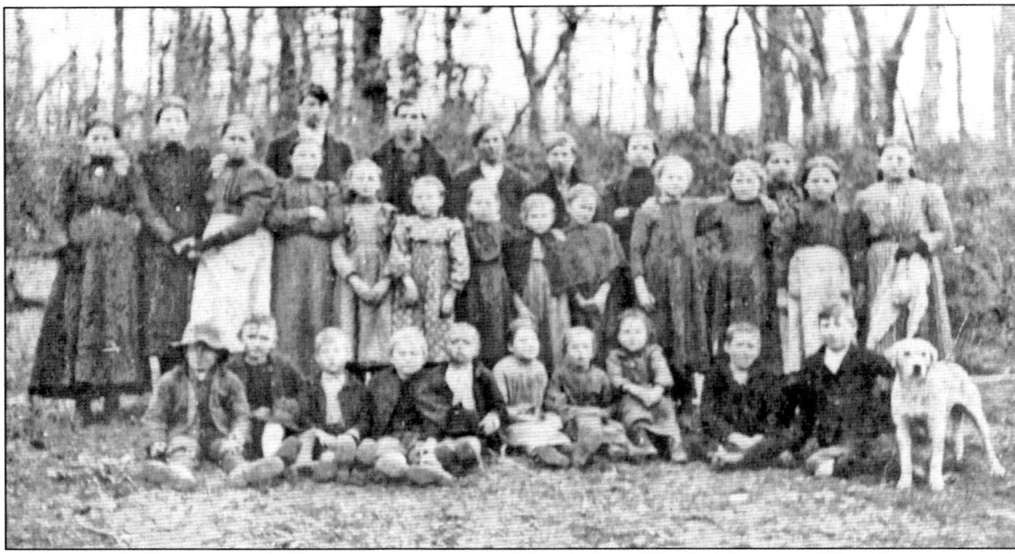

Ada Greenlee was the teacher for this group of students in 1909. This school was located in the Halltown community. The teacher in a community school was responsible for every student's education, from the youngest to the oldest, all in the same room. Even the dog came to school on this day. (Courtesy of Elizabeth Davenport.)

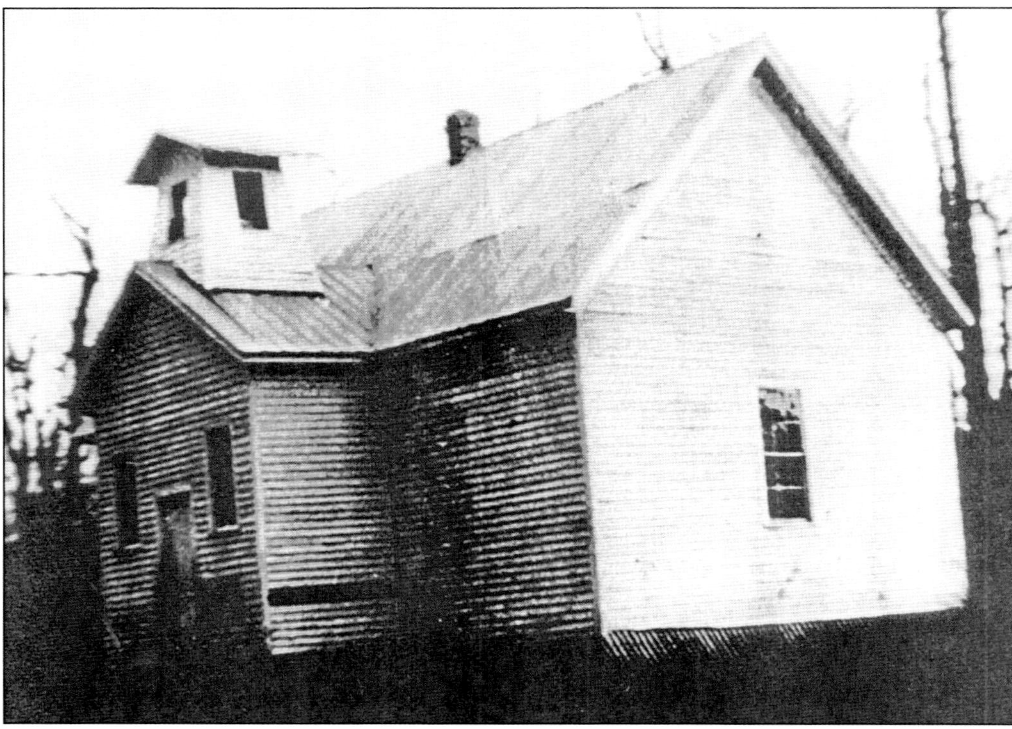

The Wiseman School was located near the intersection of Dula and Dale Roads in the Grassy Creek community, south of Spruce Pine. In 1939, there were 14 such schools in Mitchell County. The building in this picture was typical of a small community school of that time. (Courtesy of Max Gouge.)

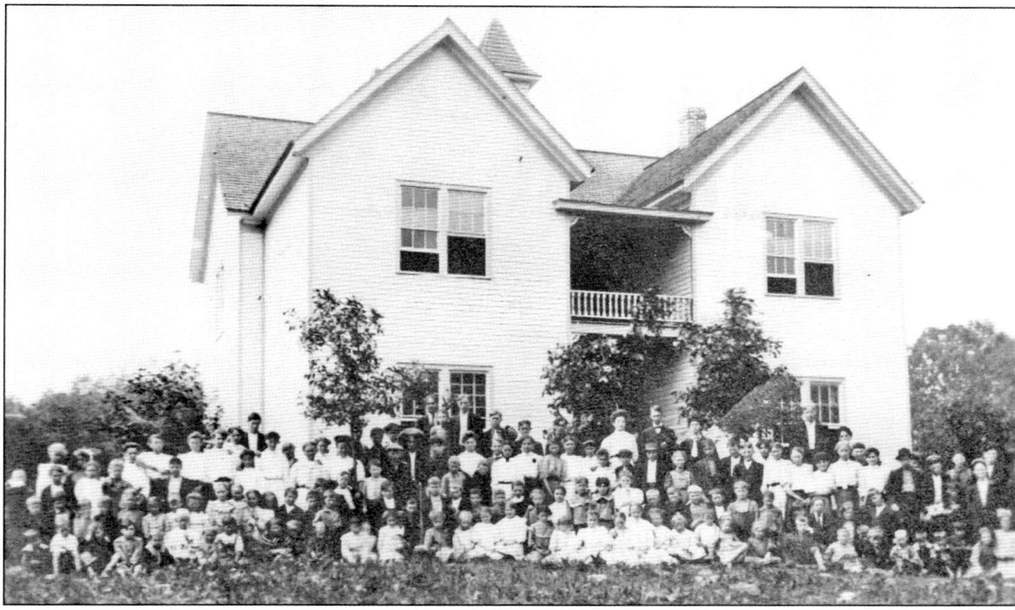

These images show Spruce Pine School in 1907 (above) and 1917 (below). After the coming of the railroad in 1903, Spruce Pine grew into a sizeable town. During this time, it would develop its own school system. The first public high school in Mitchell County, as well as an elementary school, were erected in Spruce Pine when the town was incorporated in 1907. A 2-acre plot was sold to school officials for $25 by T. A. English and J. L English, Isaac English's sons, on which the building in this picture was constructed. Before this time, about 100 students attended a school that had been situated near the English Inn and aided by the Presbyterian church. (Above, courtesy of Elvira Bryant; below, courtesy of Elizabeth Davenport.)

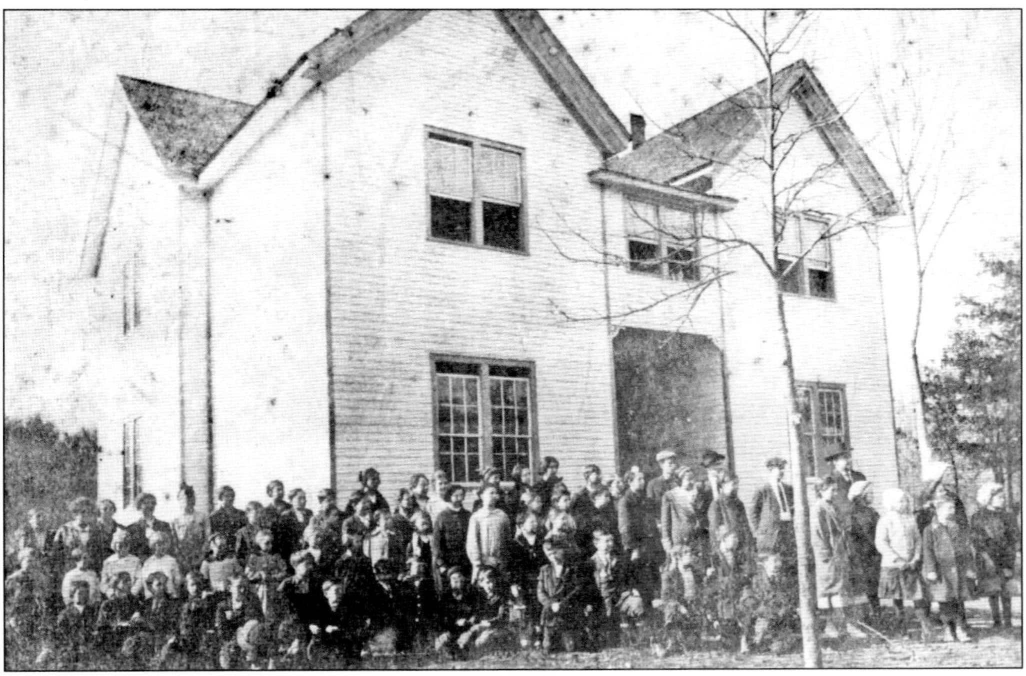

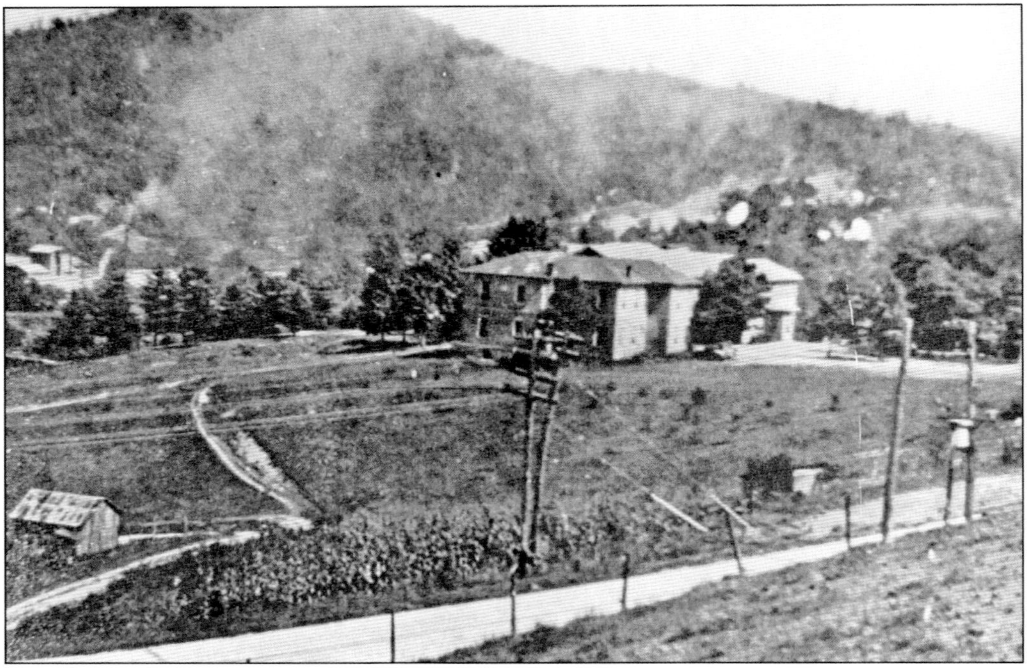

With the growth of the town, there arose a need for land on which to build a new and larger school. Col. C. J. Harris donated a 10.5-acre tract surrounding the existing school plot, which was part of his mining interest, across the river from the town on which to build the new school. Several large brick structures were constructed as part of the Harris School complex over the years. At first glance, it would seem that the new school would take its name from its benefactor—C. J. Harris. However this would not be the case. Colonel Harris and his family requested that the school be named in honor of his brother Dr. William Torrey Harris, who had died in 1909. The Pinebridge complex is located there today. (Above, courtesy of Elivra Bryant; below, courtesy of Geraldine Canipe.)

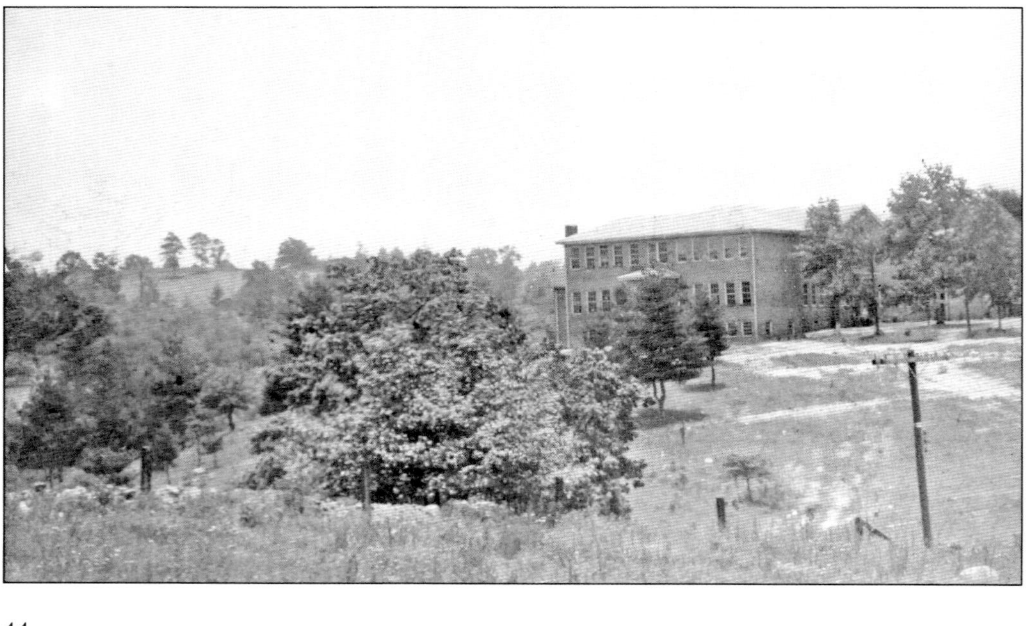

Dr. William Torrey Harris (1835–1909) was born in North Killingly, Connecticut. He was appointed U.S. commissioner of education in 1889. He was known for innovation in education while serving as superintendent of the St. Louis, Missouri, schools, establishing America's first permanent public kindergarten there in 1873. He also edited the *Webster's International Dictionary* from 1900 to 1909 and helped produce the Appleton series of schoolbooks. (Courtesy of Chris Hollifield.)

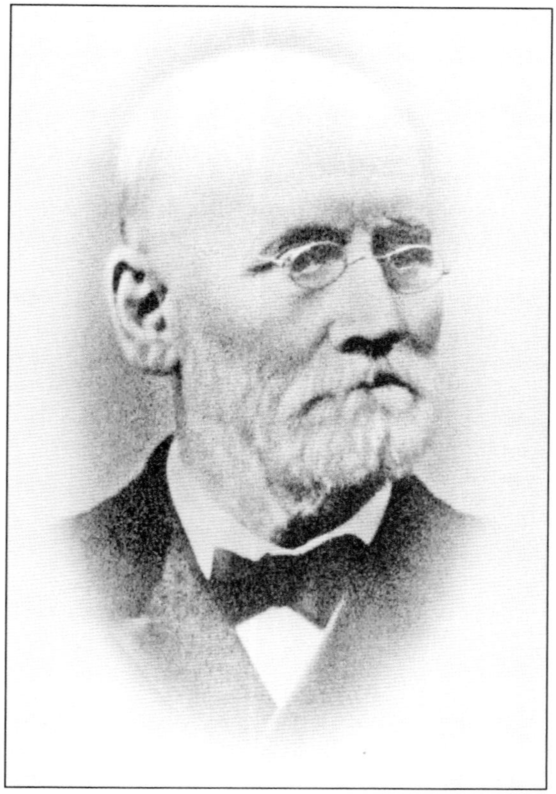

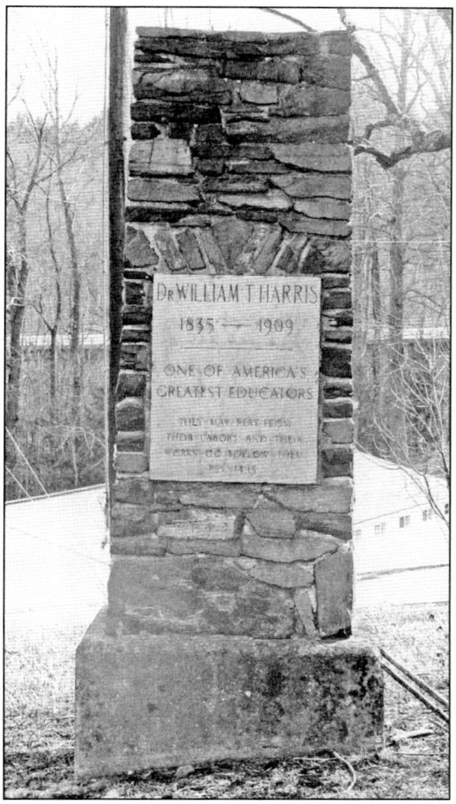


When Charles J. Harris agreed to donate land to expand the Spruce Pine School, he and his family requested that the new campus take the name of his brother William Torrey Harris. Today a monument in Harris's honor stands on the site of the school, the present location of Pinebridge. It was erected in 1925 and dedicated at a ceremony honoring Harris and his contributions. (Courtesy of David Biddix.)

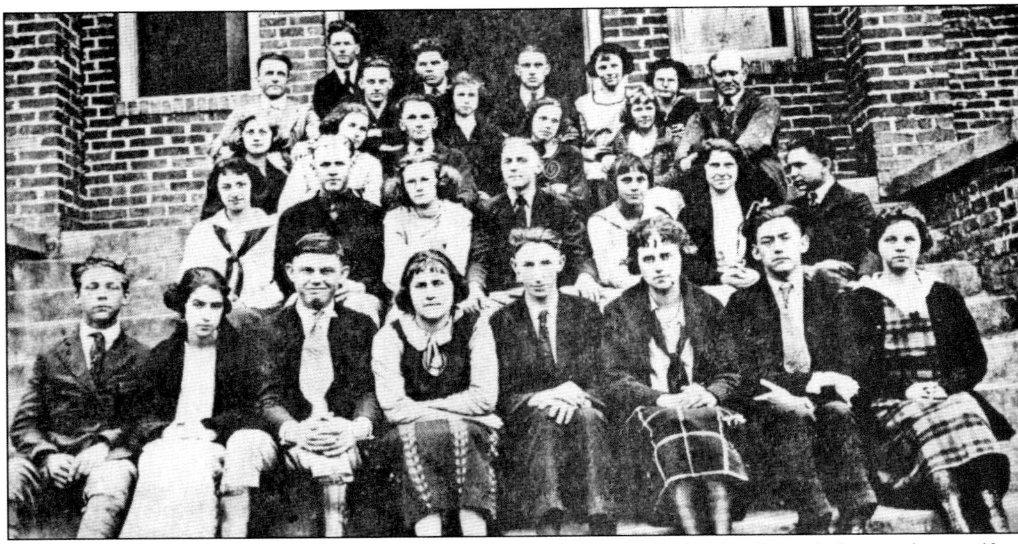

The Harris High School student body is pictured in the spring of 1922. From left to right are (first row) Guy Wiseman, Josephine McCullough, Ed Fortner, Elizabeth Lawson, Lewis McCullough, a Miss Cochran (teacher), William Hickey, and Jane McKinney; (second row) Agnes English, Bill McKinney, Lois Dodson, Robert Phillips, Lillian Wiseman, Belle Sparks, and David Farr; (third row) Roberto Renfro, Neva Lovin, Sam English, Bertie Wilkie, Blanche Buchanan, Willie Dodson, and Carson Lawson (teacher); (fourth row) Sherman Holloway (principal), Conley Hollifield, Caesar Gardner, Tom Sullins, Otto Poteat, Pearl Wright, and Anna Hickey. (Courtesy of Chris Hollifield.)

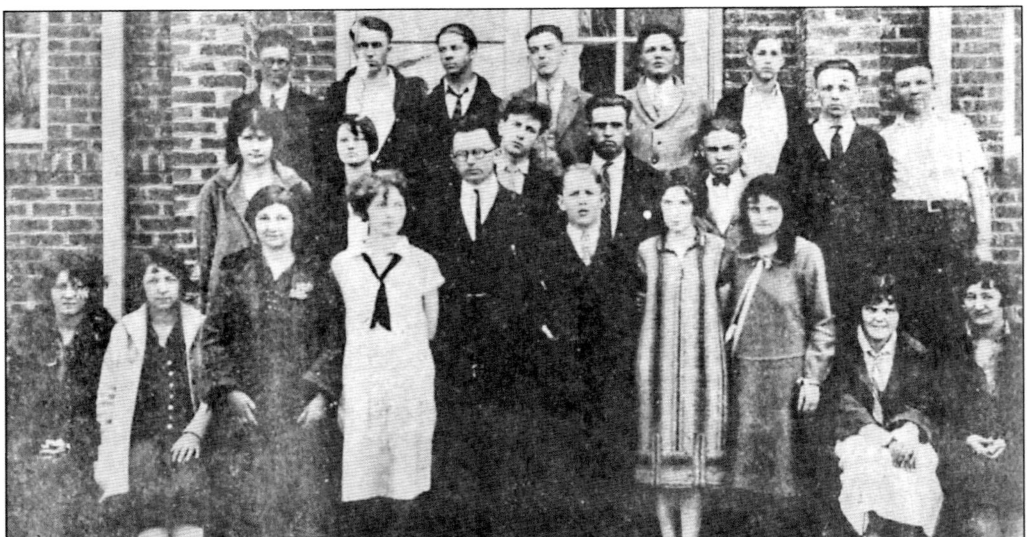

The 1925–1926 Harris sophomores are pictured here. From left to right are (first row) a Miss Davis and a Miss McIntire (teachers), Retta Willis, Hazel Turbyfield, Edd Warrick (principal), Albert Cannon, Mary McCoulough, Nell Buchanan, a Miss Parter (teacher), and a Miss Chestnut (teacher); (second row) Ruth Loven, Mae McBee, Hall Houch, Brown Buchanan, Carl Gunter Sr., Roy Gunter, and Scott Hickey; (third Row) Waldo Presnell, Milt Young, Jack Tappan, Jack Burleson, Rom Sparks, and Lawrence Stewart. (Courtesy of Chris Hollifield.)

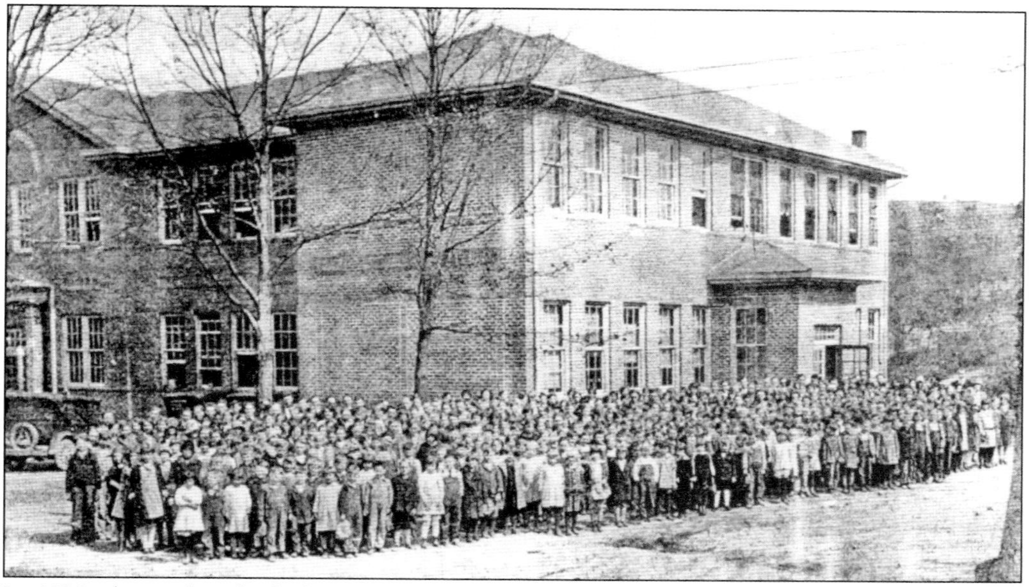

In 1928, the student body (pictured above) and faculty (shown below) of the Harris School posed for these photographs. There were 13 students in the graduating class. They were the first Harris class to have a yearbook and to take a trip to Washington, D.C. The faculty (not in order of the image) included Jason Deyton, William Hickey, E. W. Mease, Caroline Lee Young, Edith Wedekind, Emma Allison, Robert Phillips, Amelia Greenlee, Ruby Deyton, Virginia Person, Helen Johnson, Ann Lawrence, Earle Hill, Elva Ellis, Mary Hunter Cross, Lois Dodson, Anna Hickey, Mrs. C. B. Hollifield, Sarah Kathryn Leary, Mrs. Sam Knight, Rev. W. R. Smith, Rev. J. E. B. Houser, Pearl Pritchard, and Mrs. Roy Weld. They boasted impressive educational credentials. (Both, courtesy of Chris Hollifield.)

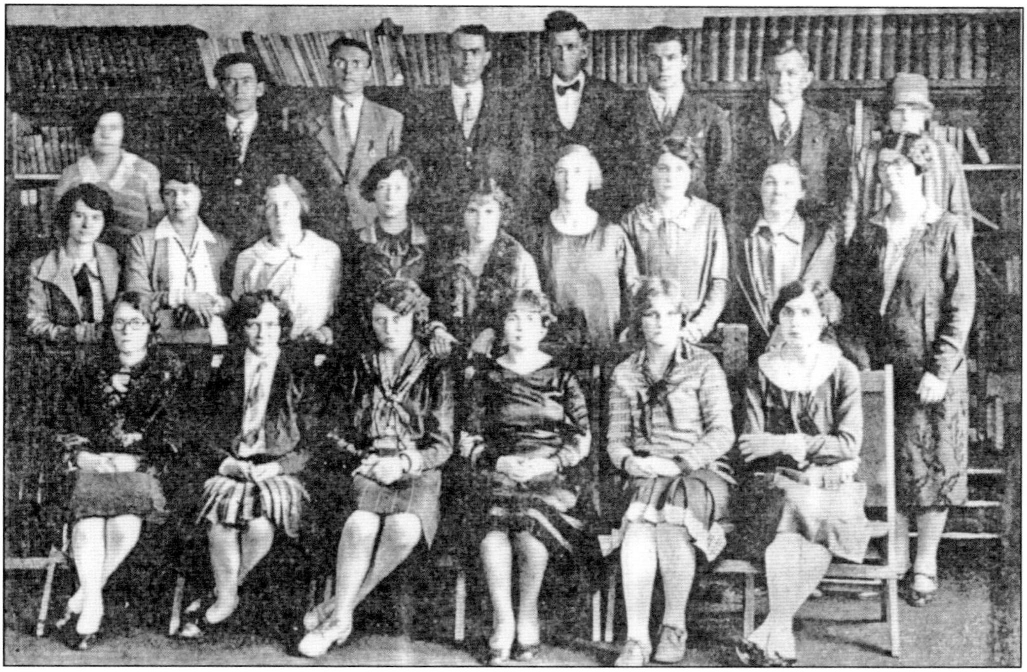

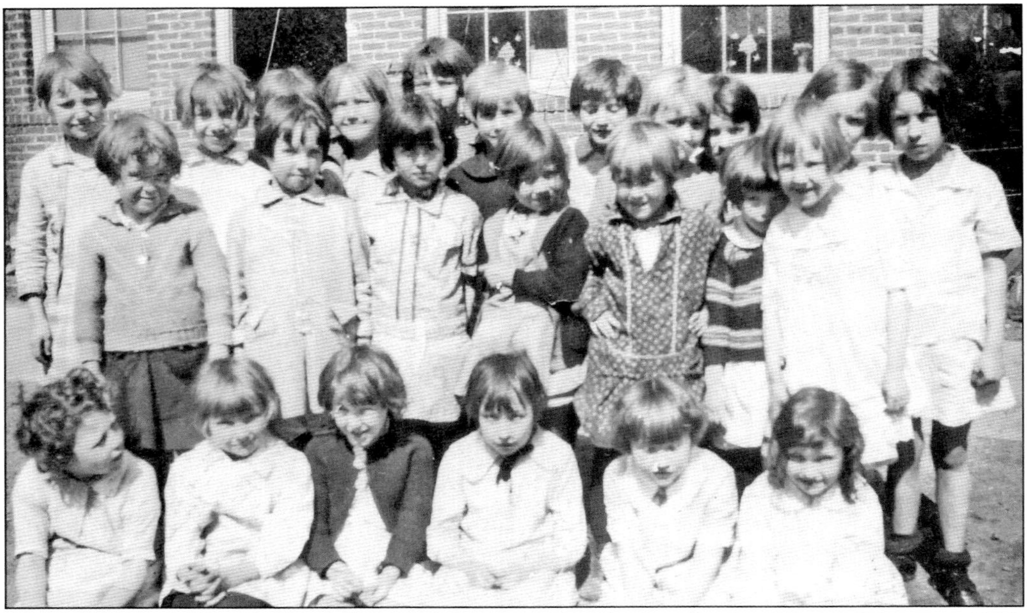

Jennie Willis Collis welcomed this motley crew to her first grade classroom at Harris in 1929. There are several unidentified children. Among the girls (pictured above) are, from left to right, (first row) Jennie Ellis, Mary Lee Snipes, Mary Lee Love, Helen Autrey, Mary Louise Phillips, and Mildred McNeil; (second row) Melba Young, Josephine Cox, Jewel McKinney, Lucille Sullins, Bell Riddle, Mary Riddle, Marie Pittman, and Madge Young; (third row) Lois Richardson at the far right. Among the boys (shown below) are, from left to right, (second row) Morrison Gunter, Ed Riddle, Claude Riddle second through fourth from the left, and a boy with the first name Pyatt second from right; (third row) Charles Sullins second from right and Lamar Rose at right. (Above, courtesy of Mary Lee Cuthbertson; below, courtesy of Richard and Peggy Riddle.)

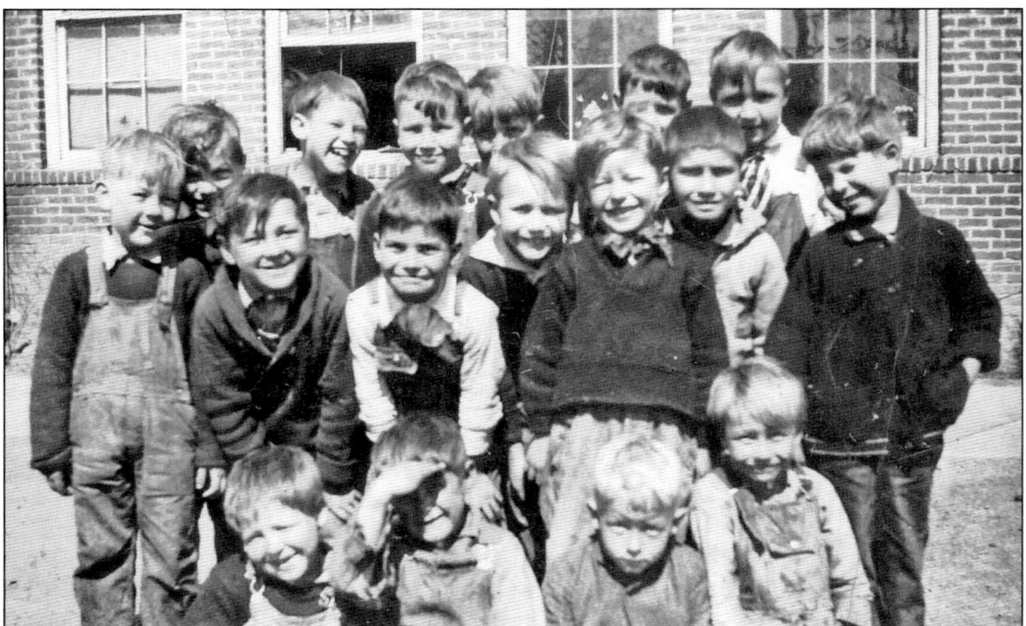

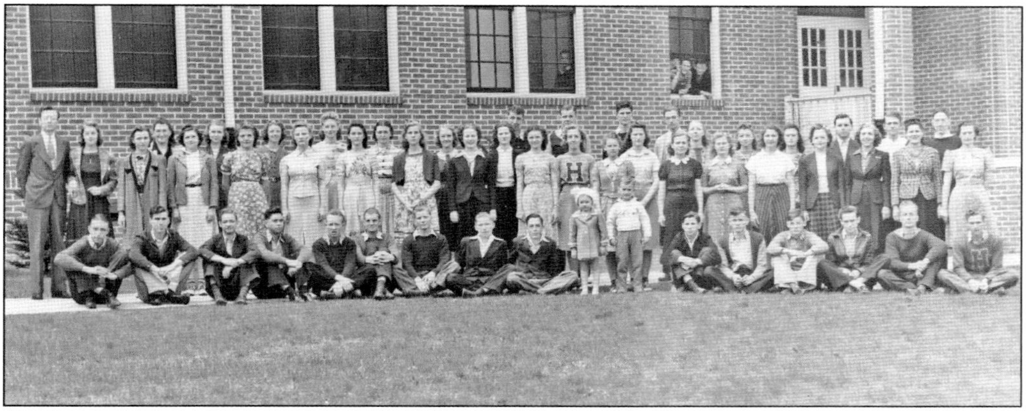

Eleven years after the photographs on the left, those students graduated as part of the Harris High class of 1940. Pictured above, from left to right, are (first row) Lamar Rose, Lee Lentz, Bill Queen, Robert Glass, Lee Dale, Charles Phillips, Bob Taylor, Harold Riddle, Jack Pendley, Jean Johnson (mascot), ? Wilson, Bill Pittman, Bill Dale, Rex McKinney, Paul Wilson, Paul Young, and Bill Burleson; (second row) principal Robert Phillips, Dr. Elizabeth Phillips, Marjorie McKinney, Lucy Glenn, June Garland, Myrtle Smith, Alice Rhyne, Marie Pittman, Marjorie Vance, Ruby McKinney, Mildred McNeil, Frankie Hall, Mary Carolyn Murray, Callie Brown, Wanda Brinkley, Oma Baker, Charles Sullins, Helen Bell, Fred Garland, Lois Lee Richards ("H"), unidentified, Clifford Pittman, Mary Louise Phillips, Reed Queen, Lucille Sullins, Emma Wright, Belle Riddle, Mary Lee Snipes, Minnie McGee, Sue Dale, Virginia Queen, Bill Wilkie, Wanda Hawley, Albert Smith, Gladys Buchanan, Jolly Duncan, and Pauline Ballew. Alvin Hollifield is in the window at the far right. The class appears in caps and gowns below. (Above, courtesy of Lucille Hovis; below, courtesy of Mary Lee Cuthbertson.)

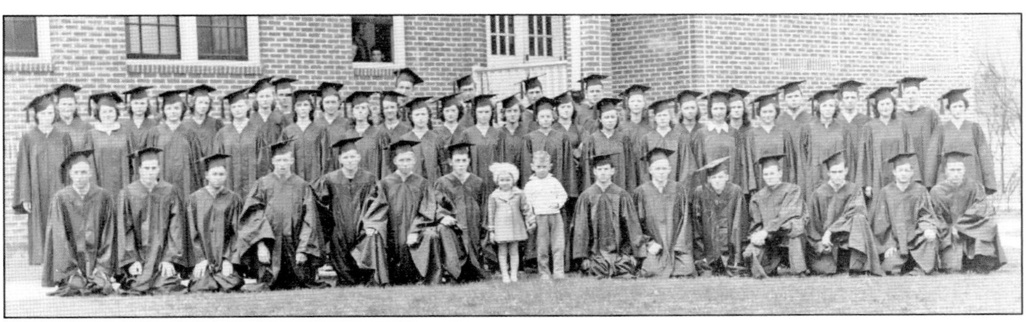

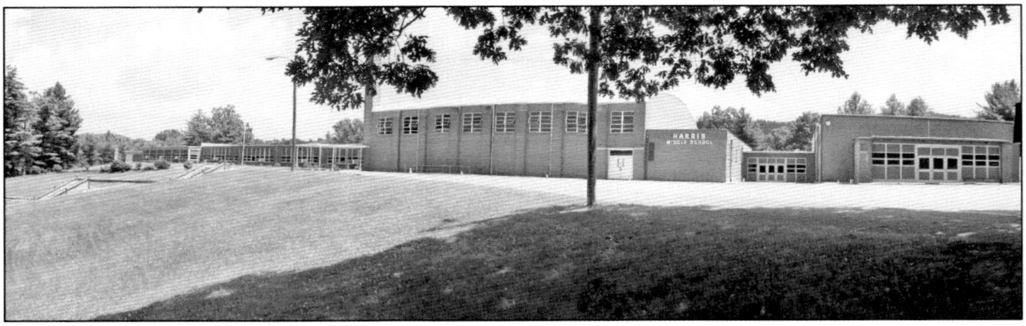

The Harris School campus is a familiar scene to most Spruce Pine residents who either attended high school or middle school in this location. The school opened to grades 9 through 12 in January 1951 and graduated 28 classes. The opening of Mitchell High School in 1978 converted it to a middle school, which it remains today. (Courtesy of Chris Hollifield.)

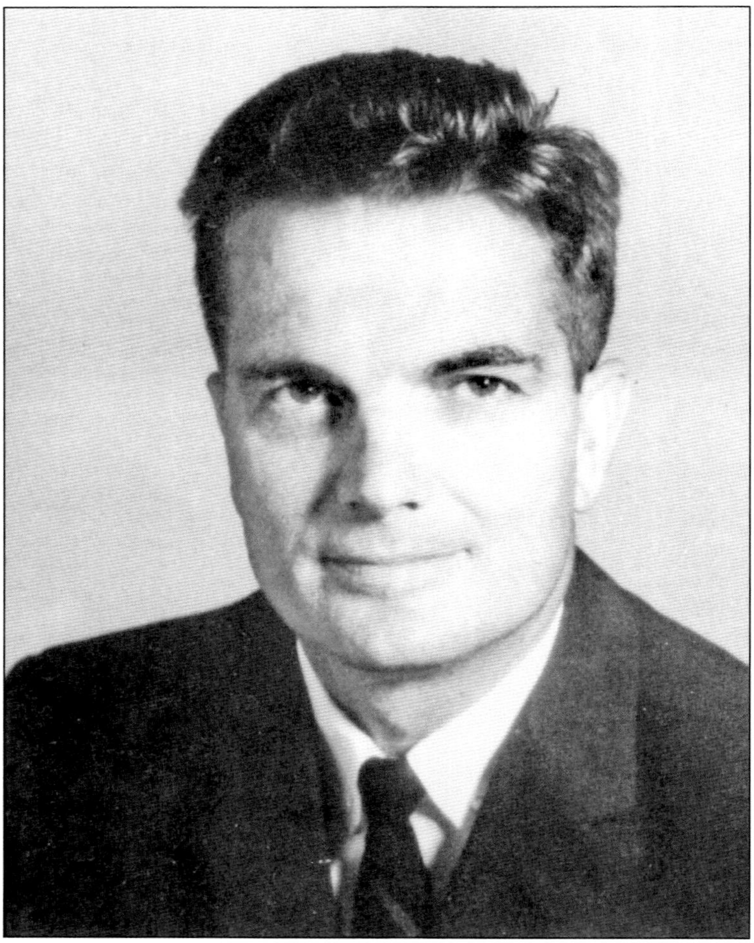

Bob Young served as principal of Harris High School from 1963 to 1978. He had a reputation of being firm but fair as principal, and the school prospered under his leadership. He later went on to serve as superintendent of Mitchell County Schools and as a member of the Mitchell County Board of Education and the Mayland Community College Board of Trustees. (Courtesy of David Biddix.)

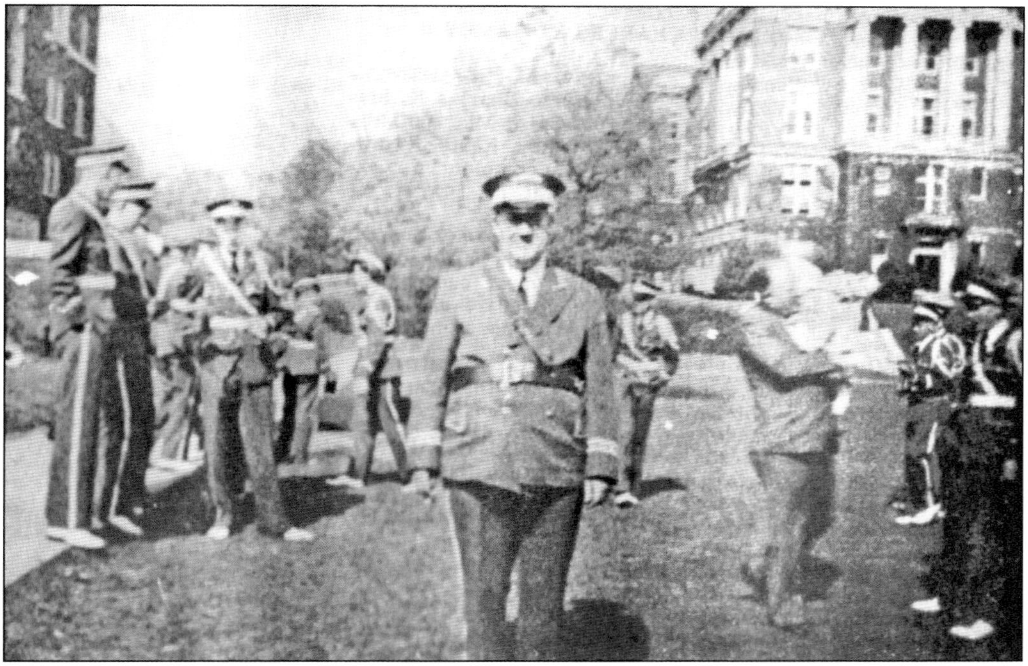

On April 27, 1939, the Harris High School Band, under the direction of J. I. "Doc" White, won the state championship in Greensboro. White is pictured here with the band at the competition. The victory was bittersweet because White passed away on June 18, 1939, just six weeks after the win. (Courtesy of the *Mitchell News-Journal.*)

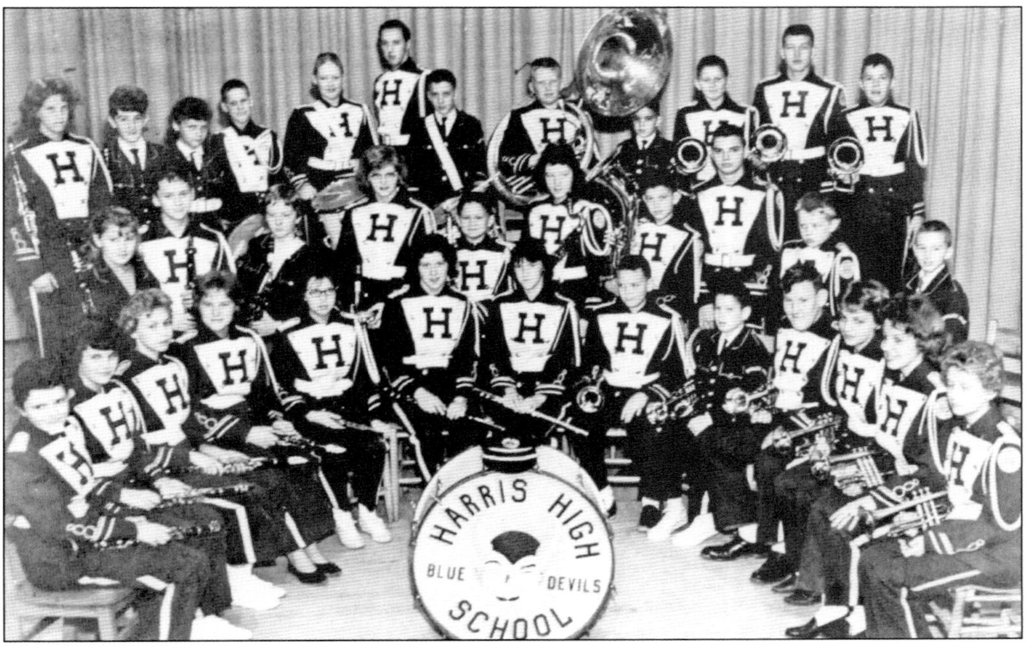


The 1962 Harris High Band poses for the camera. Directed by James Hall, the band performed at sports events and parades, and gave concerts to the community. With the prominent *H* on their chests, they led school spirit and pep for Harris teams and events. (Courtesy of David Biddix.)

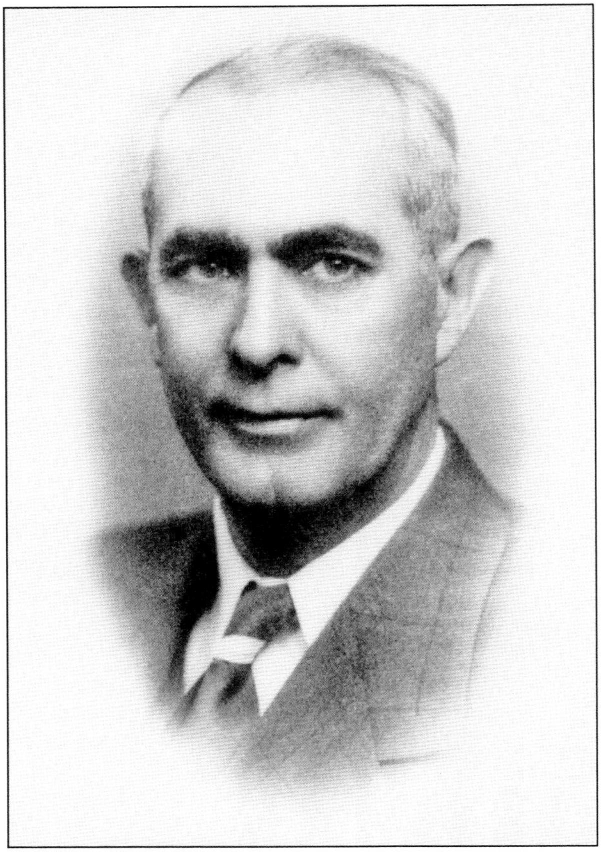

Jason B. Deyton was a noted educator. A graduate of schools in Mitchell County, Deyton held a degree from the University of North Carolina at Chapel Hill and did graduate work at Columbia University and Syracuse University. He served on the faculty and as principal of Harris High School, and was also superintendent of Mitchell County Schools. A noted historian, Deyton published *The History of the Toe River Valley to 1865*. (Courtesy of Chris Hollifield.)

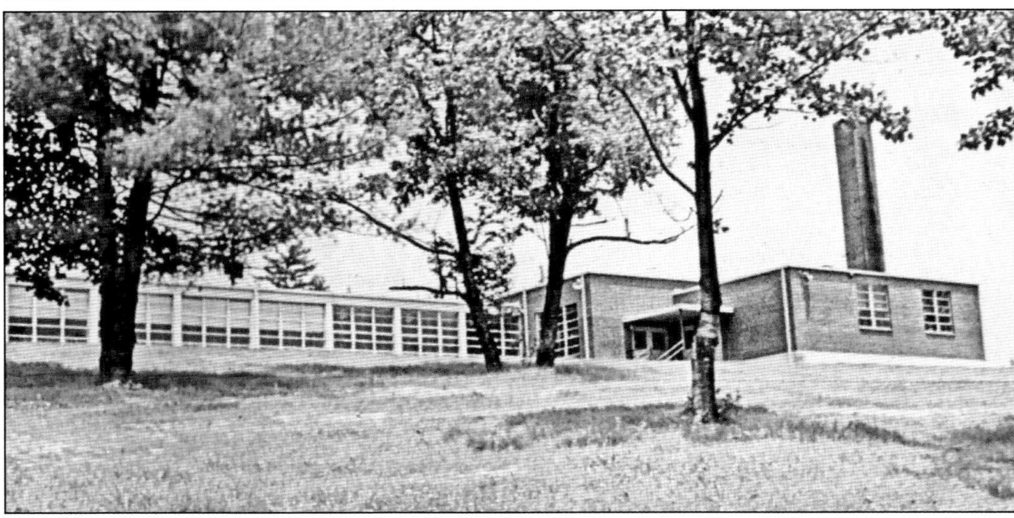

Named for Jason Deyton, the Deyton Elementary School opened in March 1957. It began with only the seventh and eighth grades, expanding in 1961 by adding fifth and sixth grades. In 1968, a gymnatorium was constructed. It served grades five through eight until 1978, when the opening of Mitchell High School prompted the move of grades kindergarten through third to Deyton and the creation of the Harris Middle School. (Courtesy of Chris Hollifield.)

Amelia Mears arrived in Spruce Pine in 1913 to teach at the new mission school at Grassy Creek Presbyterian Church. She married Sam Greenlee, son of one of the community's earliest settlers. She began working for Mitchell County Schools and was the first Mitchell County teacher to receive state retirement benefits in 1947. She was nominated for State Mother of the Year in 1958. (Courtesy of Elvira Bryant.)

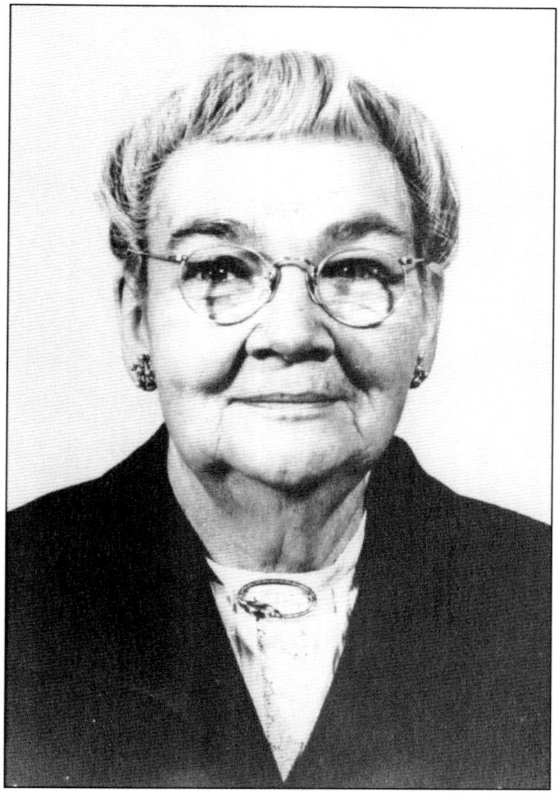

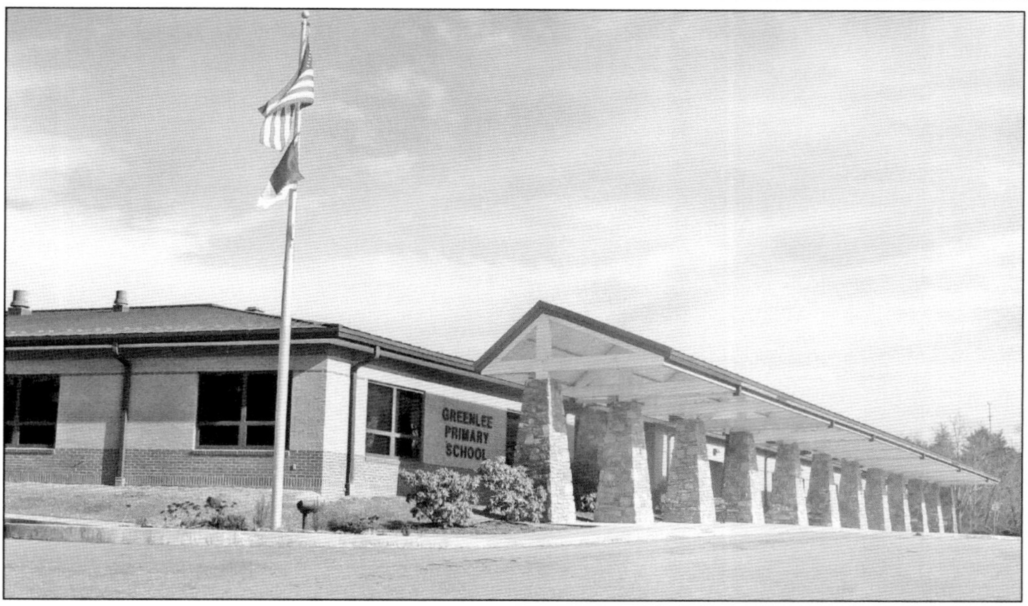


Greenlee Primary School, named for Amelia Greenlee, opened for kindergarten through second grade in 2001. Built to alleviate overcrowding at Harris and Deyton schools, Greenlee was constructed in the Grassy Creek community south of Spruce Pine, a departure from having schools inside the Spruce Pine city limits for nearly 100 years. (Courtesy of David Biddix.)

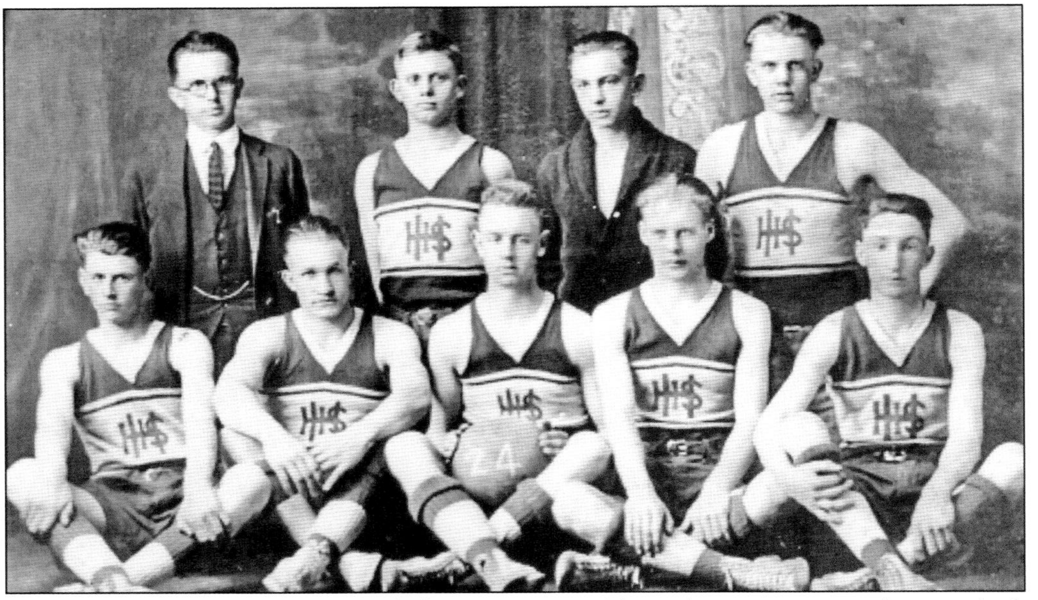

The 1924 Harris High School basketball team was one of the earliest sports teams photographed. Pictured, from left to right, are (first row) Beverly Loven, Ted Braswell, Lee Swann, Fletcher Phillips, and Louis McCullough; (second row) Edd Warrick (principal and coach), Frank Ellis, David Farr, and Claude Ellis. (Courtesy of Chris Hollifield.)

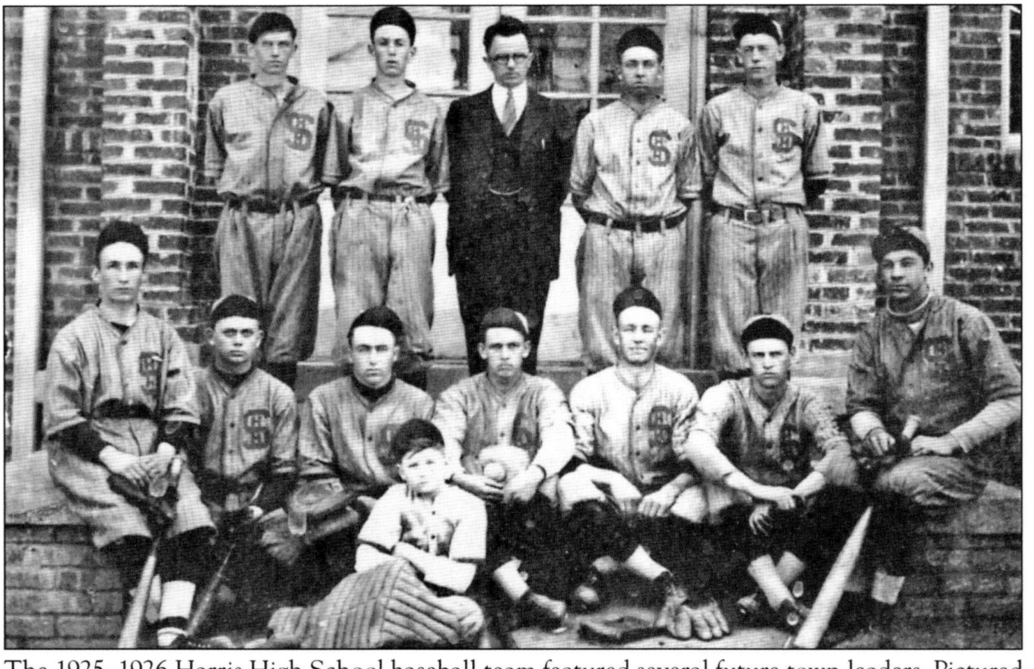

The 1925–1926 Harris High School baseball team featured several future town leaders. Pictured from left to right are (first row) Brown Willis, Frank Ellis, Milt Young, Brown Buchanan, Lee Swann, Beverly Loven, and Jack Tappan; (second row) Bill Hall, Ottis Greene, Edd Warrick (coach and principal), Edd Swann, and Howard Glenn. The batboy is Howard Burleson. (Courtesy of Chris Hollifield.)

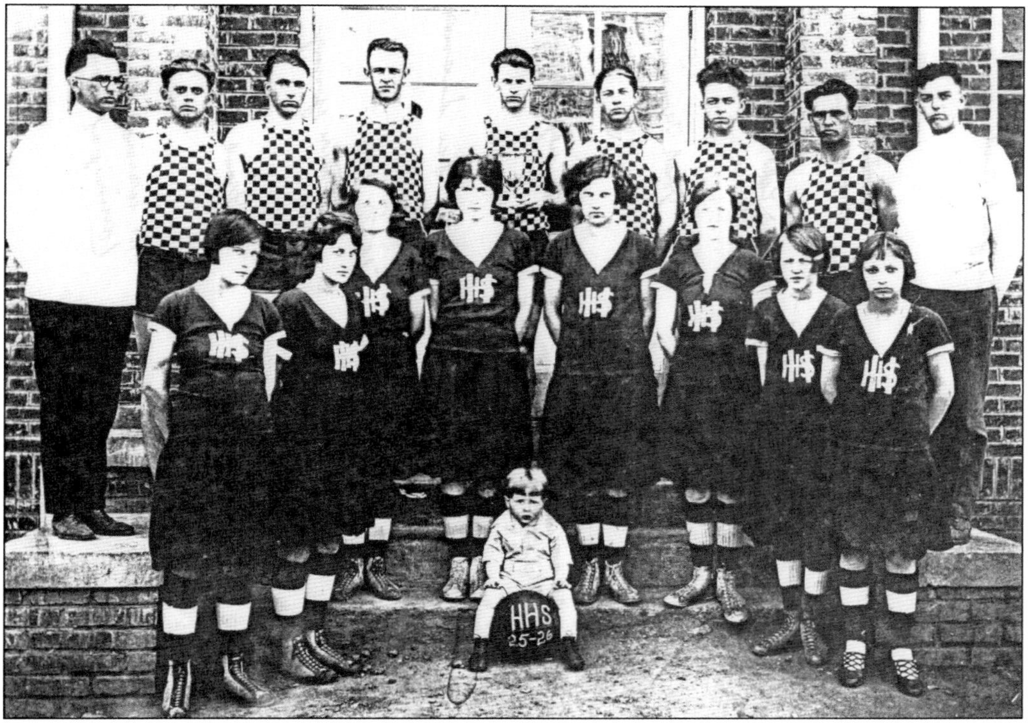


The 1925–1926 Harris High girls' and boys' basketball teams are pictured. From left to right are (first row) Georgia Wright, Lillian Turbyfill, Lena Phillips, Ruth Loven, Nola Houck, Marjorie Ward, Grace Davenport, and Maude Young; (second row) Edd Warrick (principal and coach), Frank Ellis, Milt Young, Lee Swann, Beverly Loven, Jack Tappan, Edd Swann, Brown Buchanan, and Jack Burleson. The mascot was Edward Warrick Jr. (Courtesy of Chris Hollifield.)

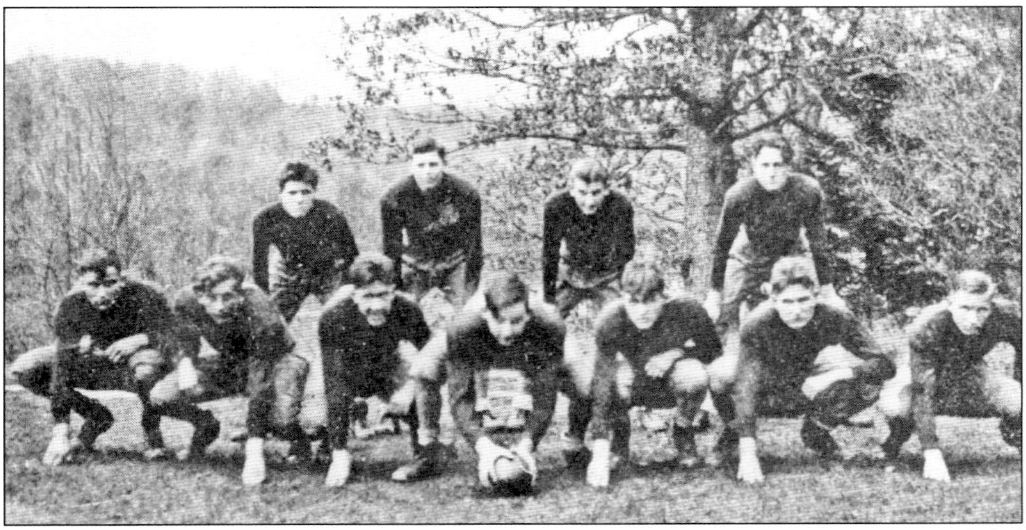

The 1927 Harris High football team was the first one fielded by the school. Team members included Paul Gouge, George Bartlett, Otto Sullins, J. W. Gilbert, Stokes Henry, Lawrence Buchanan, Norman Berry, Dick Reid, Bob Gilbert, George Ellis, and Phillip Young. The 1928 team won all six of its games and the Tri-County Conference championship. (Courtesy of Chris Hollifield.)

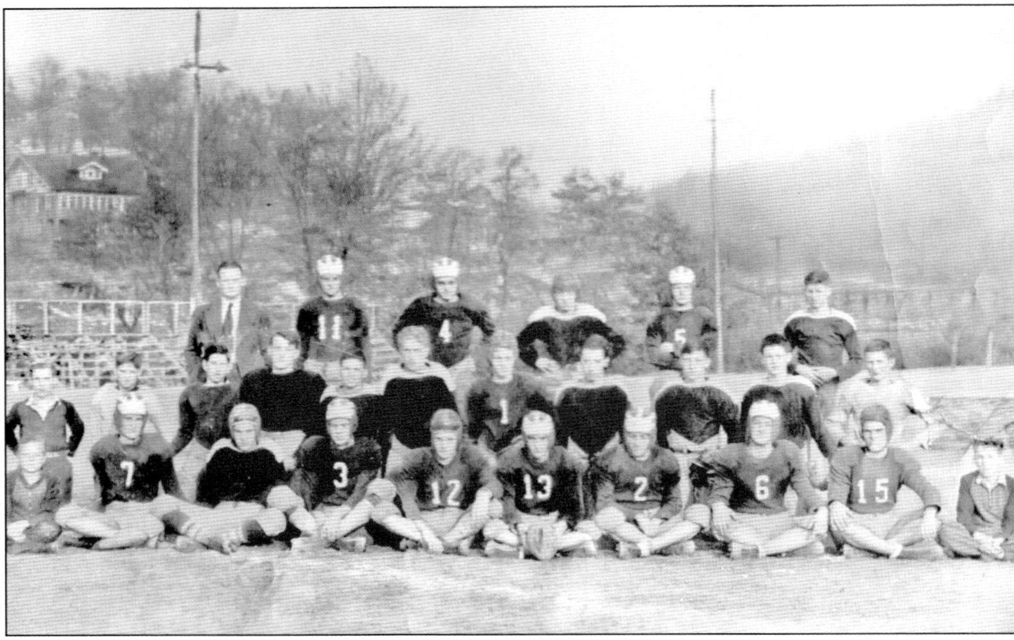

The 1939 Harris High School football team faced Charlie "Choo-Choo" Justice and the Lee Edwards High School Cougars. C. A. "Chauncey" Humphries was the coach. The photograph was taken on the old Deyton Field in downtown Spruce Pine, now Riverside Park. (Courtesy of Richard and Peggy Riddle.)

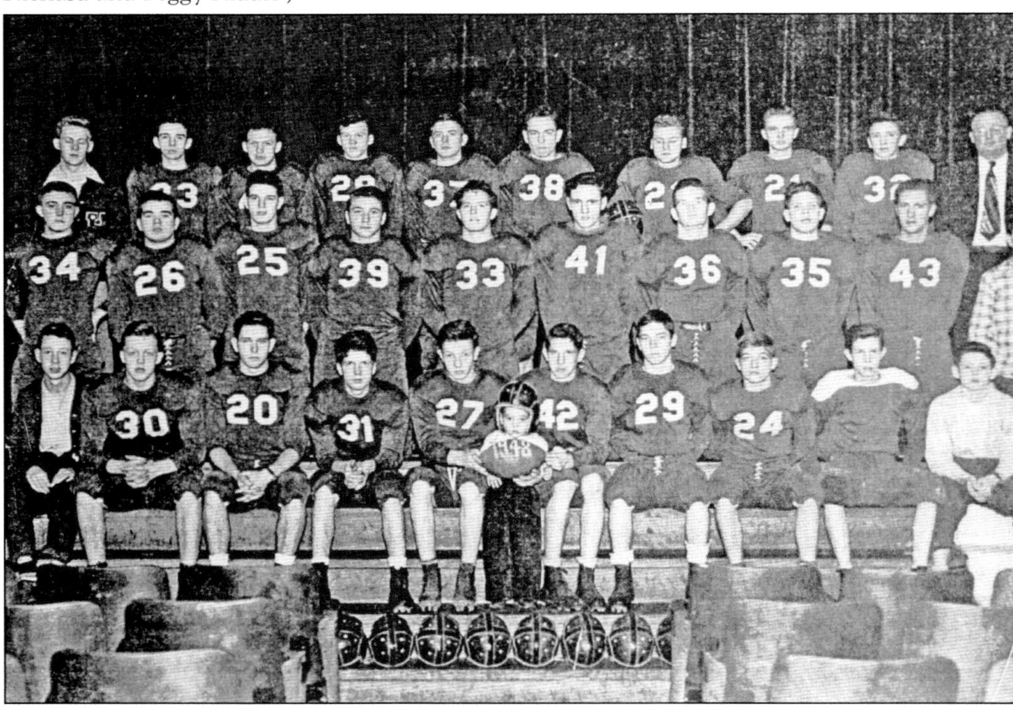

The 1948 Harris High School football team is pictured on the stage of the old auditorium. C. A. "Chauncey" Humphries was also coach of this team. (Courtesy of Guss McKinney.)

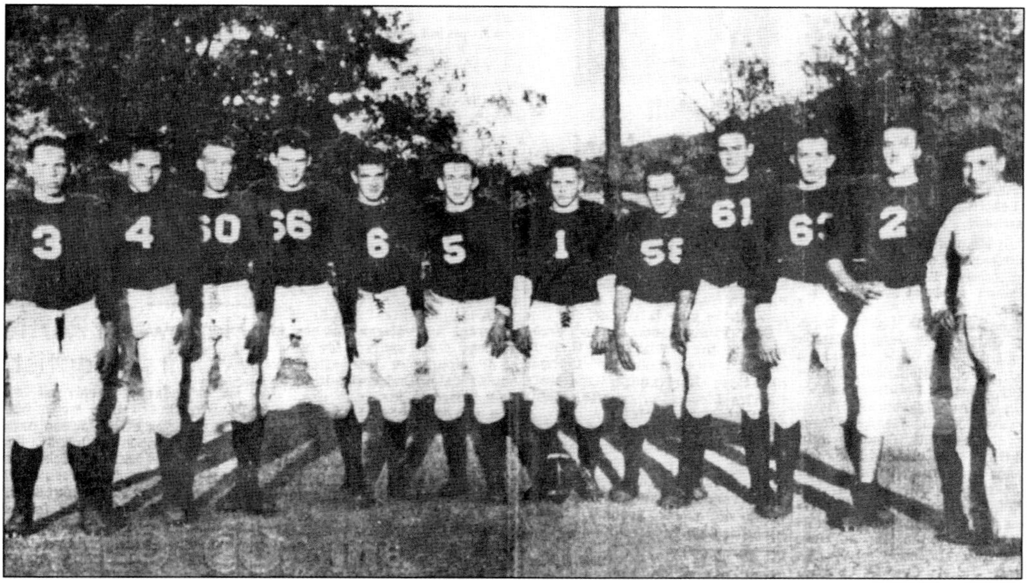

Coach Lee Willis's 1954–1955 Harris High squad secured the Skyline Conference championship with a 25-0 win over Glen Alpine. The first-string players, from left to right, are Clarence Hise, Jimmy Phillips, Wayne Pitman, Charles Boone, Fred Medford, Charles Sproles, Buzzy Henline, Harrison Glenn, Marion Swann, Gary McAllister, Gaylon Hefner, and coach Lee Willis. (Courtesy of Spruce Pine Public Library.)

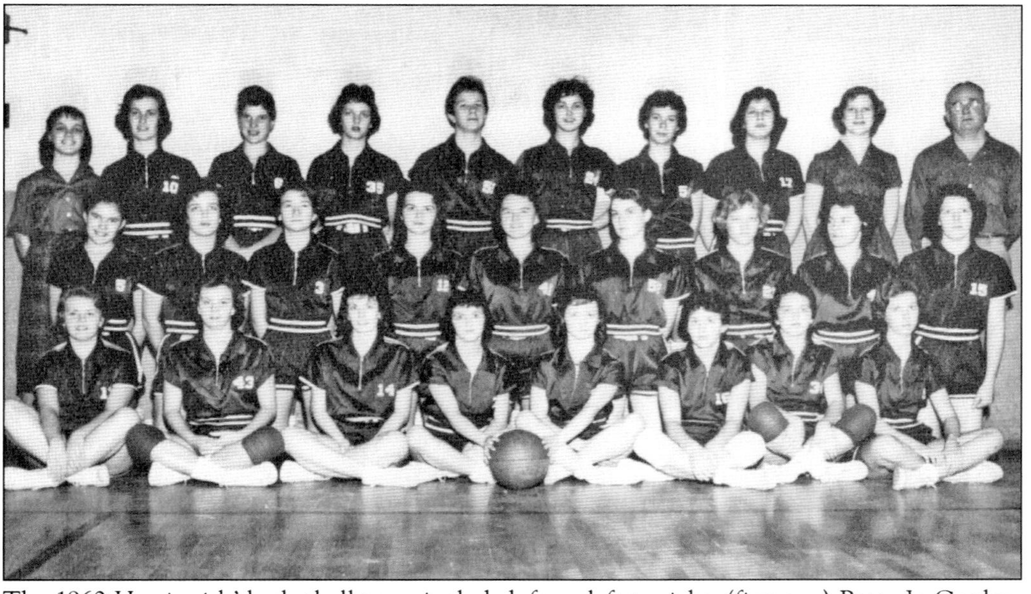

The 1960 Harris girls' basketball team included, from left to right, (first row) Betty Jo Garden, Melinda Hall, Edith Wyatt, Patsy Carpenter, Sammie Parsley, Janice Holtsclaw, Connie Taylor, and Beverly Sparks; (second row) Sara Williams, Gay Cox, Myrtle McKinney, Beth Bartlett, Kathy Bartlett, Loretta Cox, Gail Biddix, Angie Burleson, and Shirley Burleson; (third row) Kay Aldridge (manager), Carolyn Stout, Joan Phillips, Linda Buchanan, Mary Tappan, Judy Swann, Jean McKinney, Corena Dayton, Nancy Peterson (manager), and C. A. Humphries (coach). (Courtesy of Richard and Peggy Riddle.)

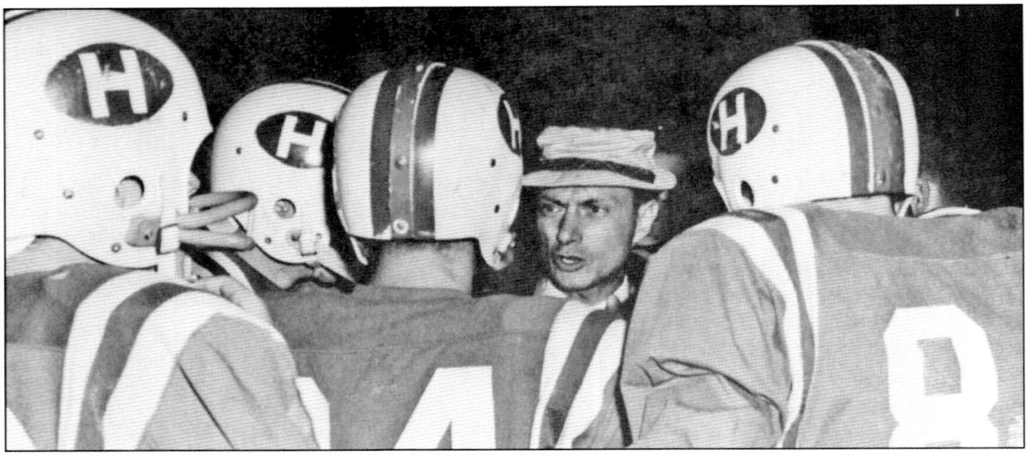

Doug Greene took over the reins of Harris football in 1963, winning Appalachian and Blue Ridge Conference championships in the late 1960s and losing in the Western State championship games to Robbinsville and to Murphy. Pictured below are assistant coaches Leland Riddle, Randy Buchanan, Harry Anderson, and Phil McKinney with coach Greene in the 1970s. He retired from coaching in 1979, later becoming Mitchell County Schools superintendent. (Courtesy of David Biddix.)

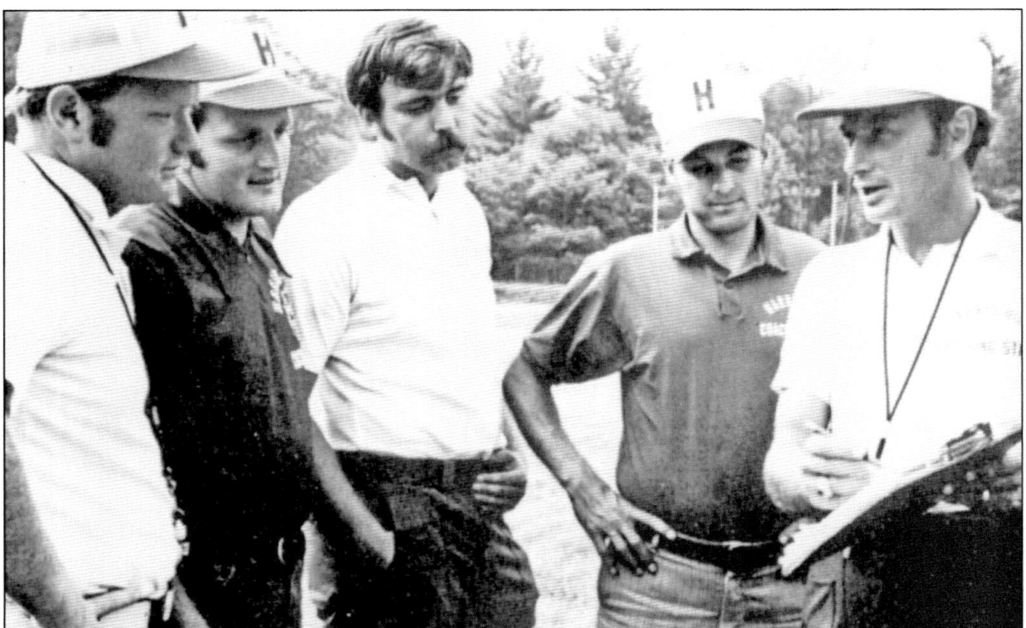

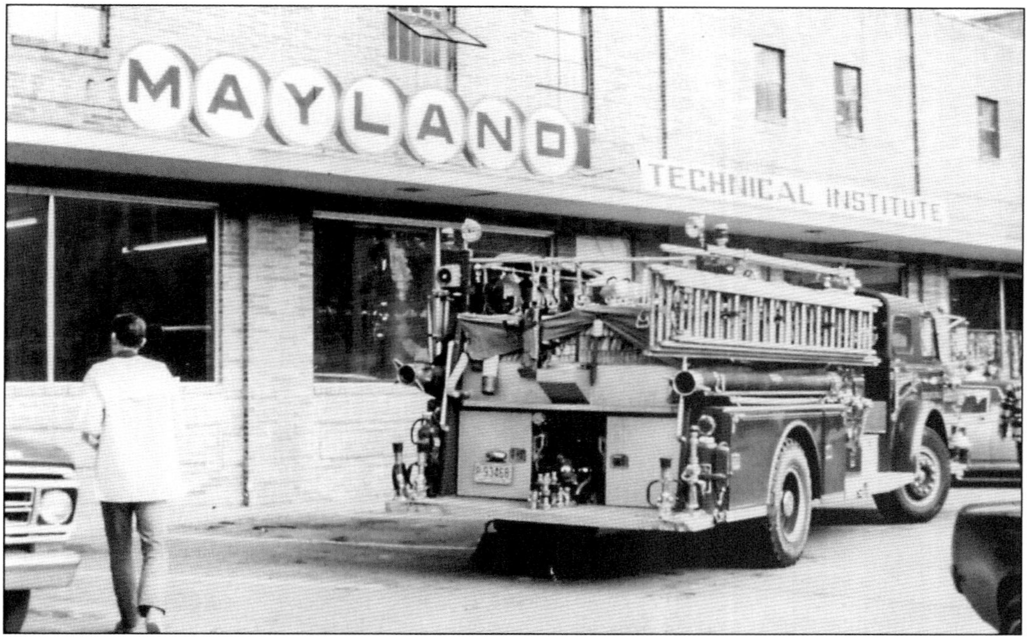


Opening in 1971 in space rented from the Northwestern Bank, the Mayland Technical Institute (MTI) became the first (and only) community college serving three counties in North Carolina. Named for the region it serves (Mitchell, Avery, and Yancey, with *land* on the end), Mayland used rented space on Upper Street while a campus was being constructed. The old Mayland Foods building was where the cosmetology and construction programs were housed. (Courtesy of Mayland Community College.)

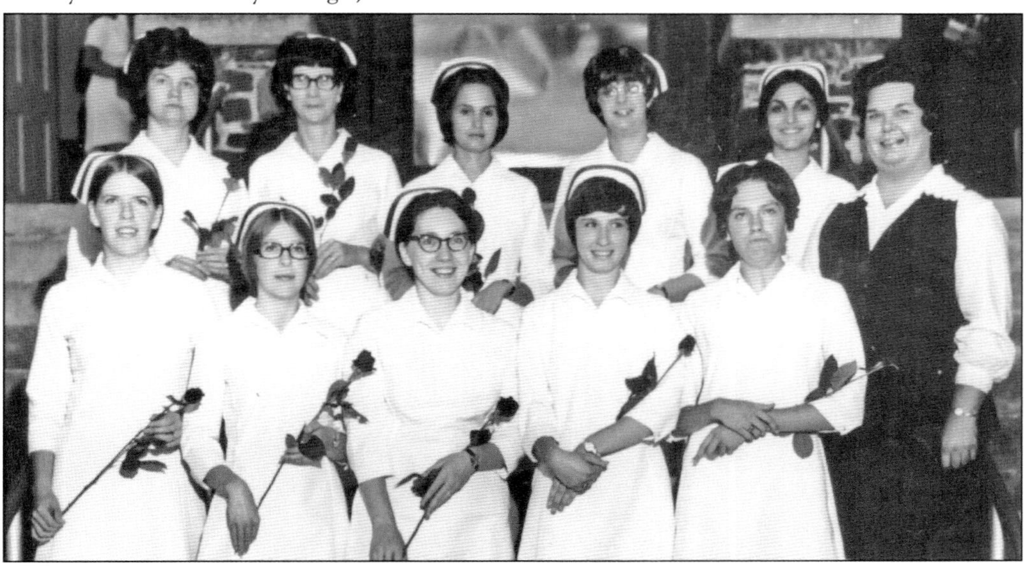

The first graduating nursing class of Mayland Technical Institute is pictured above. From left to right are (first row) Sheilah Puckett Banner, Doris Weatherman Biggs, Lynda M. Freshour, Beverly Ann Greer Isaccs, and Juanita Nash; (second row) Rosemary A. Nefos, Beverly Gragg Ollis, Barbara Ann McKinney, Patricia Cox Silver, Linda Kaye Townsend, and Irene Blevins, program head. (Courtesy of Mayland Community College.)

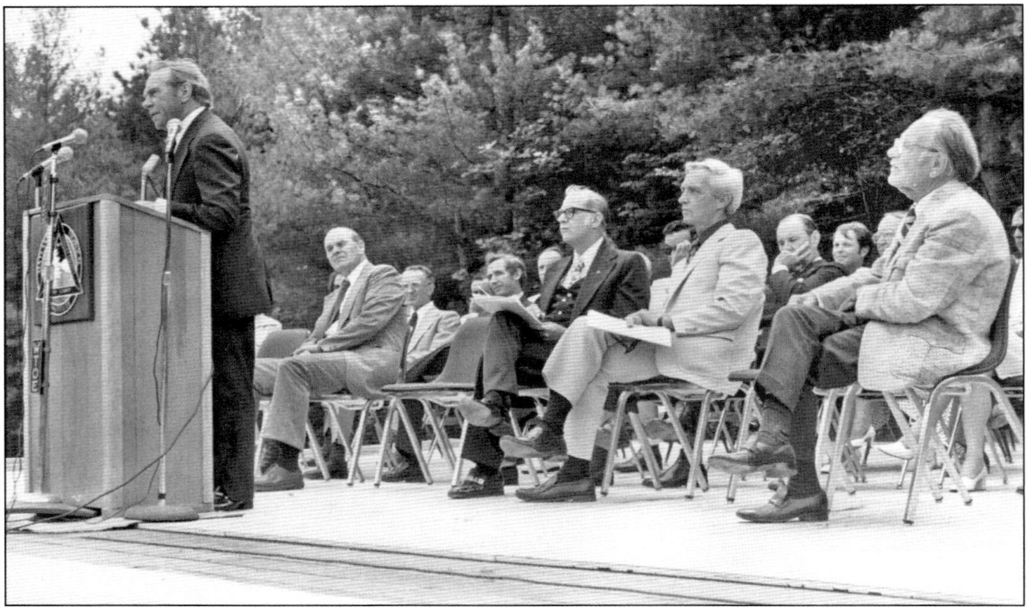

North Carolina lieutenant governor Jimmy Green speaks at the dedication of the new Mayland Technical Institute campus on Highway 19-E at the Avery and Mitchell County line on May 22, 1977. Pictured behind Green, from left to right, are Rev. R. M. Cassity, MTI president O. M. Blake, board of trustees chair Bill Wilkins, and board member O. V. "Bud" Talley. (Courtesy of Mayland Community College.)

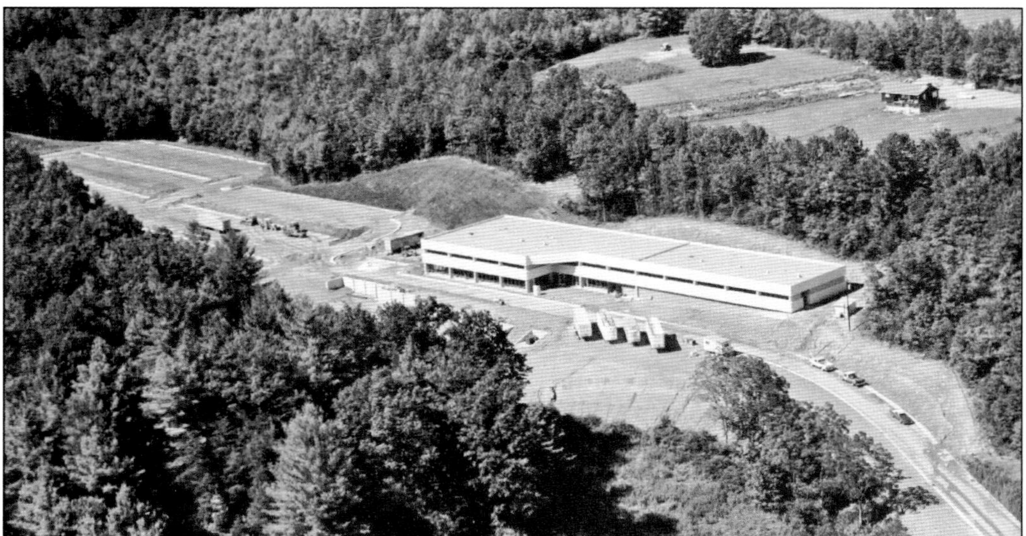

The finishing touches are being made on the new campus for Mayland Technical Institute. MTI changed its name to Mayland Technical College in 1979 and to Mayland Community College in 1988. The campus serves more than 6,000 residents of the region annually. Presidents of Mayland include O. M. Blake (1971–1986), Virginia Foxx (1987–1993), Nathan Hodges (1994–1996), Tommy Williams (1997–2005), and Suzanne Owens (2005–present). (Courtesy of Mayland Community College.)

# *Four*

# Hidden Treasures

## A Mountain of Opportunity

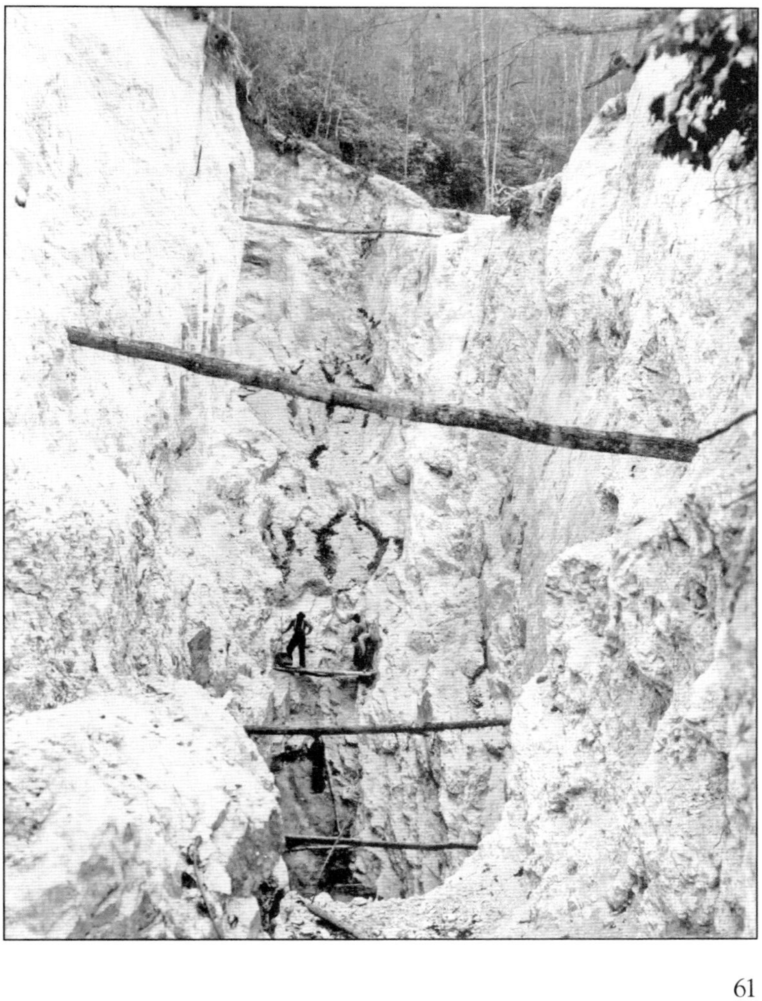

The Wiseman Mine on Beaver Creek was owned by M. D. and Matilda Wiseman. Mica was mined commercially in the region starting in the 1870s. The mineral was a good insulator for electrical and mechanical devices. The work was hard and dangerous, but men needed regular work, and the mines provided it. (Courtesy of Alan Schabilion.)

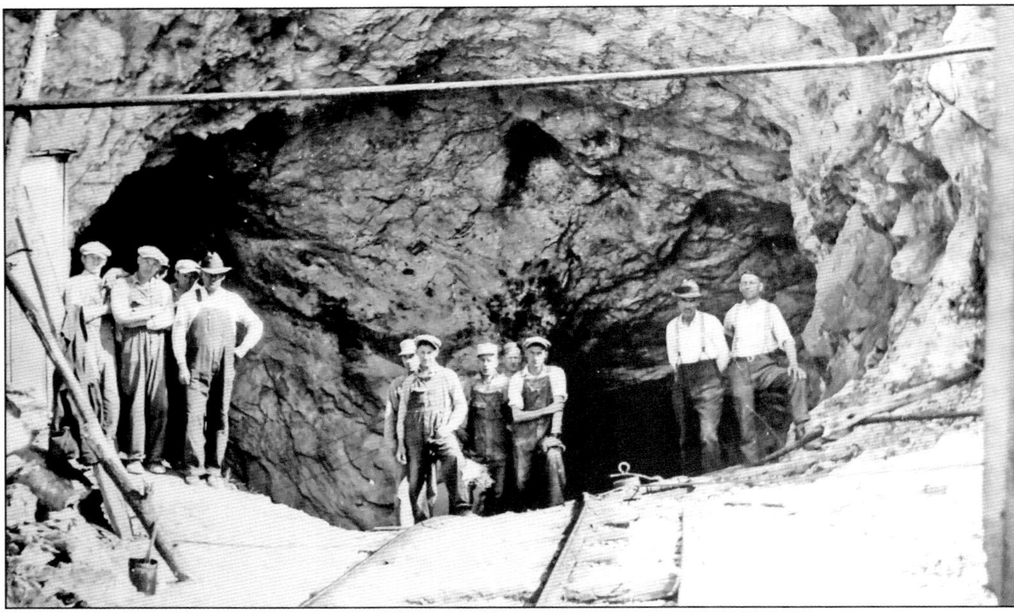

The Chestnut Flat Mine, located in the Ledger community, was first mined in about 1913. It produced prodigious amounts of feldspar and quartz for approximately 40 years before it was closed because of safety issues. Pictured here, from left to right, are workers Ed Turbyfill, Arnold Blackburn, Jeff Willis, Merritt Sparks, John Duncan, Newland Sparks, Landon Pitman, Walter Buchanan, Ike Grindstaff, Roe Duncan, and Bob Duncan. (Courtesy of Wayne Ward.)

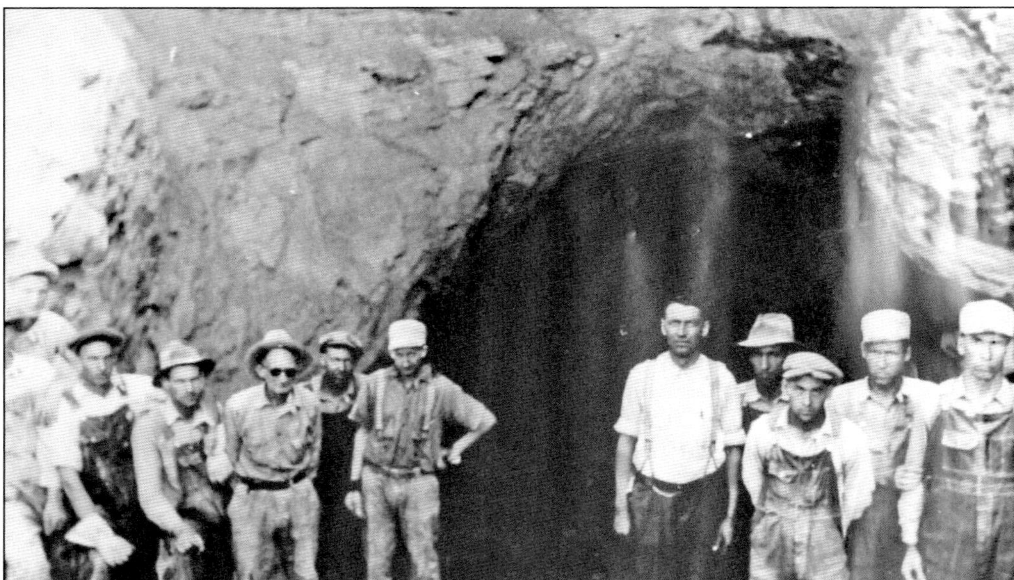

This photograph of the Chestnut Flat Mine, taken around 1930, shows, from left to right, Fred Duncan, Carrol Buchanan, Emmett Duncan, Paul Duncan, Mardie Sparks, George Davis, Carrol Sparks, Bob Duncan, Raymond Pitman, Dale Harris, Paul Stewart, and Avery Stewart. The mine produced the ore used to shape the mirror for the famous Hale Telescope at Palomar Mountain, California. (Courtesy of Buster Sparks.)

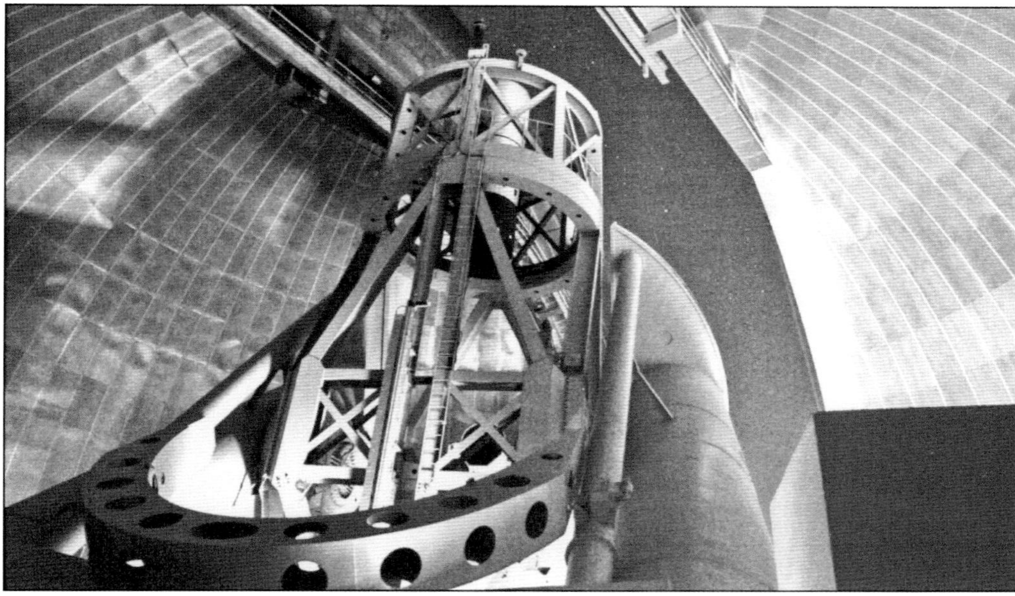

The Chestnut Flat Mine produced ultrapure quartz that was used to cast the 200-inch mirror for the Hale Telescope at Palomar Mountain in California. At the time, it was the largest piece of glass ever cast, and the telescope was the largest and most effective in the world from 1949 until 1993. The quartz was taken by railcar to the Corning Glass Works factory in New York where, in 1934, the Pyrex mirror blank was cast. After cooling for more than 10 months, the 20-ton disc was transported to California, where it was ground and polished. The project was interrupted by World War II, delaying the mirror's arrival to Palomar Mountain until 1947. The mirror's honeycombed underside can be seen below. (Both, courtesy of Palomar Observatory, California Institute of Technology.)

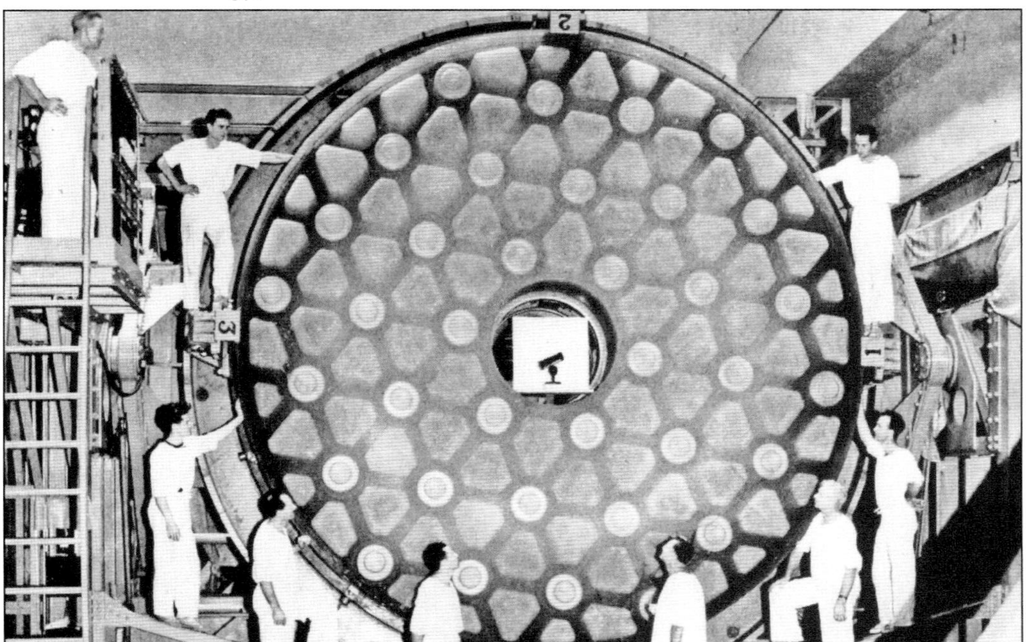

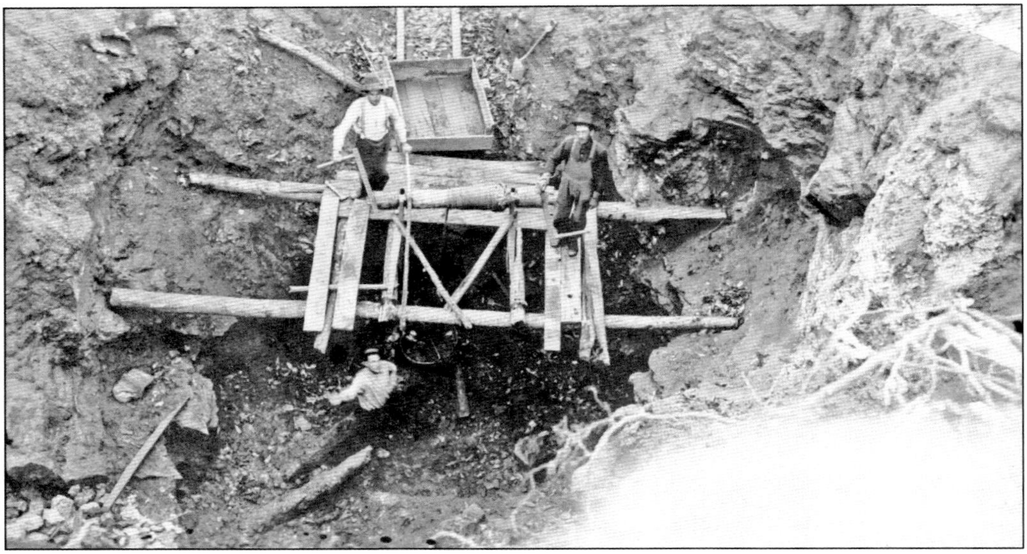

The Hoot Owl Mine (pictured below) was located in the Estatoe community. It was engaged in the mining of feldspar. The Gopher Hole Mine, pictured above, is located above the Hoot Owl Mine. The unidentified miners in these photographs dug the spar and loaded it onto a narrow-gauge railroad, the "Dinky," which then transported it to the train station at Penland, transferring it to the main Clinchfield line for shipment. (Both, courtesy of Eddie McGee.)

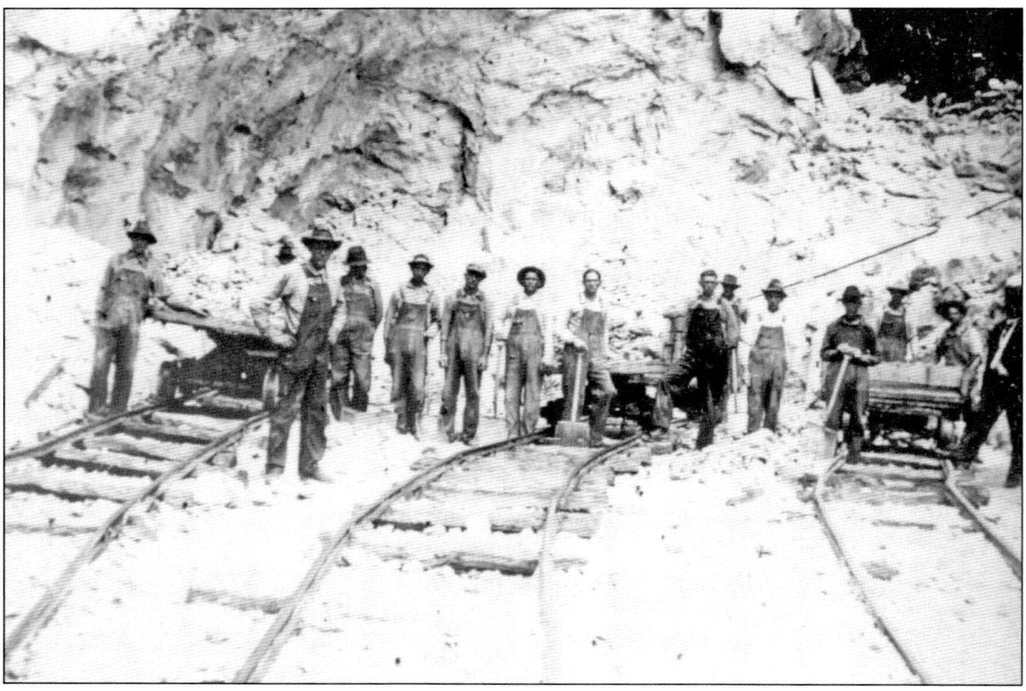

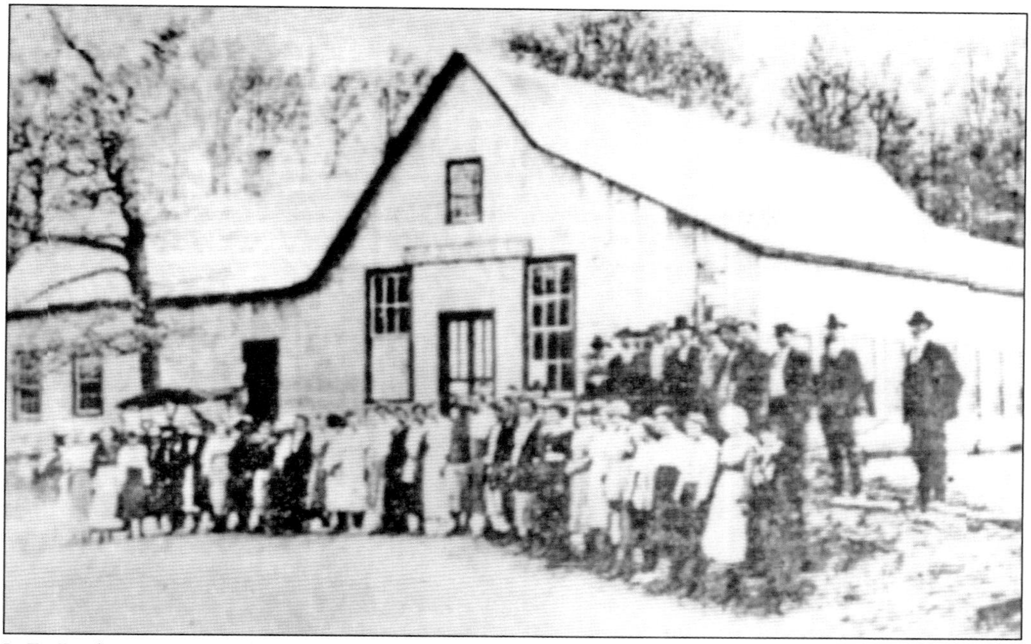

J. E. Burleson operated this mica house atop Burleson Hill, the location of the current town cemetery. Burleson began opening mica mines in 1894, and ground mica beginning in the 1900s. He was the largest individual mica operator in the region. (Courtesy of Mitchell County Historical Society.)

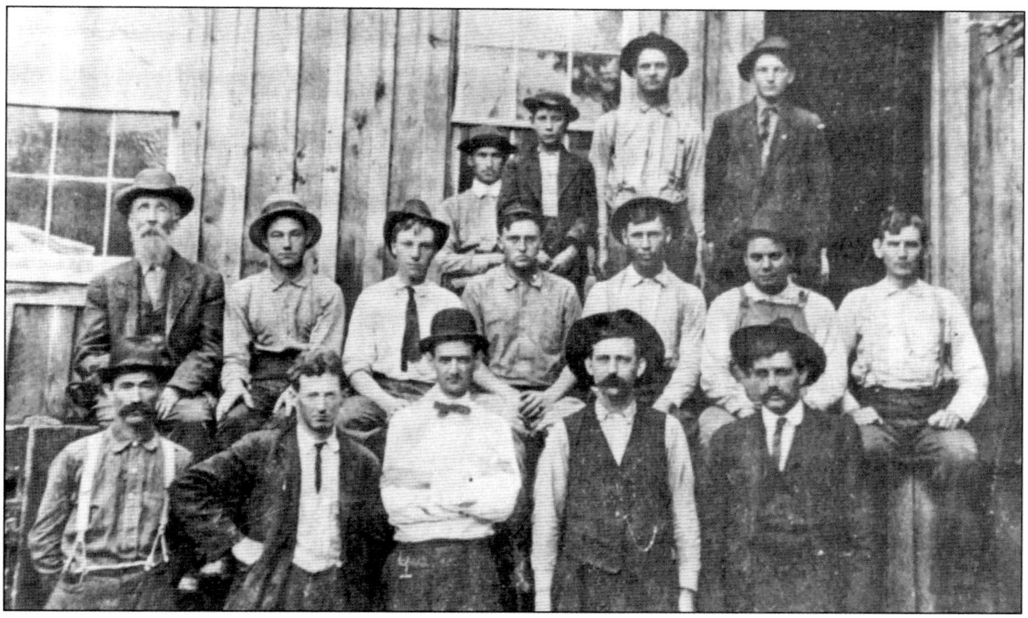

This 1912 photograph features employees of the J. E. Burleson Mica House. They are, from left to right, (first row) Newton Willis, Mack Burleson, Lat Young, Calhoun Smith, and Isom Wilson; (second row) Dock Biggerstaff, Pete Biddix, Rasmus Greene, Joe Murphy, Milton Ellis, W. D. Carpenter, and Lynn Young; (third row) Charles Dale, Fred Carpenter, Charlie Biddix, and unidentified. (Courtesy of Guss McKinney.)

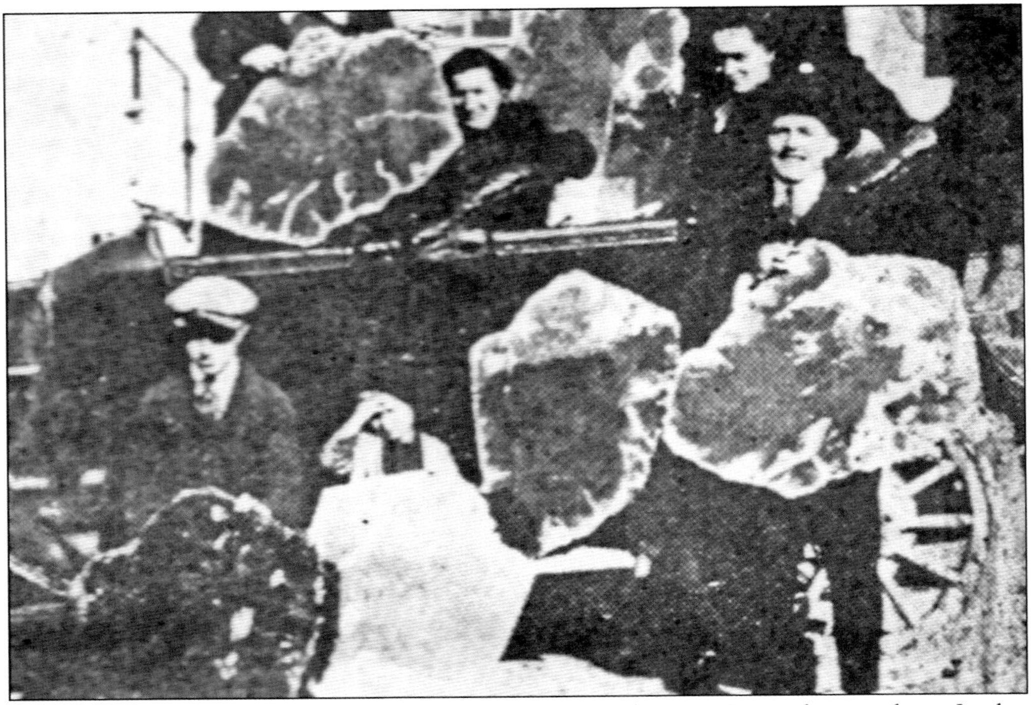

One of the first cars in Spruce Pine belonged to J. E. Burleson, a Carter friction drive. In this 1915 photograph, it is featured with, from left to right, Joe Mayberry, Mrs. Walter Laughridge (Viola Burleson), Mrs. J. A. Mayberry (Estelle Burleson), and a young man from Pittsburgh. The car ran on the only road from the train depot to the mica plant, approximately 1 mile in length. (Courtesy of the *Mitchell News-Journal*.)

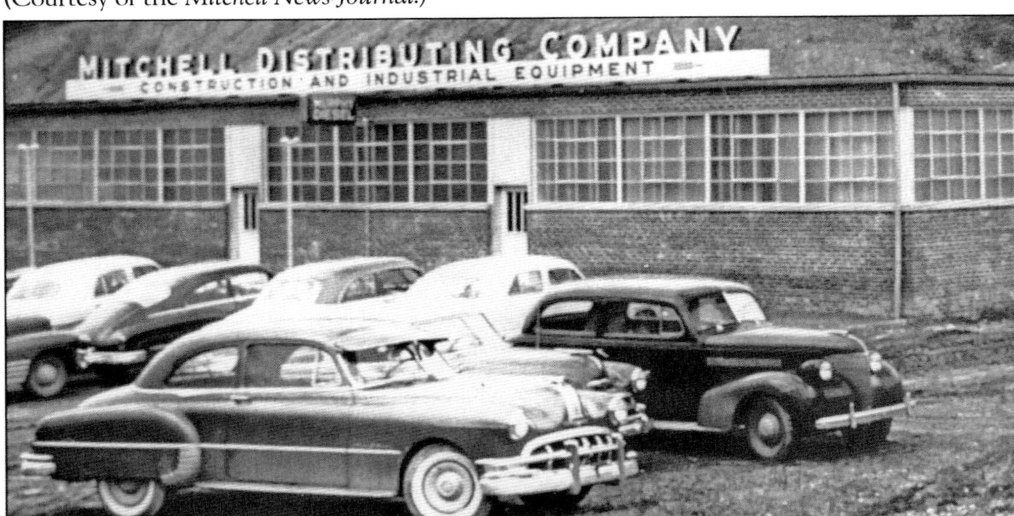


Mitchell Distributing Company (MDC) began in Spruce Pine in the late 1930s, providing equipment for the mining industry. George Greene and Ed Boone were principals in the business, with Rom Sparks running day-to-day operations. MDC grew and moved in the 1940s into this building on the Newland Highway, which housed a knitting mill. It grew into an international business, with its headquarters moving to Charlotte, North Carolina. (Courtesy of John Wellborn.)

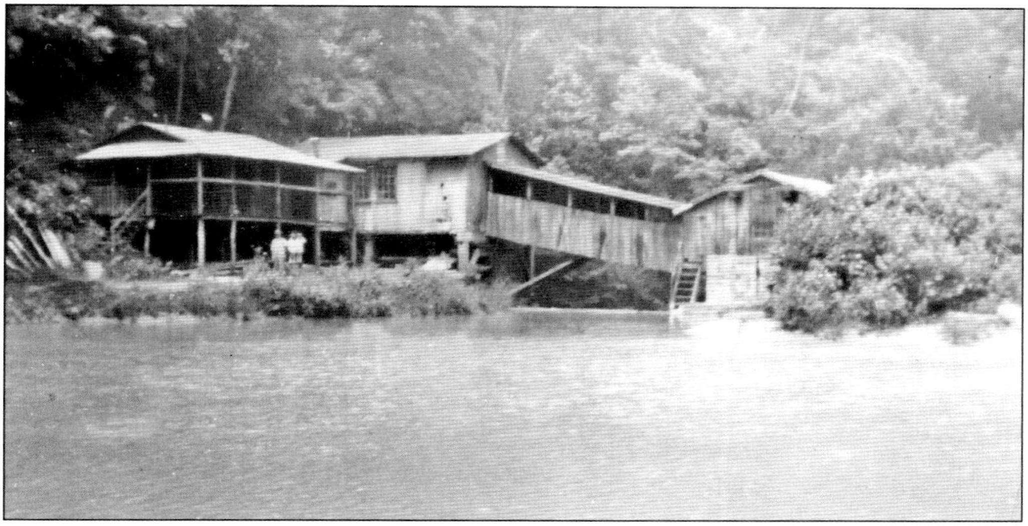

The Harris Mining Company brought electricity to Spruce Pine in 1918, with both steam and hydroelectric generating plants being constructed. The hydroelectric plant pictured above was built on the river just west of Spruce Pine near Minpro. Pictured below in front of the dam is Jesse Rhyne, who operated the water powerhouse. Other Harris Mining employees helped residents wire their homes for electricity. Arnold Ellis, one of the workers who wired many homes, noted that "it cost $1.15 a month to use all the 'juice' they wanted to" in a newspaper article in 1981. The plants provided electricity for the entire community until Carolina Power and Light began operations in 1927. (Both, courtesy of Doris Thompson.)

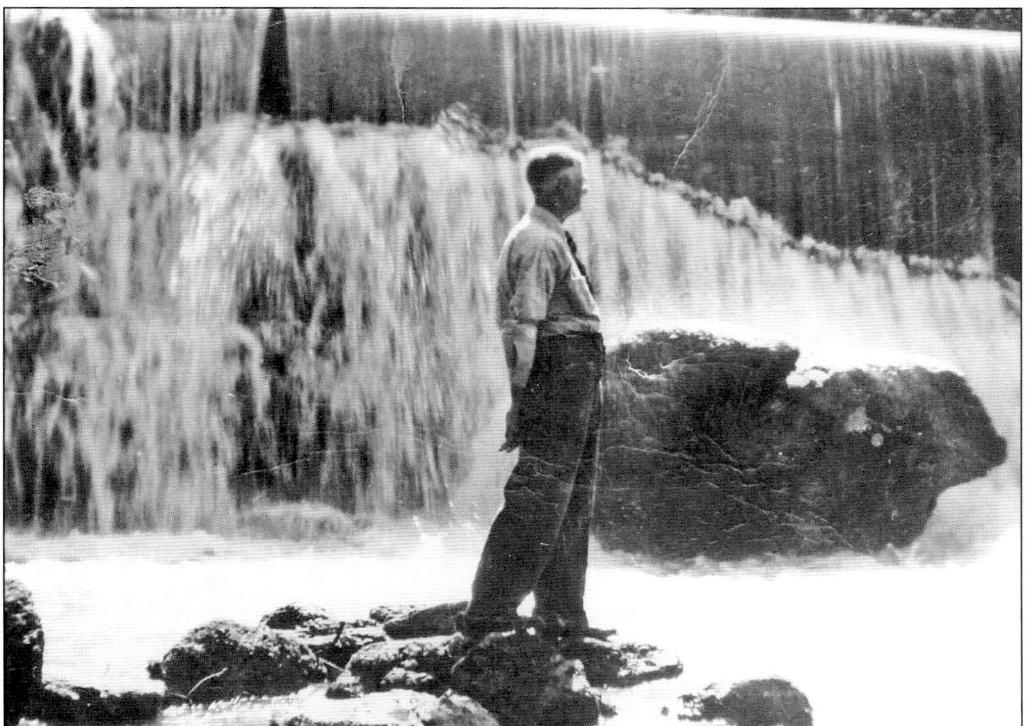

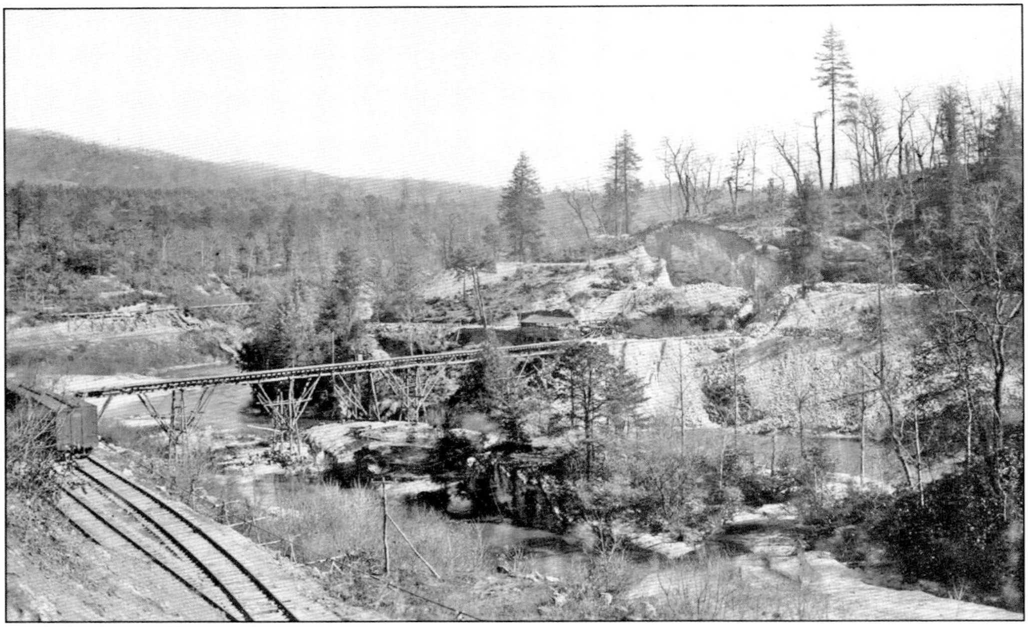

William Dibbell of Baltimore, Maryland, became interested in waste piles of feldspar discarded by early miners around Spruce Pine. He organized the Carolina Minerals Company of Penland and started shipping feldspar from a mine in the Deer Park area in 1911. Deer Park also produced mica, which is used for electrical insulation, in paint for automobiles, in women's makeup, and as an additive in plastics. These photographs of the Deer Park mines show how the railroad was used to transport the ore and how it was mined from shafts below ground to be sent to Erwin, Tennessee, for processing via railcars. Indians mined for mica in the area 2,000 years ago, trading it as far away as the Ohio River Valley with the Spanish visiting in 1540 to explore the area's treasures. (Above, courtesy of Alan Schabilion; below, courtesy of Sheila Grindstaff.)

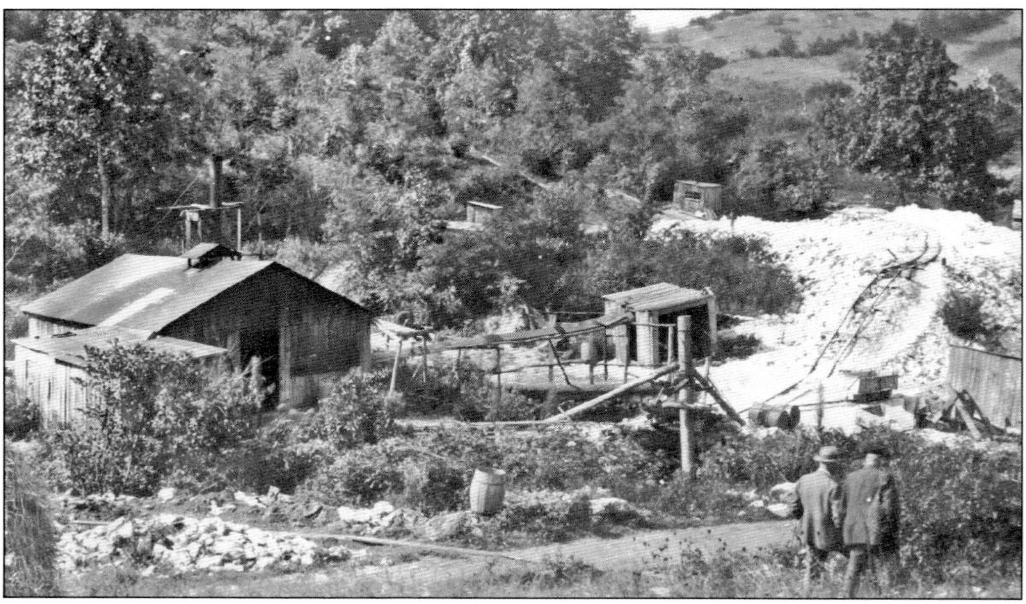

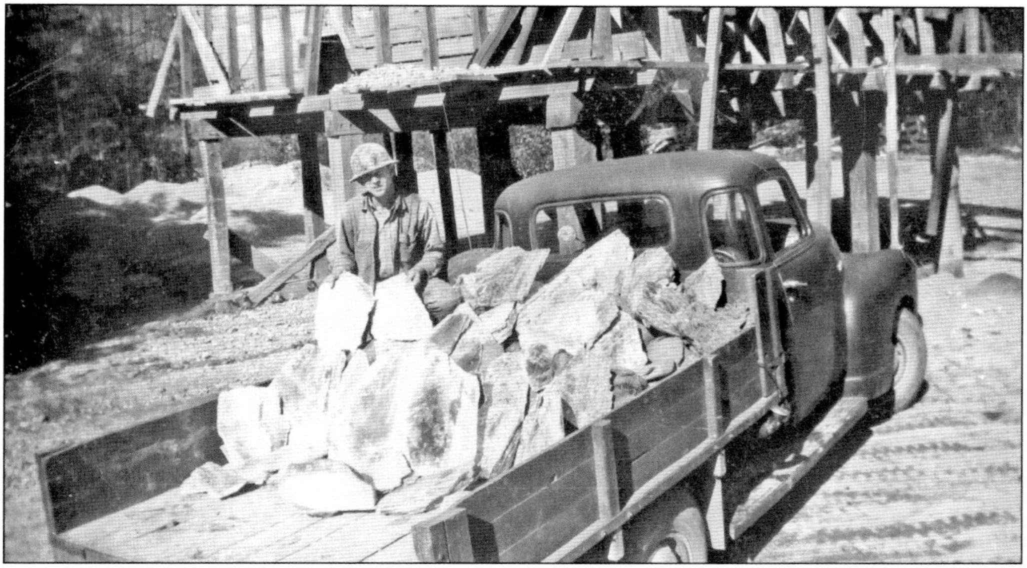

The Deer Park mines had two productive eras. Following the Carolina Minerals Company, Sam and Ben Blalock reopened the mines in the 1930s for sheet mica production and continued to operate the mine until the 1950s. The books of mica pictured above were dug out of the pegmatite and transported for processing to mica houses. Below, Sam (left) and Ben are pictured with some of the books. (Courtesy of Sheila Grindstaff.)

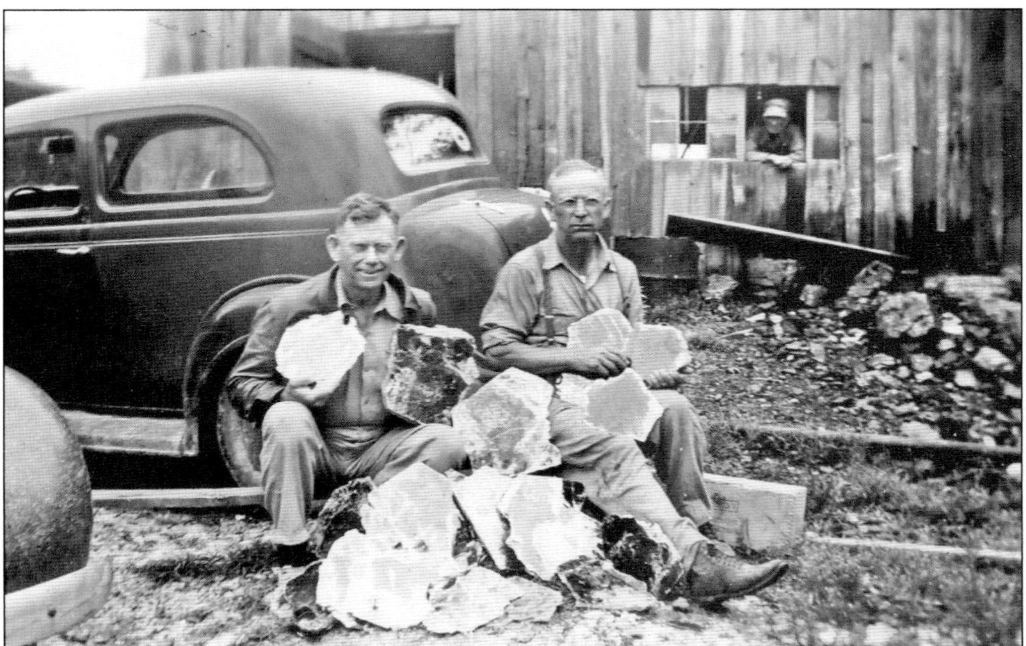

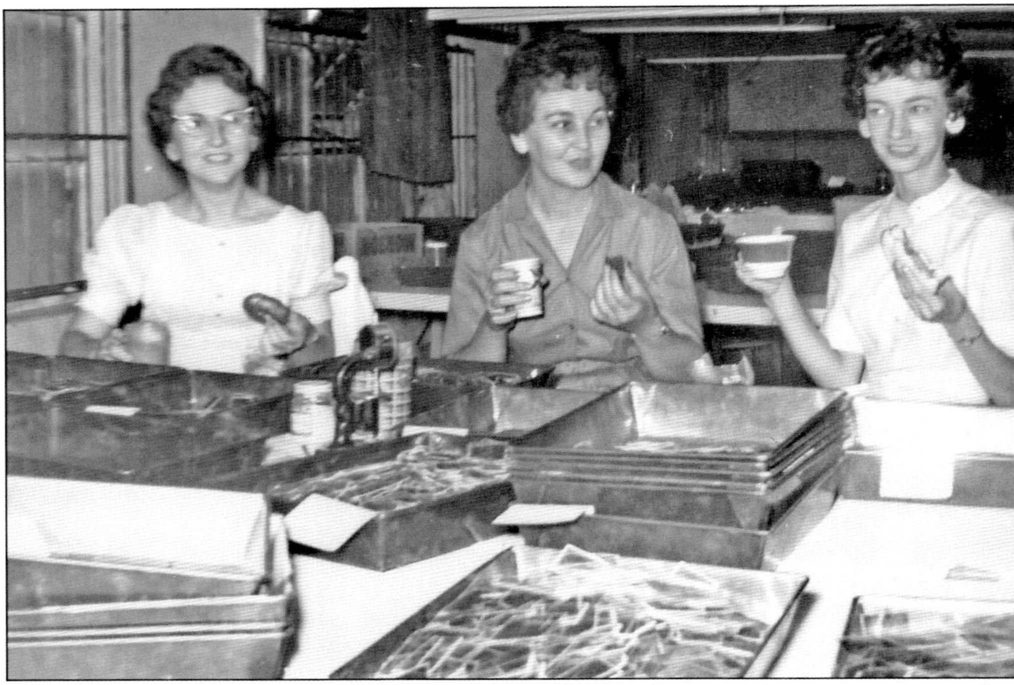

At one time, 1,500 experienced people graded and sheeted mica in Spruce Pine, more than in any other place in the world. They split it into sheets 1/1,000 of an inch in thickness and trimmed the cracked edges. Pictured above, from left to right, are Barbara Young, Vera Huskins, and Rachel Greene taking a break from their work qualifying mica at the U.S. government mica depot. (Courtesy of Rachel Greene.)

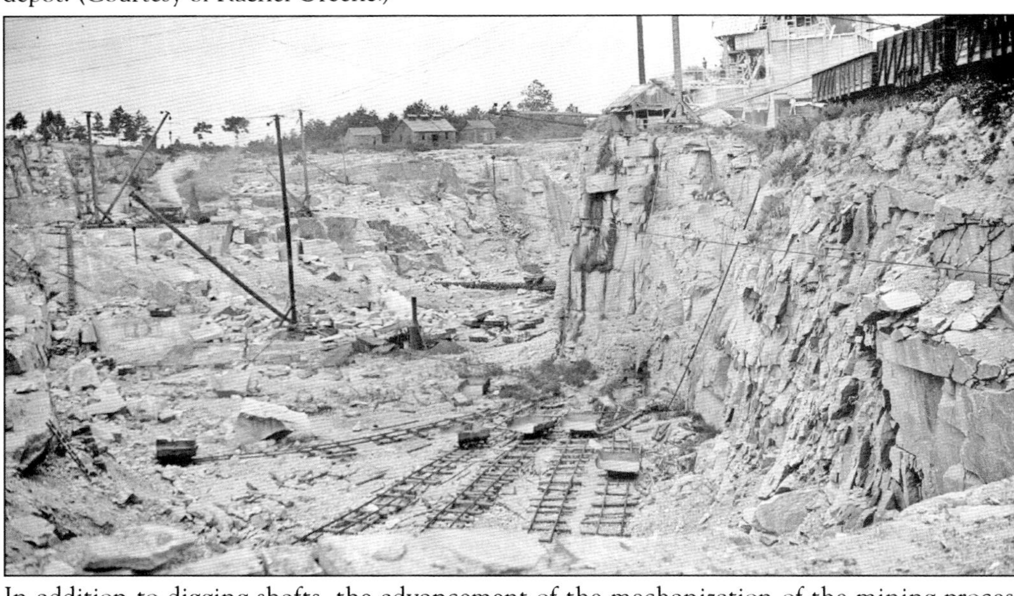

In addition to digging shafts, the advancement of the mechanization of the mining process permitted the use of strip-mining techniques for removal of ore. Miniature railroads ran into the pits, where they were loaded with raw ore to be transported to the railroad siding for transfer into cars for refinement. (Courtesy of Alan Schabilion.)

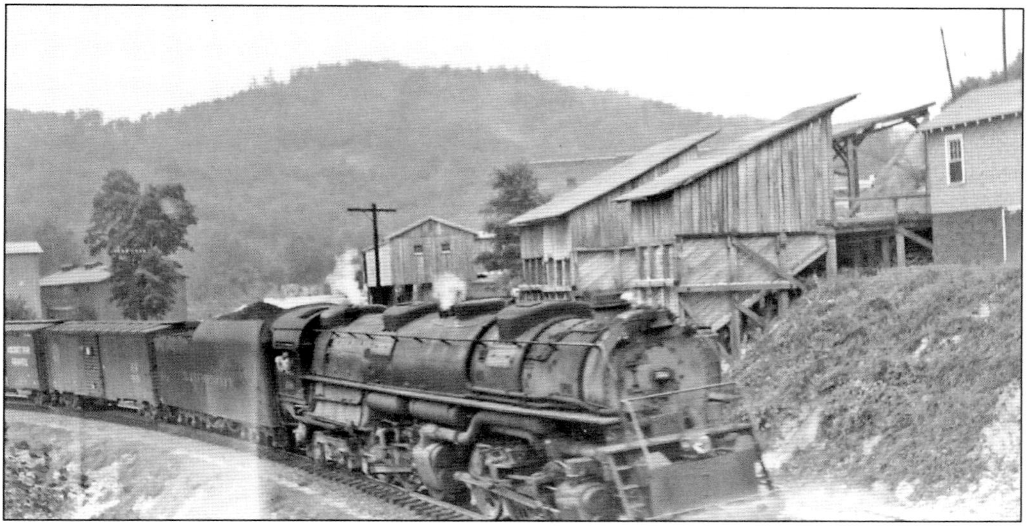

The railroad and mining interests worked closely together, even in the downtown area. This photograph shows a Clinchfield train passing the chutes where ore was loaded onto cars for transport. They were located on Oak Avenue, near the current location of Central Baptist Church. (Courtesy of Daniel Barron.)

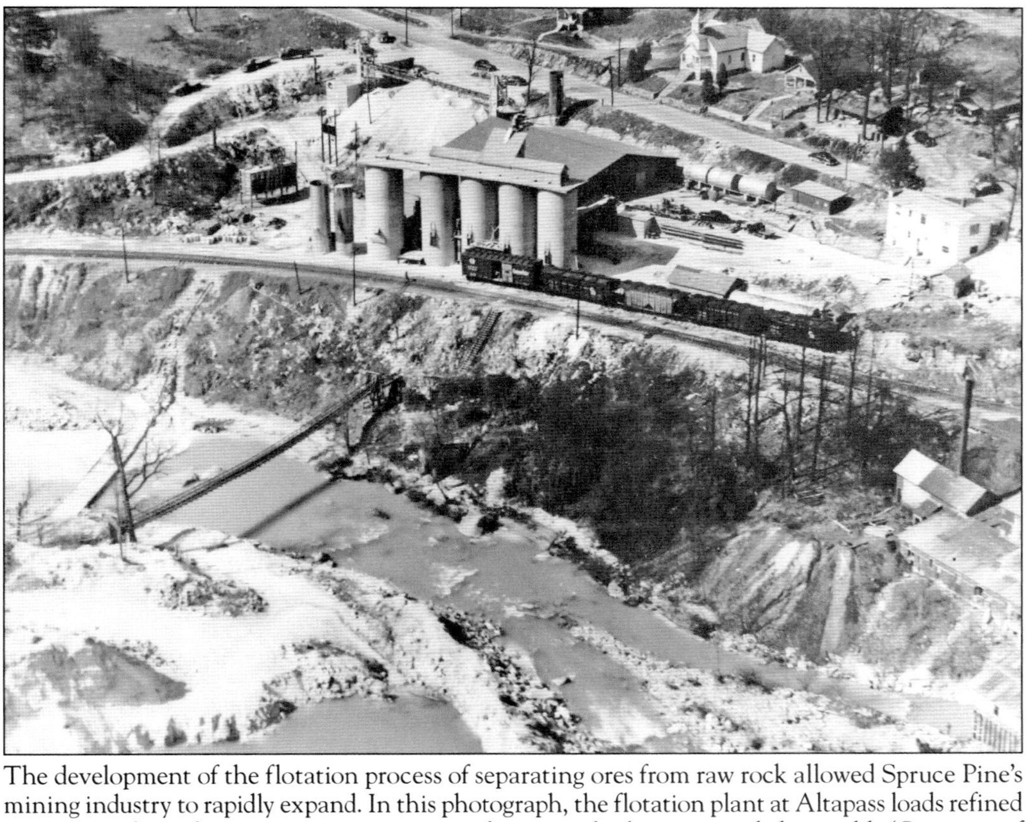

The development of the flotation process of separating ores from raw rock allowed Spruce Pine's mining industry to rapidly expand. In this photograph, the flotation plant at Altapass loads refined ore onto railcars for transportation to manufacturing facilities around the world. (Courtesy of Guss McKinney.)

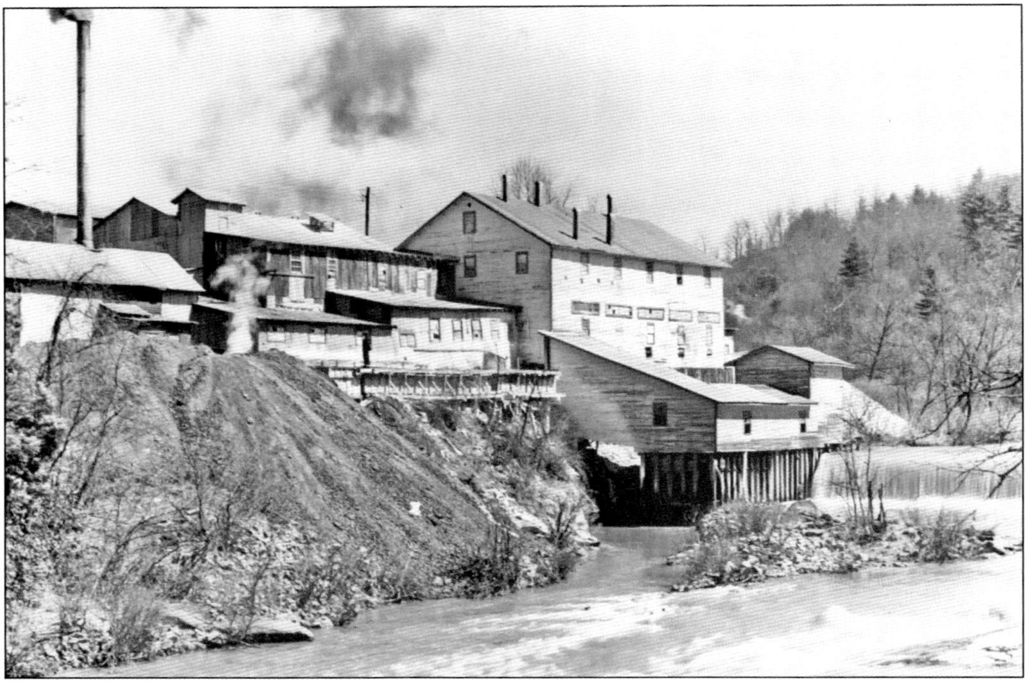

James Gere and Isaac English began mining mica in the late 1800s in the Spruce Pine area. They eventually formed the English Mica Company in 1908 to develop and sell their wares. It was later operated by Charles Gunter. The plant was on the banks of the Toe River in the Altapass community. Only the foundations of the building remain. (Courtesy of Brannon and Bryson Young.)

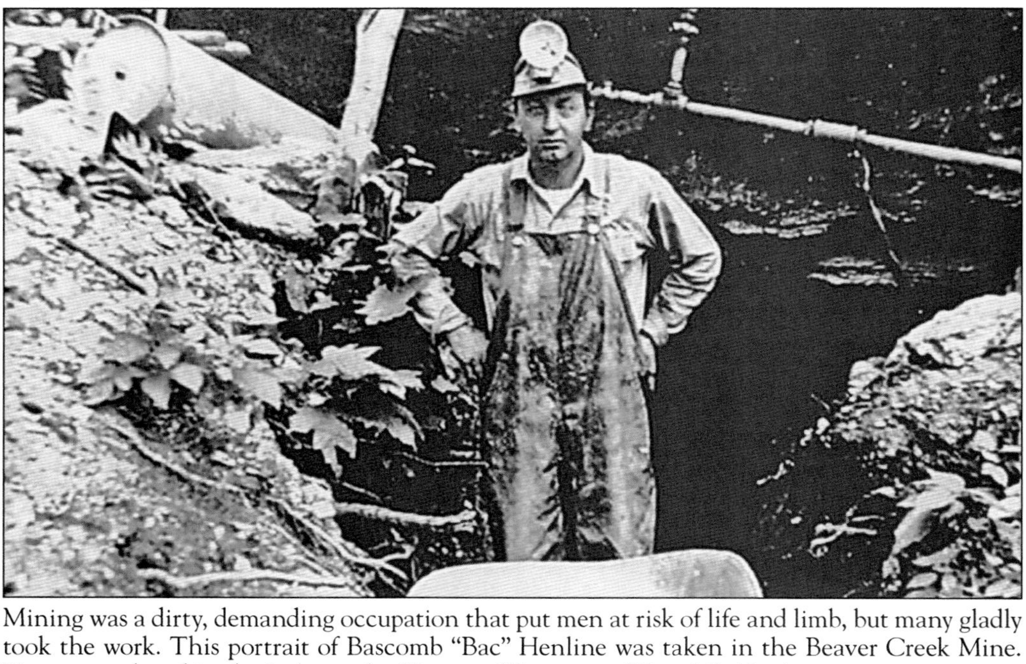

Mining was a dirty, demanding occupation that put men at risk of life and limb, but many gladly took the work. This portrait of Bascomb "Bac" Henline was taken in the Beaver Creek Mine. He was employed in the industry for 35 years. (Courtesy of David Biddix.)

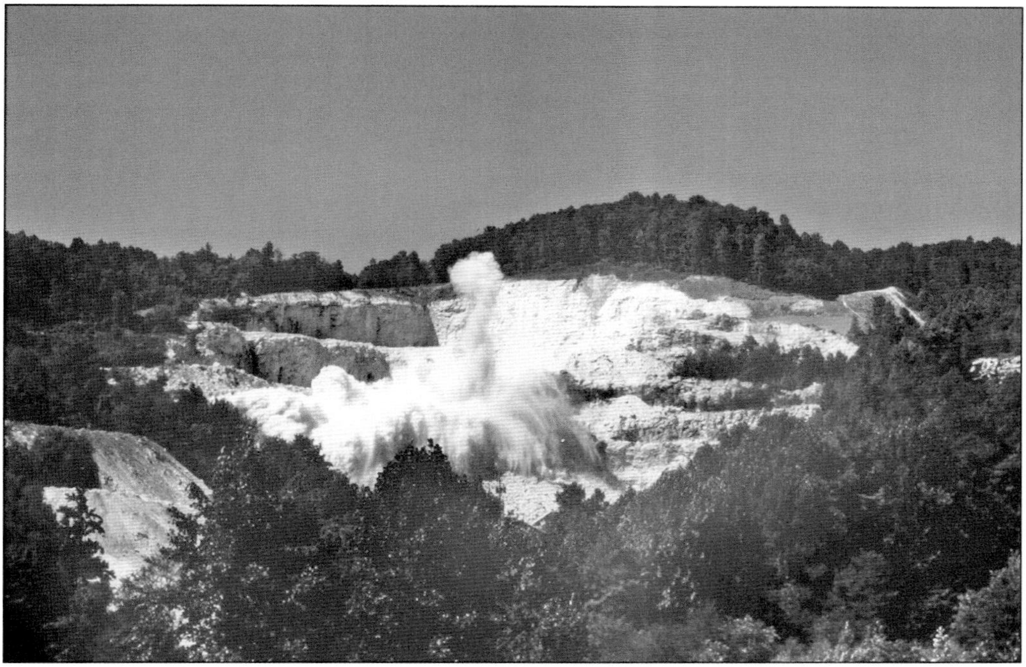

One of the more spectacular sights at a mine is when dynamite is used to loosen material for processing. This photograph at the Hawkins Mine shows the immediate aftermath of the blast as materials rain down on the area. Soon machinery will move in and begin the process of loading the ore. (Courtesy of Alex Glover.)

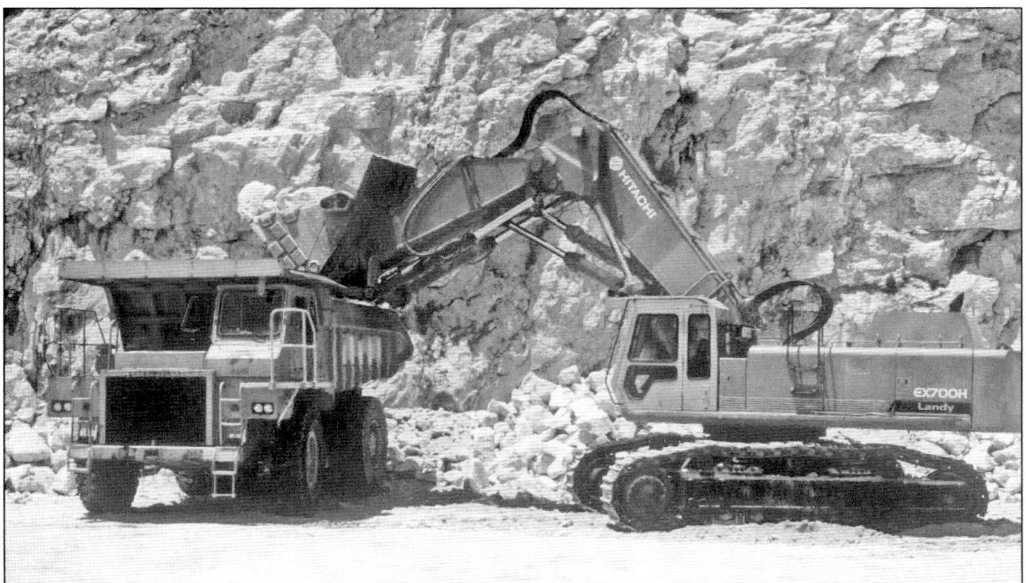


Modern mining uses large machinery to gather and move the rock to processing facilities. Uke trucks make short work of the loading and transportation. It is a far cry from when miners worked individually to break up the rock to load it on sleds or mining cars for transportation down the mountain. (Courtesy of Alex Glover.)

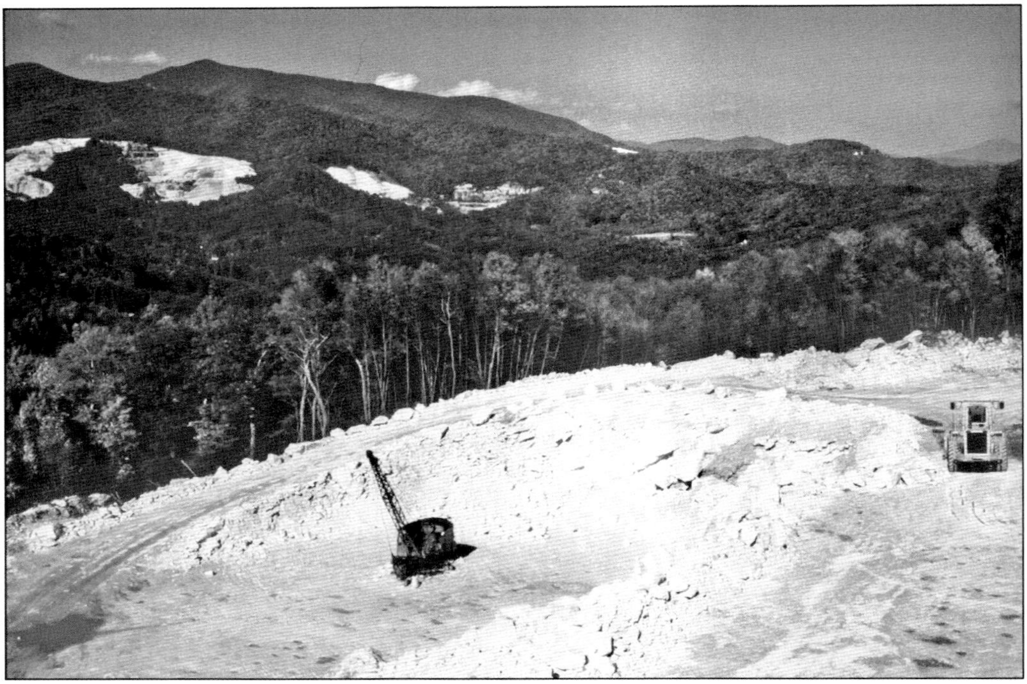

This is a familiar scene in the Spruce Pine area, as five open mine pits dot the surrounding mountain. This view from the Chalk Mountain Mine shows, from left to right, Pine Mountain, Hawkins Branch, Wiseman, and Dogwood Flats Mines, which are all currently in operation. (Courtesy of Alex Glover.)

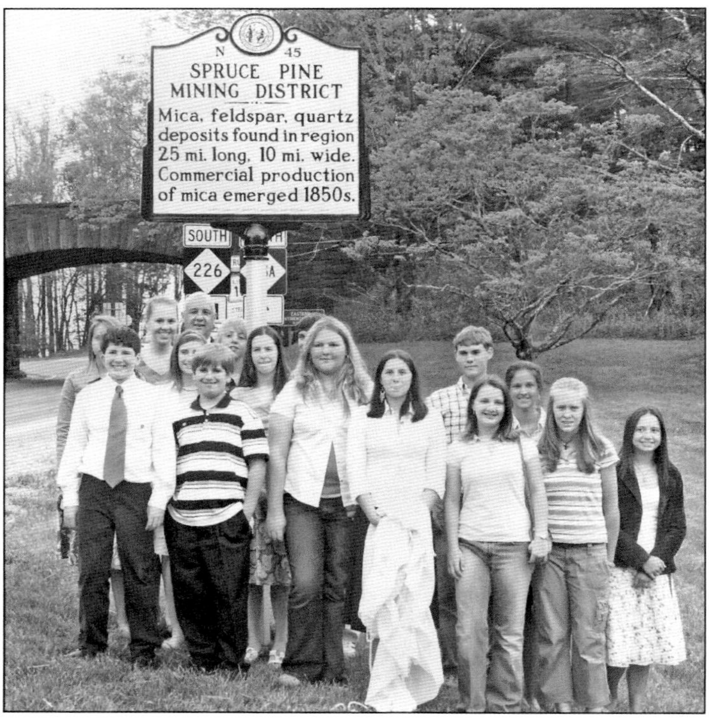


In 2005, Harris Middle School students, along with the North Carolina Department of Cultural Resources, unveiled this historical marker commemorating the Spruce Pine Mining District. Pictured from left to right are (first row) Billy Flint, Jeremy Wise, Brittany Murdock, Molly Stroup, Megan Honeycutt, Lacey McKinney, and Samantha Smith; (second row) Mariah Parsley, Brittany Calhoun, Tiffany Hall, Elias Burch, Tyler Biddix, and Emily English; (third row) Whitney Jones, Michael Barnhill, and Chris Hollifield. (Courtesy of Dana Hollifield.)

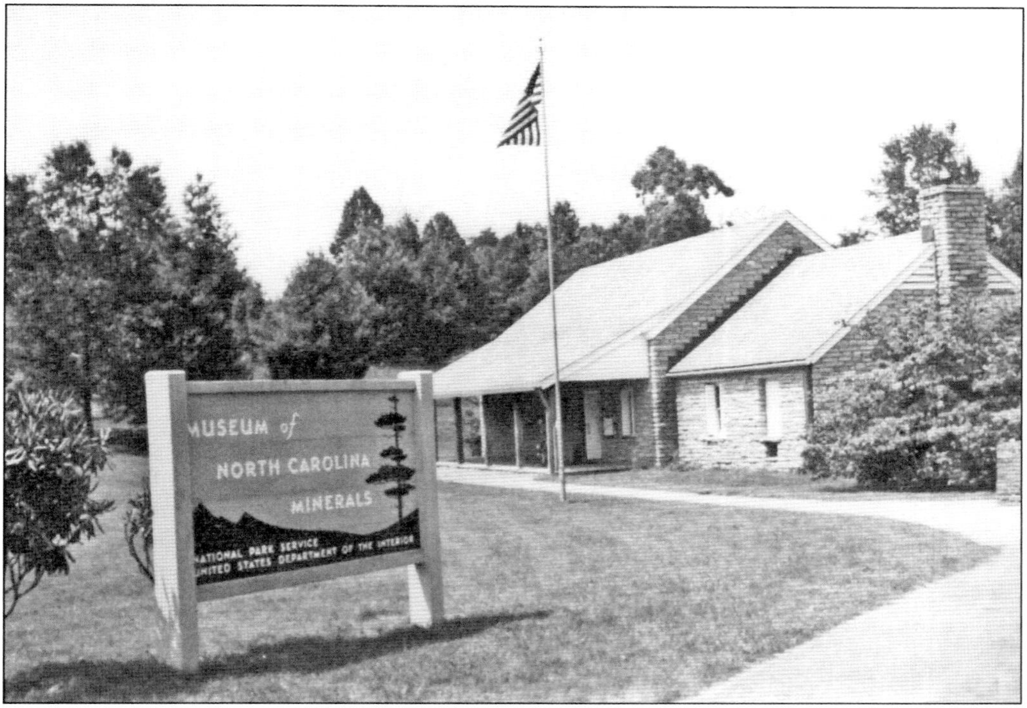


The Museum of North Carolina Minerals, located at the intersection of N.C. 226 and the Blue Ridge Parkway at milepost 331, celebrates the mineral wealth found in the Spruce Pine area with interactive exhibits and samples of minerals and gems. It is open year-round and provides visitors with information on area attractions in addition to its exhibits. An accompanying monument on the grounds commemorates the march of the Overmountain Men on their way to the Battle of Kings Mountain. Each September, the museum hosts an encampment of reenactors of the march, featuring a view of Revolutionary War life complete with mock battles, military drills, and historical interpretations. (Both, courtesy of National Park Service.)

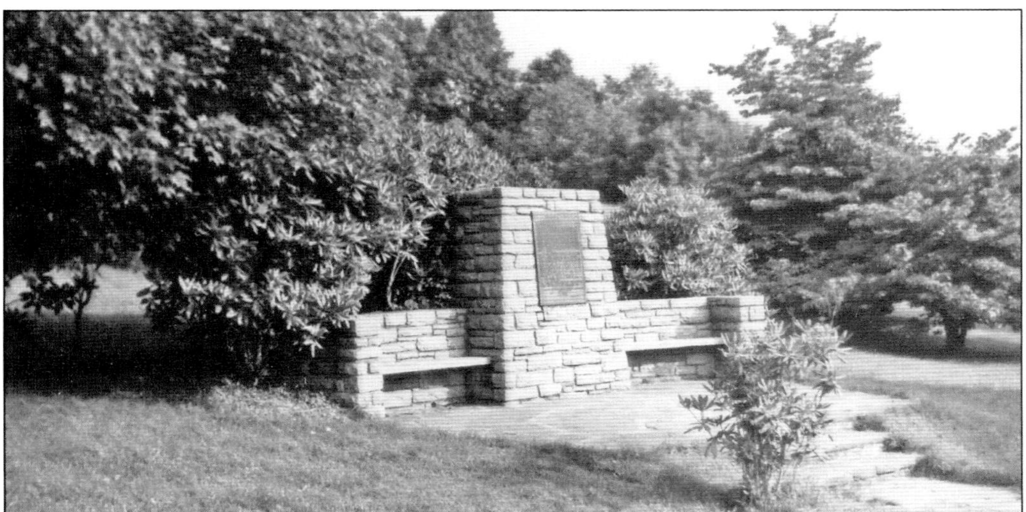

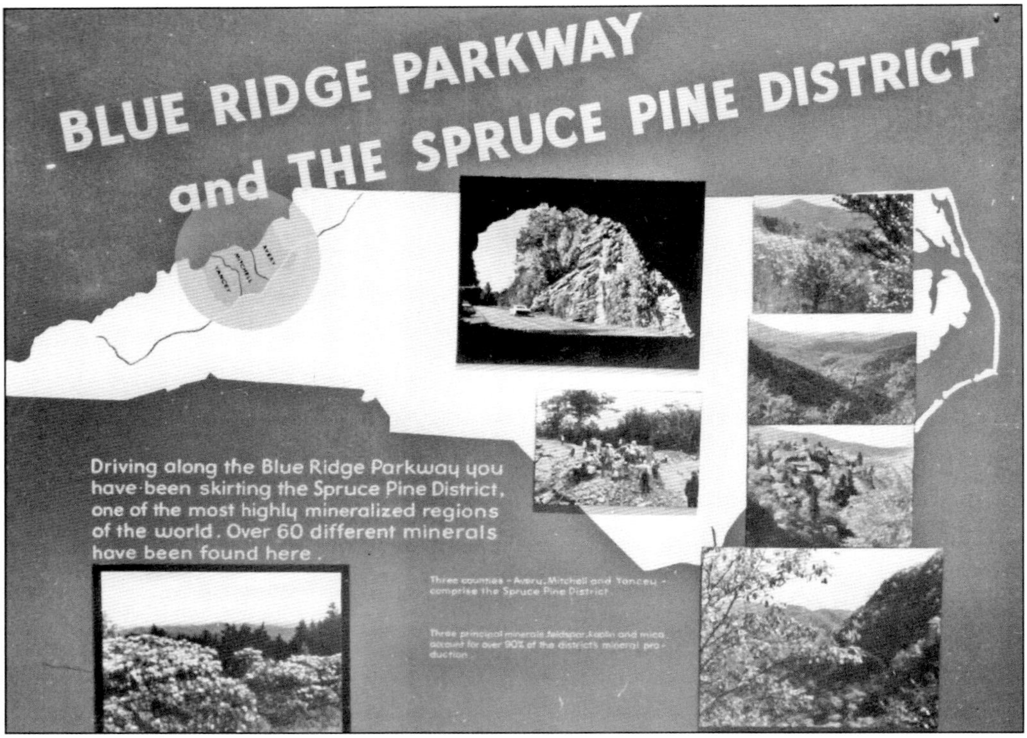


For more than a half-century, the North Carolina Minerals Museum exhibits have heralded the variety and importance of the minerals found in the 25-mile-long and 10-mile-wide Spruce Pine Mining District. In the past, visitors marveled at fluorescent minerals, a radioactive Geiger counter, and mineral collections. Today computer exhibits show how the mountains were formed, visitors can split a rock open to see embedded quartz crystals, and they can observe a model of atoms that make up the rocks. Above is an original exhibit in the museum; below is the current entrance to the museum exhibits. (Above, courtesy of National Park Service; below, courtesy of David Biddix.)

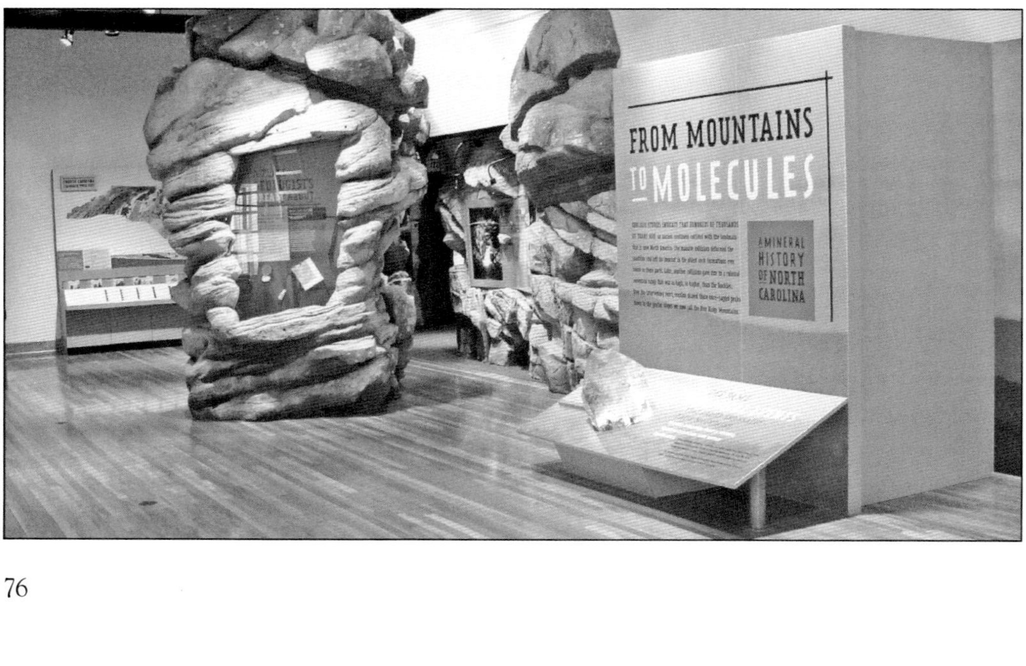

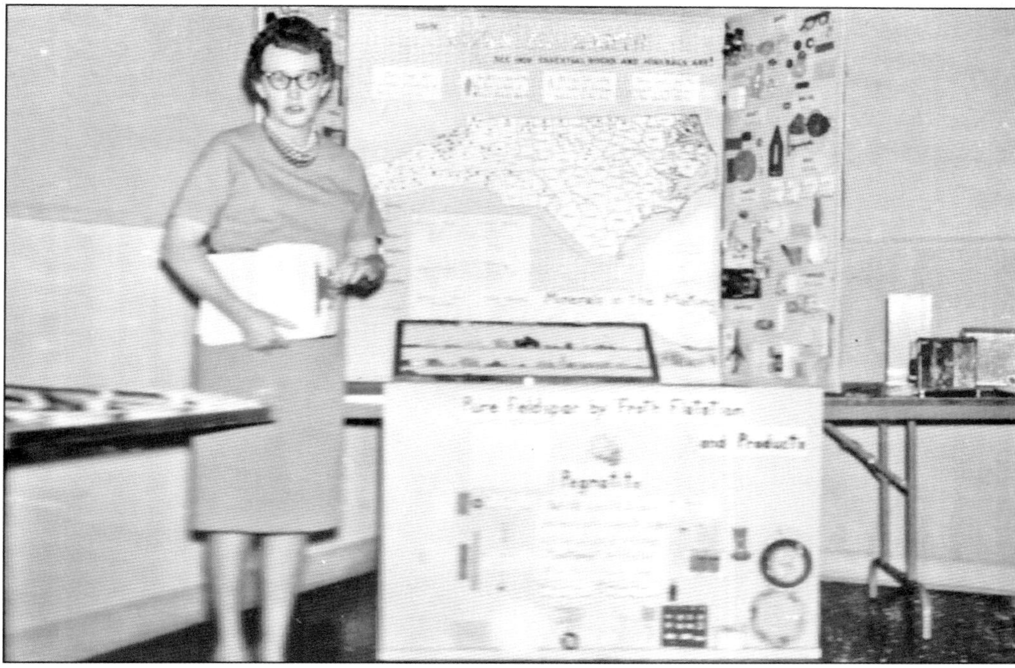

In 1957, Charlie Mae Sproles (pictured above) combined a love for mineral and gem collecting with a rising interest in the hobby to organize the North Carolina Mineral and Gem Festival. It was an immediate success, with hobbyists flocking to Spruce Pine for the chance to search for rare specimens in the mine pits in the area. Held each summer, the festival brings together dealers and thousands of rock hounds from around the world for mine tours, special collecting sessions, swap meets, and lectures. It was originally held in the Harris High School gym (pictured below). (Above, courtesy of Spruce Pine Public Library; below, courtesy of Charlie Mae Sproles.)

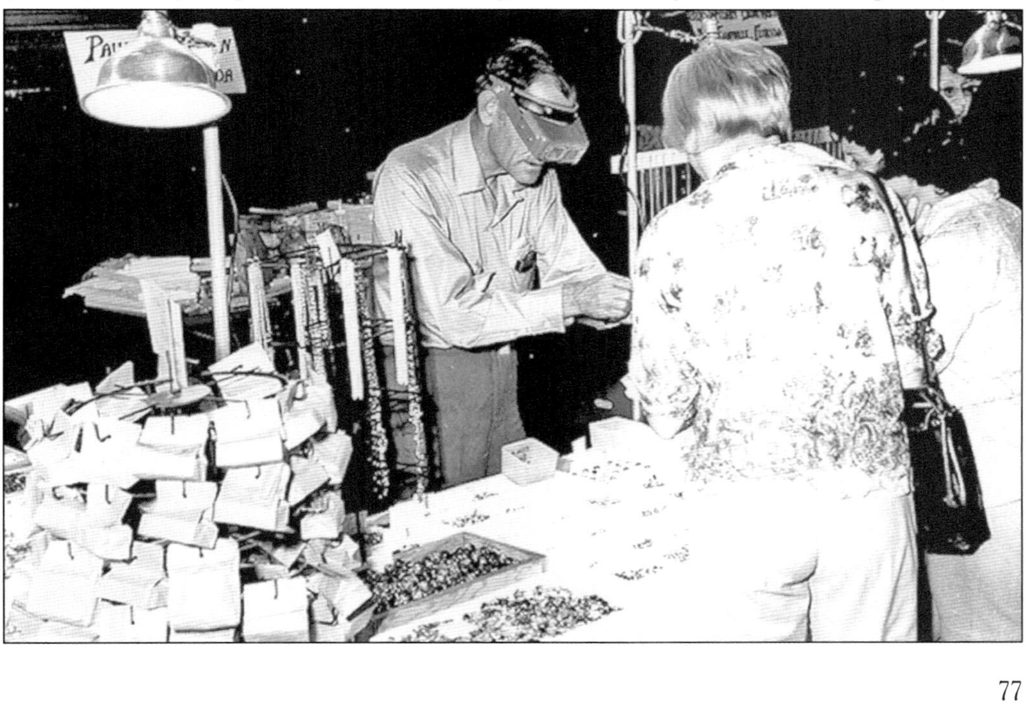

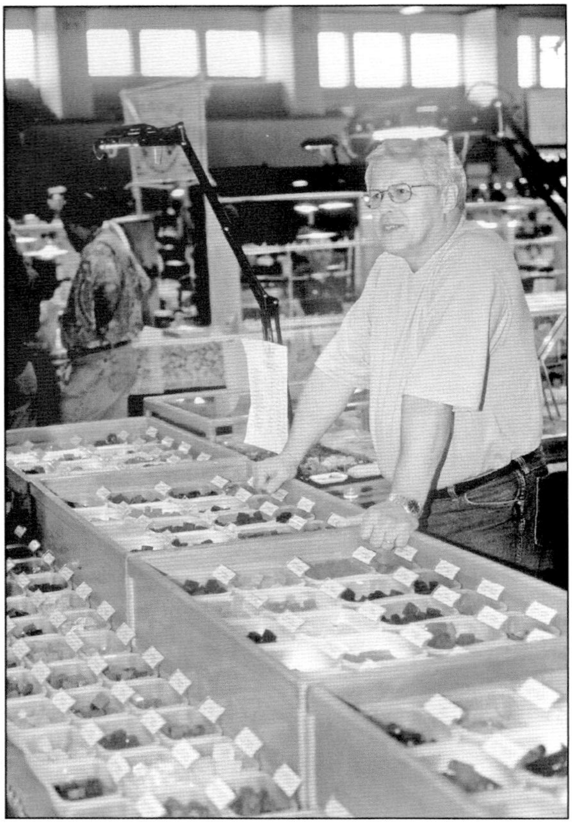

In the 1980s, the North Carolina Mineral and Gem Festival outgrew the confines of the Harris gym, and the Mitchell County Chamber of Commerce moved it to spacious quarters at the Pinebridge Coliseum in Spruce Pine. An outdoor show began at the Parkway fire department south of town and is held at the same time. Attendance to both shows continues to increase, and interest in rockhounding and geology has also continued to grow. (Both, courtesy of Alex Glover.)

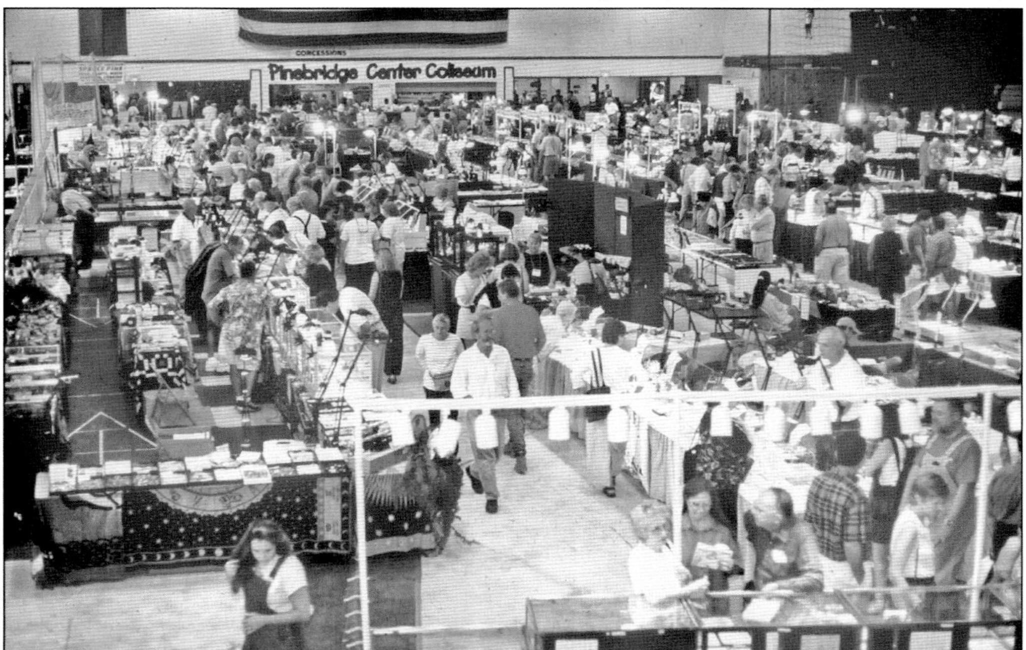

# *Five*

# How Firm a Foundation
## A Fellowship of Faith

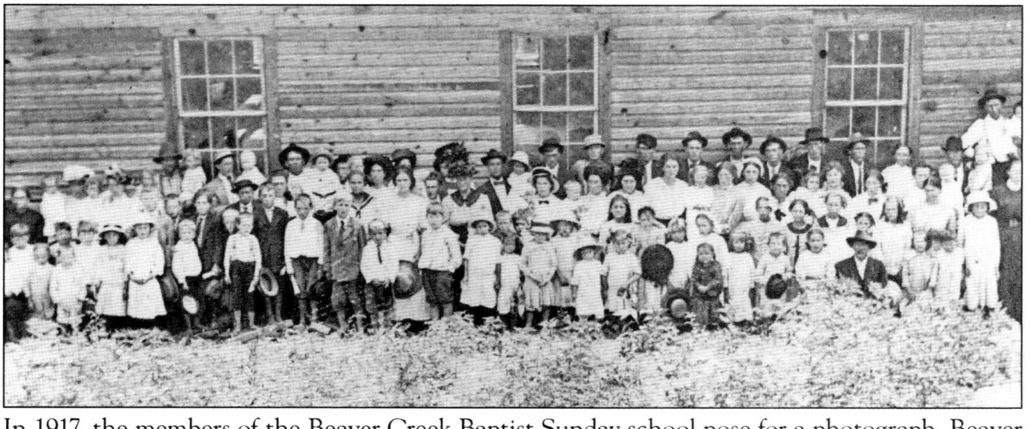

In 1917, the members of the Beaver Creek Baptist Sunday school pose for a photograph. Beaver Creek Baptist and the Mount Vernon Church shared a common location at the Mount Vernon schoolhouse, located near the Beaver Creek Falls at the head of the creek, until the Baptists built a church and the Spruce Pine United Methodist Church was founded. (Courtesy of Roger and Sherry Pendley.)

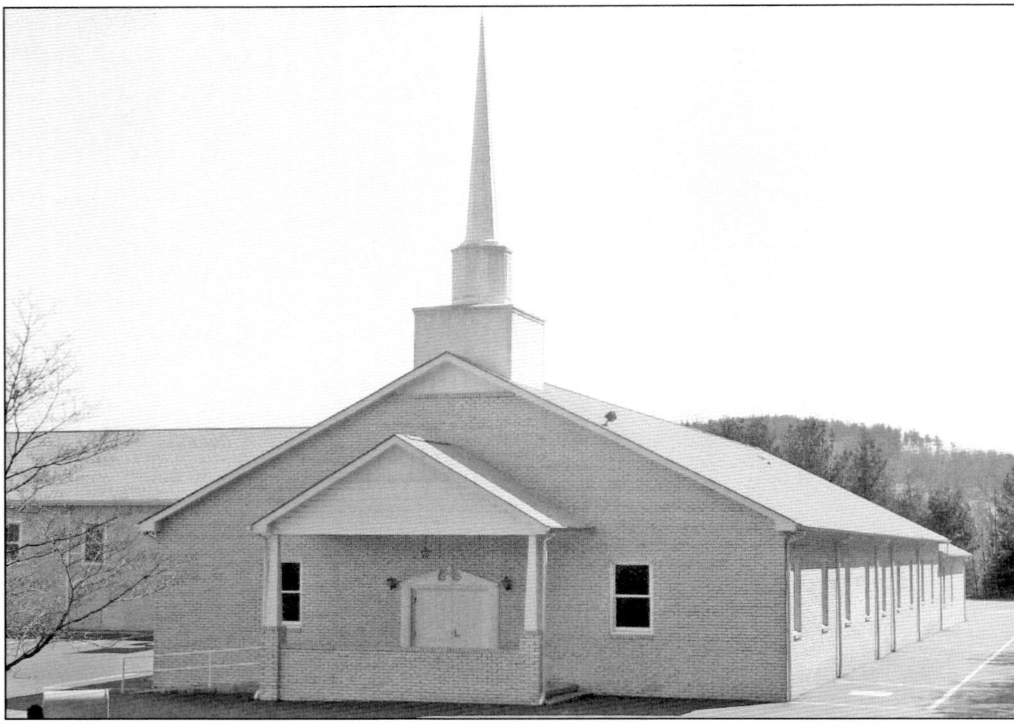

Berry Chapel Baptist Church began in 1934 when several families in the Mica Mill Flats section began meeting. Ella Berry donated land across from the feldspar flotation plant for a church, and materials from the old Beaver Creek School were used to construct it. In 1955, a new church was constructed across the road from the first, and an extension was built in 1984. (Courtesy of David Biddix.)

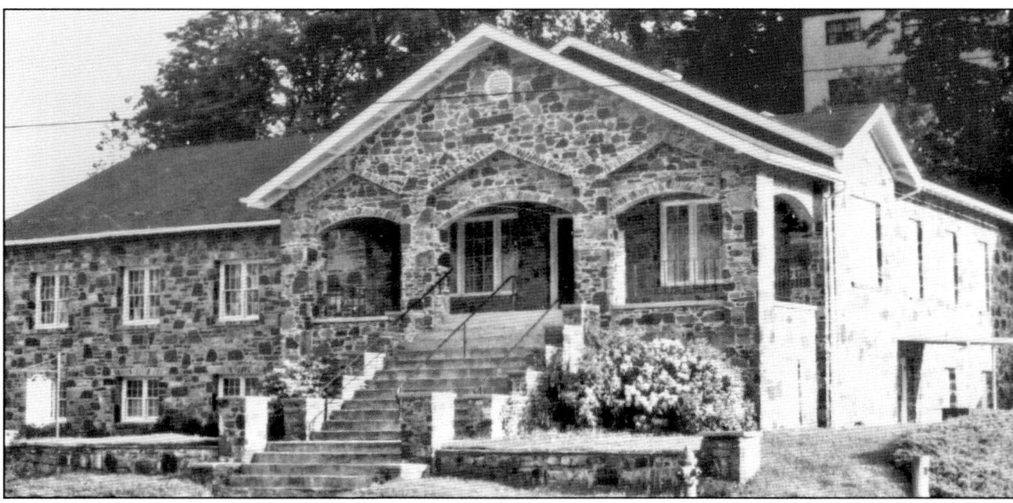

The Central Baptist Church was organized on June 23, 1932, with 68 members. The first pastor was J. T. Biddle. The church building, with stonework laid by David Greene and mined from the railroad construction in Altapass, was built on Upper Street and dedicated on June 3, 1945. A sanctuary addition was built in 1951, and a fellowship hall opened on November 20, 1994. (Courtesy of Central Baptist Church.)

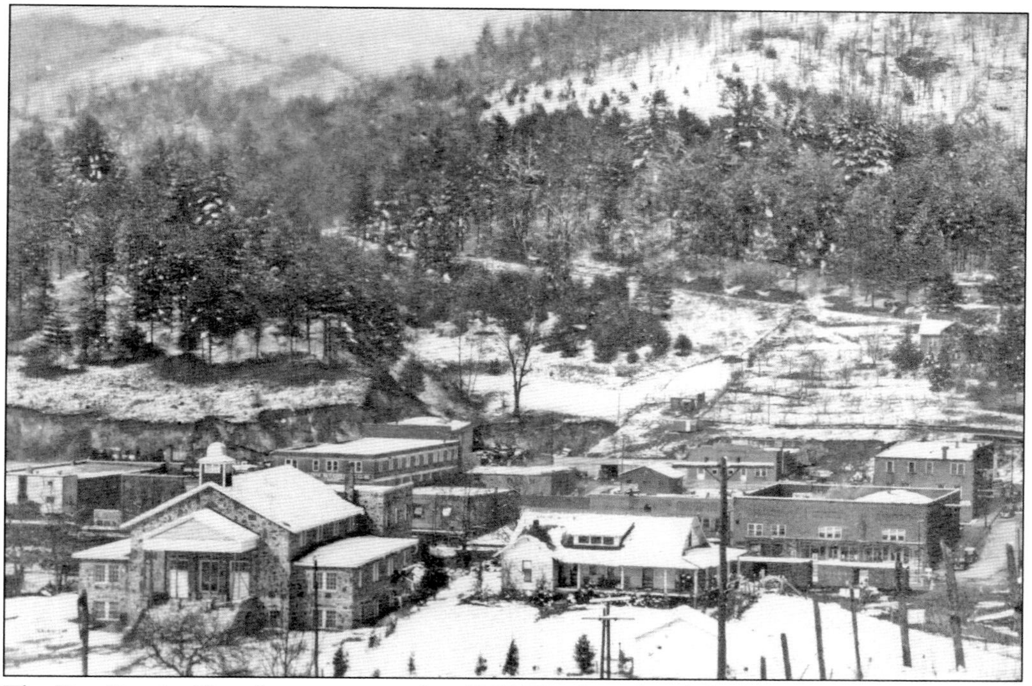

The First Baptist Church was organized in 1907. The first church building was located near the Toe River Bridge and was started in 1908. Work on the current church began in 1927, and the first service was held in 1940. Stonework was done by David Greene. This photograph is of an April 11, 1943, snowstorm with the church in the foreground and the town behind. (Courtesy of Geraldine Canipe.)

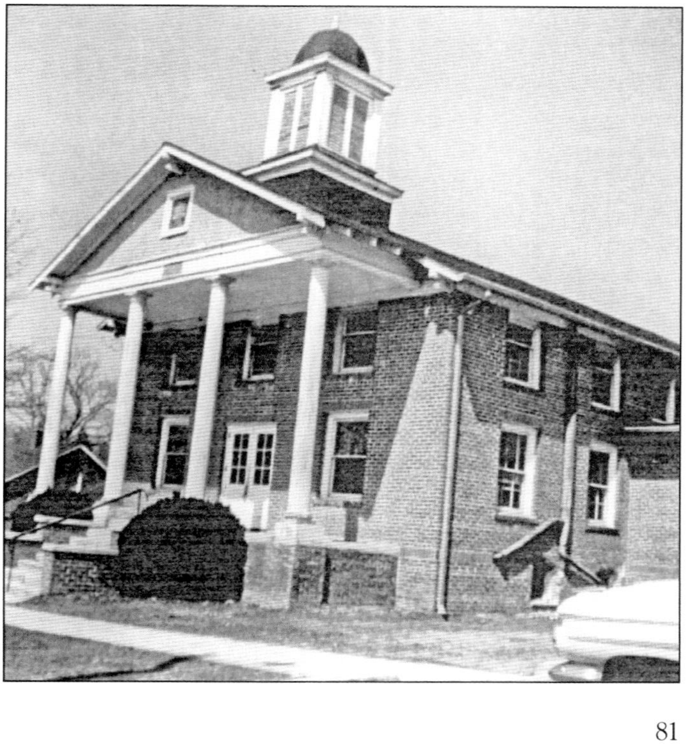

The Grassy Creek Baptist Church began sometime between 1815 and 1823 when the Caney River Baptist Church in Yancey County established a mission in the Grassy Creek community. This photograph is of the church building constructed in 1928. It was replaced with the current church in 1966. (Courtesy of Guss McKinney.)

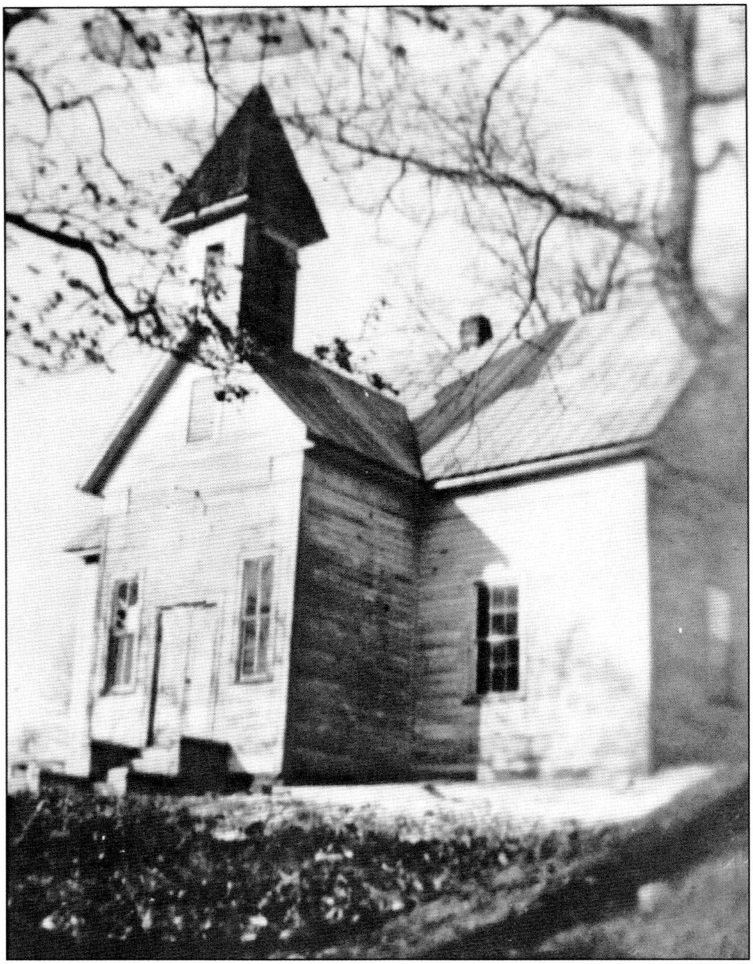

The Grassy Creek Presbyterian Church was started on March 20, 1911, by evangelist John Harris. It occupied this building, which also housed a school. Amelia Greenlee, for whom Greenlee Primary School is named, first taught there. A larger building was constructed in 1949, with additions added in 1956 and 1977. (Courtesy of Elvira Bryant.)

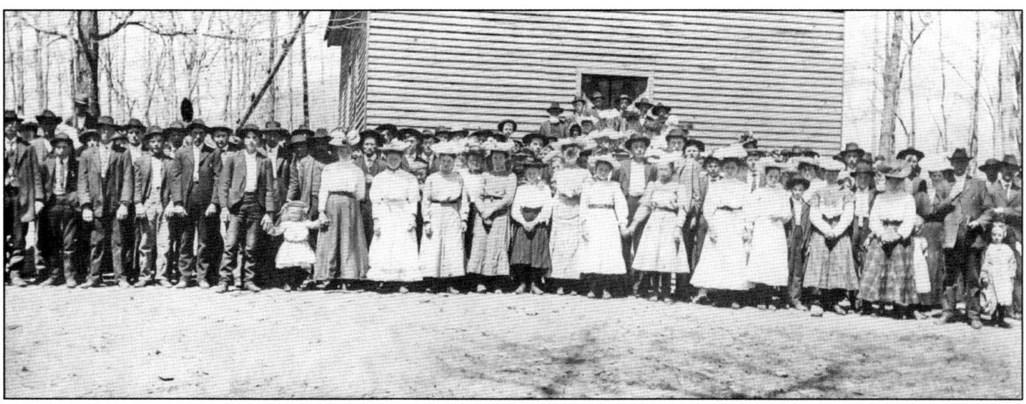

The Liberty Hill Baptist Church was organized in 1866, meeting in a building constructed in the 1840s. It moved to its present location in 1897. A structure was erected in 1926 with bricks made in Rutherford County, shipped to Spruce Pine on the train, and then brought to the site by wagon and mules. This photograph of the congregation was taken on April 12, 1908. (Courtesy of Lolita Buchanan.)

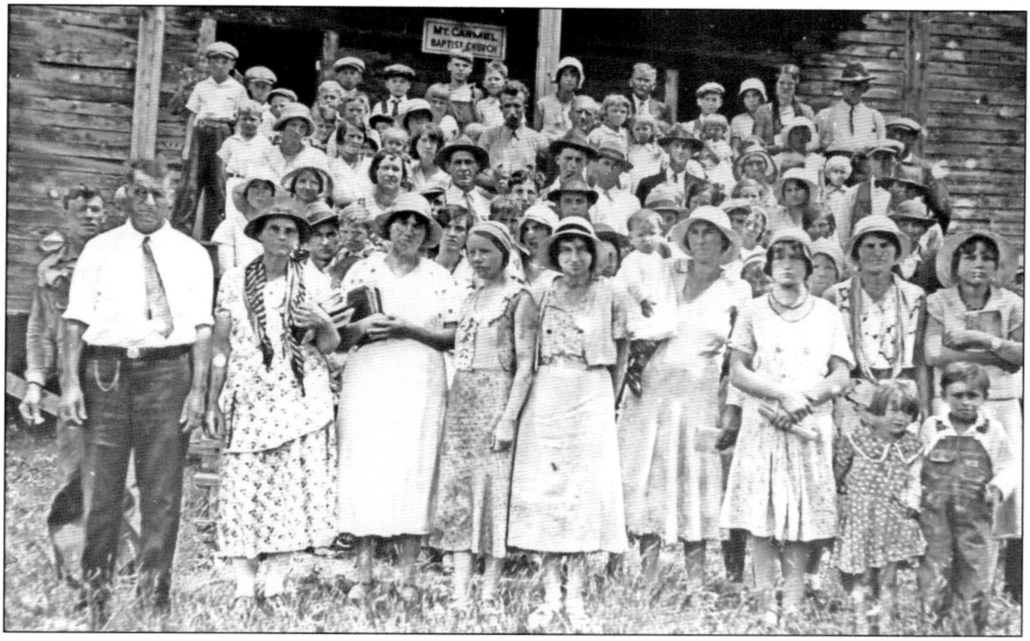


The Mount Carmel Baptist Church was founded in November 1922 at the old Sunshine School. The original building was completed in 1924, and the current church structure was finished in 1954. A fellowship hall and classrooms were added in 1976. Jesse Grindstaff was the first pastor. This photograph of the congregation was taken in the late 1920s on the church's front steps. (Courtesy of Wayne Ward.)

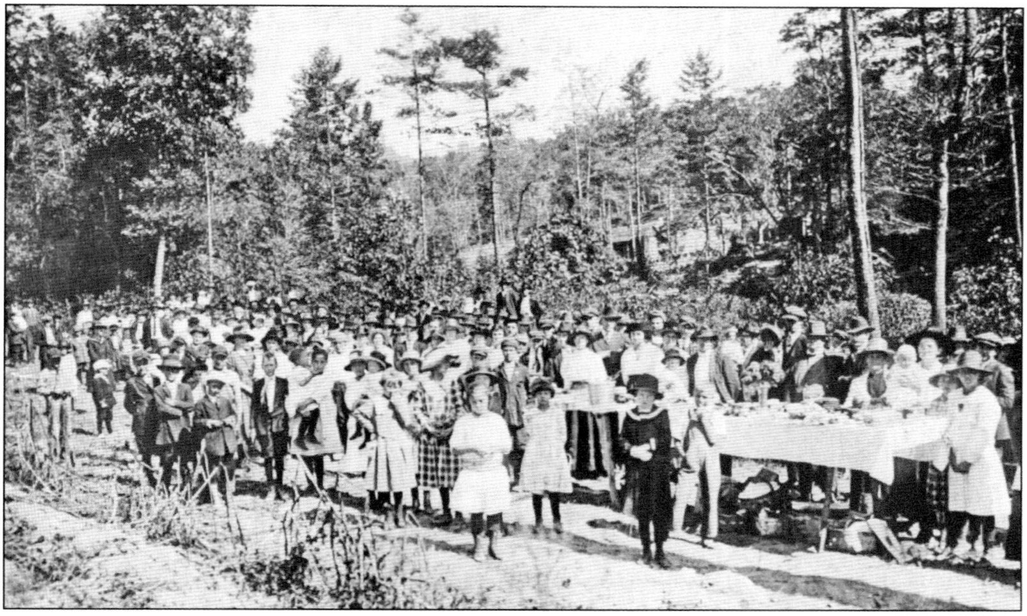

The Pine Branch Baptist Church began in 1920. Rev. Molt Buchanan founded the church, and Charlie Ellis served as its first pastor. It was originally located on property below the current church and was moved to its present location in 1948. This photograph was taken on October 17, 1920, at a picnic held to raise money on the site of the future church. (Courtesy of Chris Hollifield.)

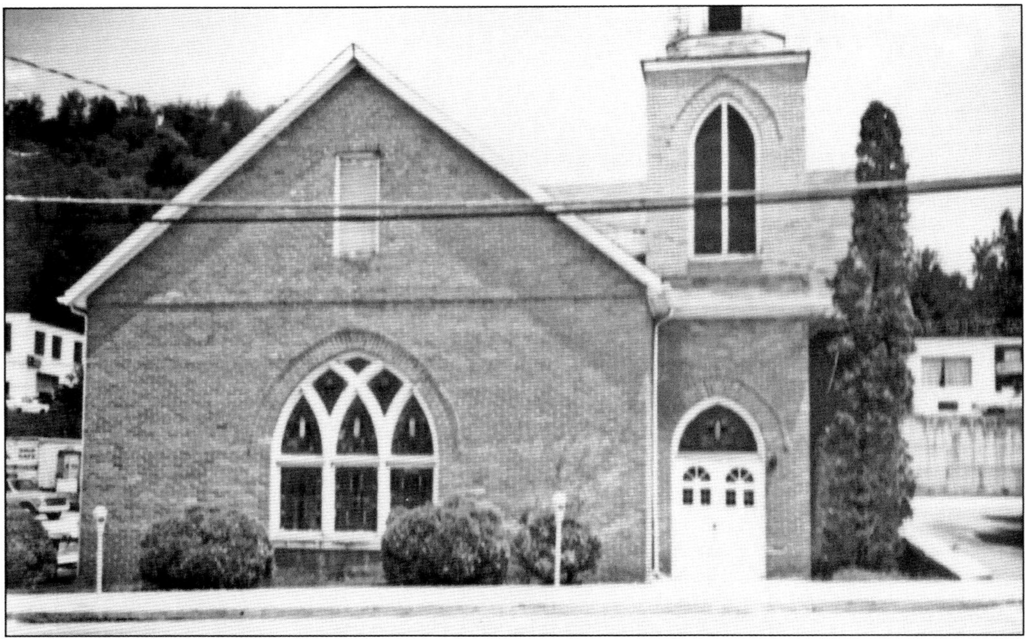

The Spruce Pine First Presbyterian Church began in 1893 on a tract of land donated by the English family. The facility served as both a school and a church. In 1918, the building pictured above was finished on Upper Street. In 1967, the church moved to its present location on Greenwood Road. Rev. Robert Payne Pell was the first pastor. (Courtesy of Mayland Community College.)

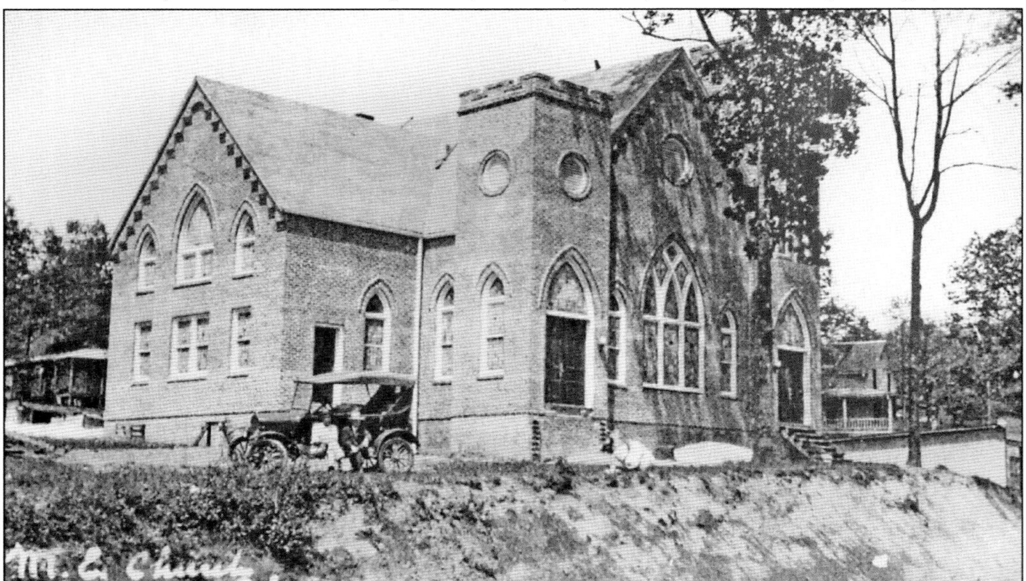


The Spruce Pine United Methodist Church was founded in 1903 when a church building was constructed on Oak Avenue, and the Mount Vernon Church moved and changed its name. In 1929, the brick structure pictured here was completed nearby, serving the congregation until it was destroyed by fire in 1965. In 1966, the current church opened on Burleson Hill. W. H. Weaver was the first pastor. (Courtesy of Evelyn Hughes.)

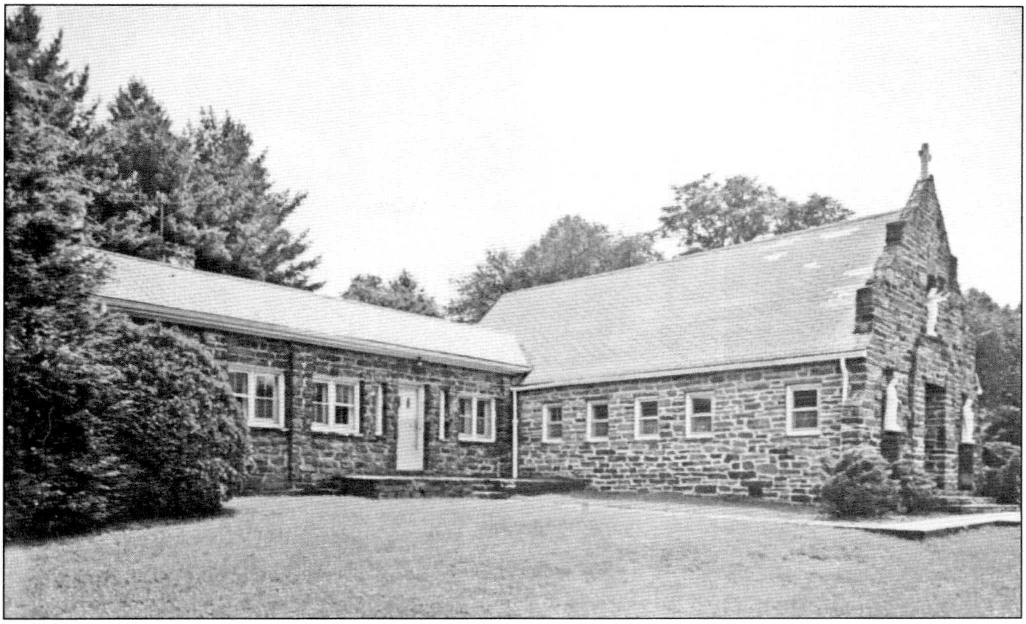

St. Lucien's Catholic Church began at the Topliff Hotel in 1928. A priest traveled from Johnson City to Spruce Pine to say Mass each week on Saturdays. Ella Clapp Thompson donated land and a house for a church in 1935, with Thomas F. Carney saying the first Mass on June 28, 1935. The church exterior was finished by mason David Greene. (Courtesy of St. Lucien's Church.)

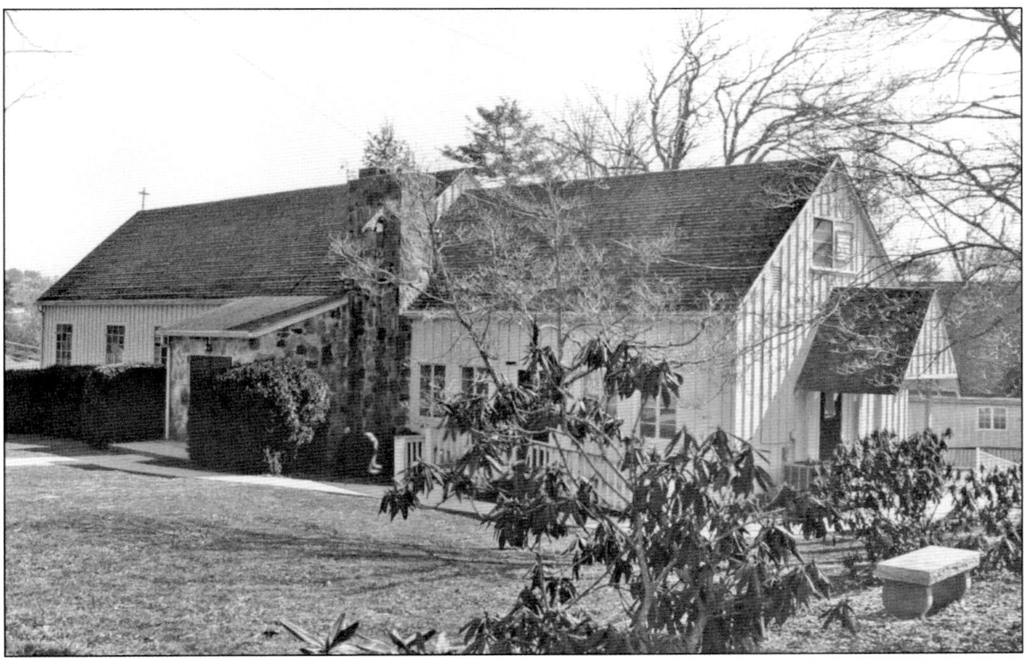

The Trinity Episcopal Church had its beginnings in 1947 at the home of Raymond Dent. A mission was established on Upper Street at the old town hall (now a gallery). This church building opened on August 12, 1955, and a parish hall was opened in 1992. The first pastor was Fr. Peter Lambert. (Courtesy of David Biddix.)

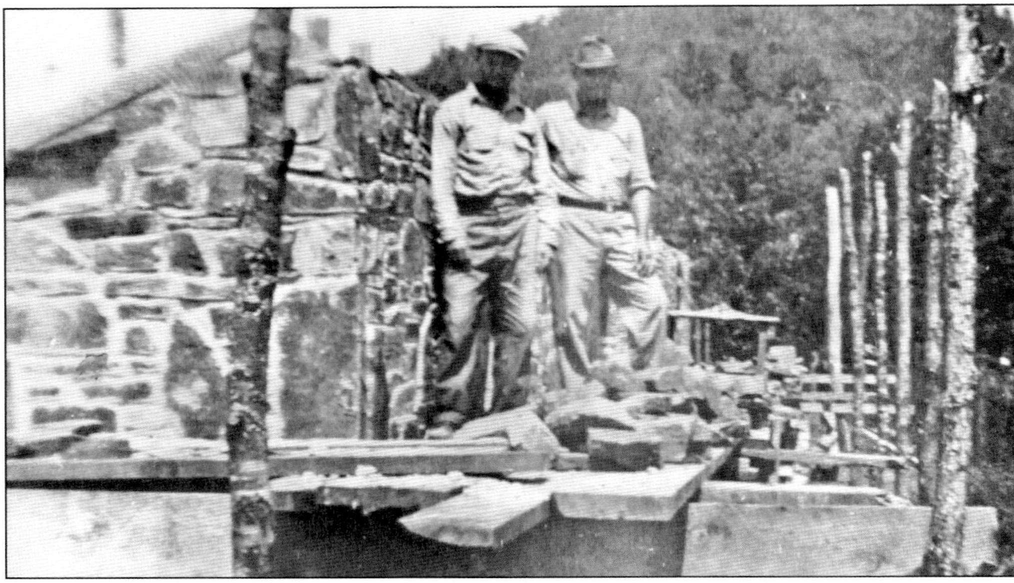

David Greene (left, pictured with Charlie Mitchell) was a mason whose work can be seen on several churches, homes, buildings, and the Harris monument in town. First Baptist, Central Baptist, and St. Lucien's, along with the Gunter building, are prominent examples of his handiwork. He also created the original Overmountain Men monument at Gillespie Gap. (Courtesy of First Baptist Church.)

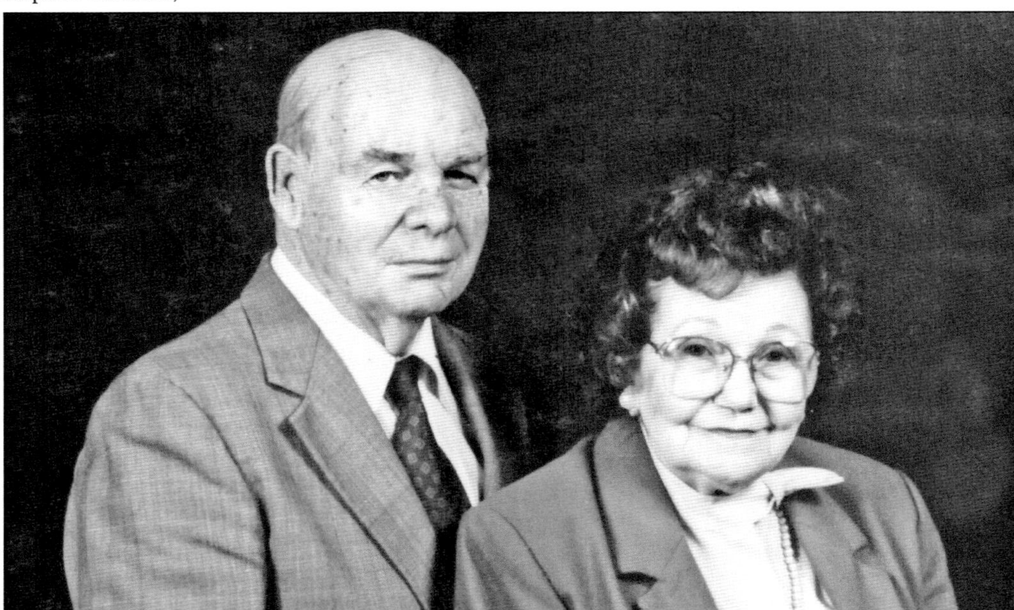

Respected and admired by all, Rev. R. M. and Nellie Cassity came to Spruce Pine in 1951. He was pastor at Beaver Creek, First Baptist, Grassy Creek, and Mount Carmel, but his influence reached far beyond these churches because he served 30 churches in the region on an interim basis. Active in civic affairs, he ministered to everyone regardless of position. He retired from the ministry in 1979. (Courtesy of Felicia Spurling.)

# *Six*

# Mountain Gems
## A Tribute to Success

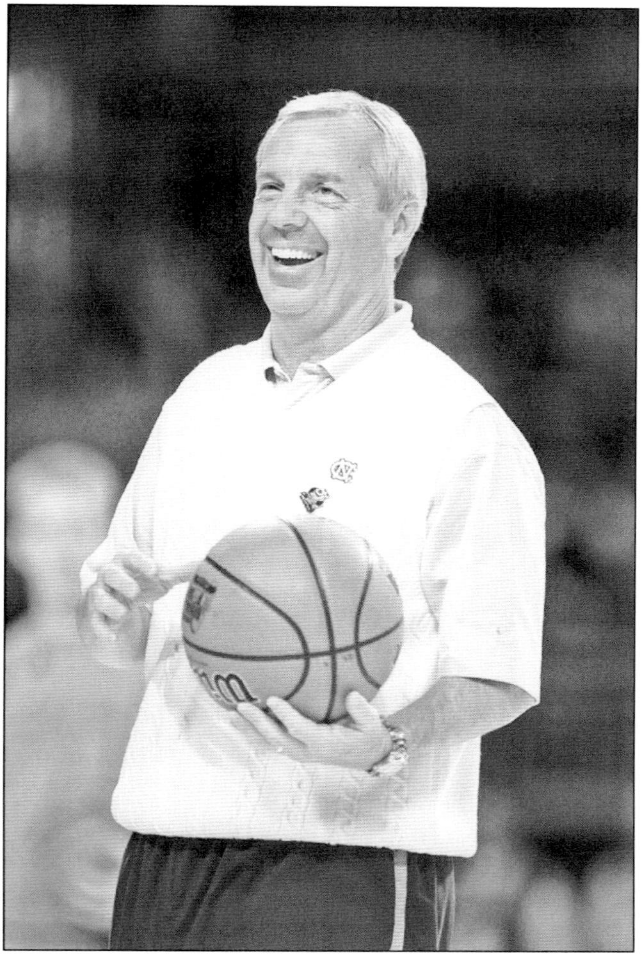

University of North Carolina (UNC) basketball coach Roy Williams lived in Spruce Pine until he was four years old, when he moved to Asheville. A member of the Basketball Hall of Fame, Williams has been named Associated Press Coach of the Year twice. He has averaged 27.5 wins per season as a head coach and won more games in the first 15 seasons of his career than anyone in NCAA history. He won the national championship at UNC in 2005 and 2009. His Kansas teams played in the Final Four three times, with his UNC teams making three appearances in the Final Four. He has coached four National Players of the Year, including Sean May and Tyler Hansbrough, and five First-Team All-Americans. (Courtesy of UNC Sports Information.)

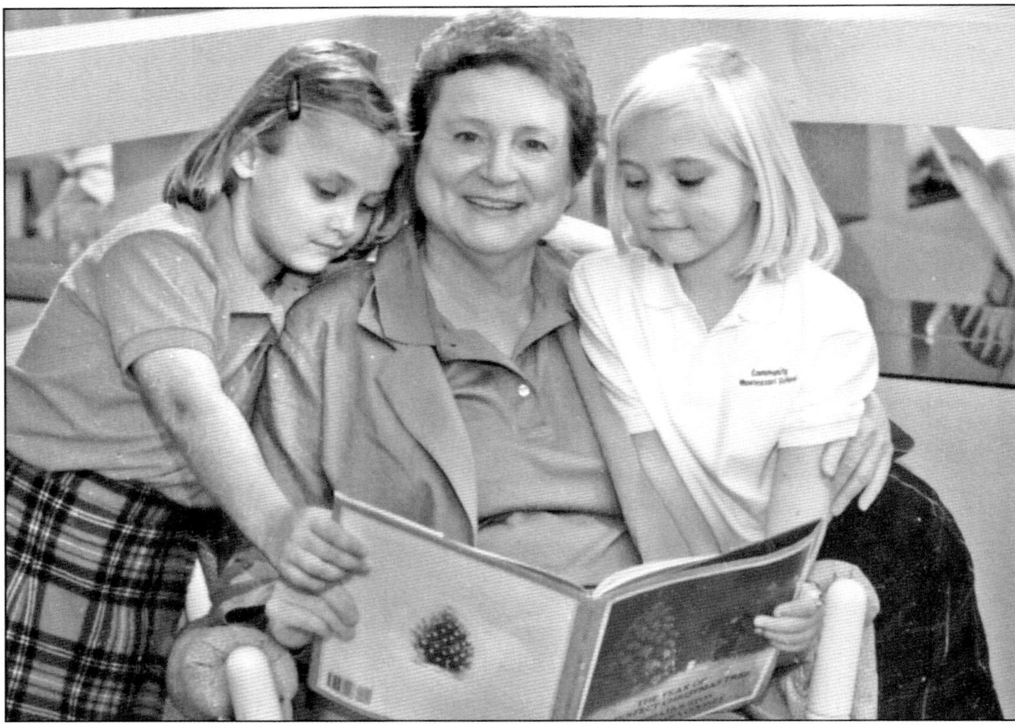

Award-winning children's author Gloria Houston calls Spruce Pine her hometown. Her books are set in Southern Appalachia and describe periods between the Civil War and the World War I era, and are loved by all ages. She is pictured reading her classic *The Year of the Perfect Christmas Tree* with her granddaughters. (Courtesy of LIFESHOTS by Lowie.)

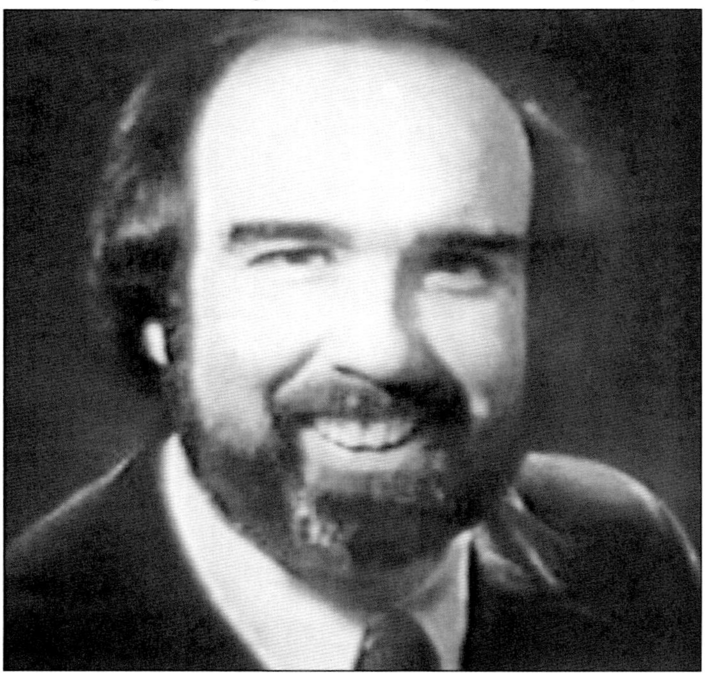

Hugh Silvis graduated from Harris High in 1962 and went on to a career in radio that spanned the nation. Starting at WTOE, he prepped for stops in Louisville, Denver, Houston, and San Francisco, where he was air personality Rick Shaw at KYUU and KIOI. Silvis passed away in 1998 and was replaced on the air by a then unknown individual by the name of Ryan Seacrest. (Courtesy of Donn St. Johnn.)

The Woody family has made chairs in Mitchell County for seven generations. Wyatt Woody moved to the region in 1800 and began the tradition. Wyatt's grandson Arthur (pictured at right) was well known for his ladder-back colonial chairs. His grandsons Paul, Walter, Arval, Frank (all pictured below from left to right), and Floyd continued on, making chairs for such notables as North Carolina governor Terry Sanford and Pres. John Kennedy. The Smithsonian Institution has a Woody rocker as part of its permanent American Crafts Collection. Today the tradition is being carried on by Jim and Scott Woody in the same location that chair making has taken place for more than a century. (Both, courtesy of Woody's Chair Shop.)

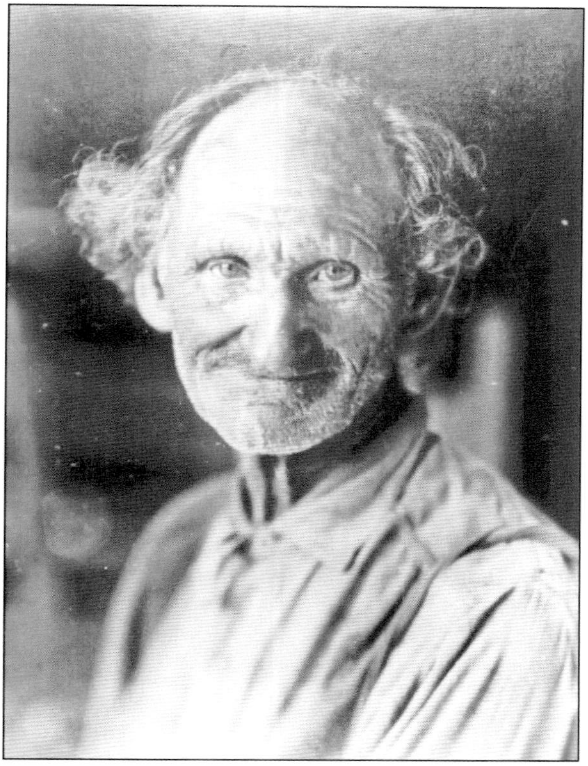

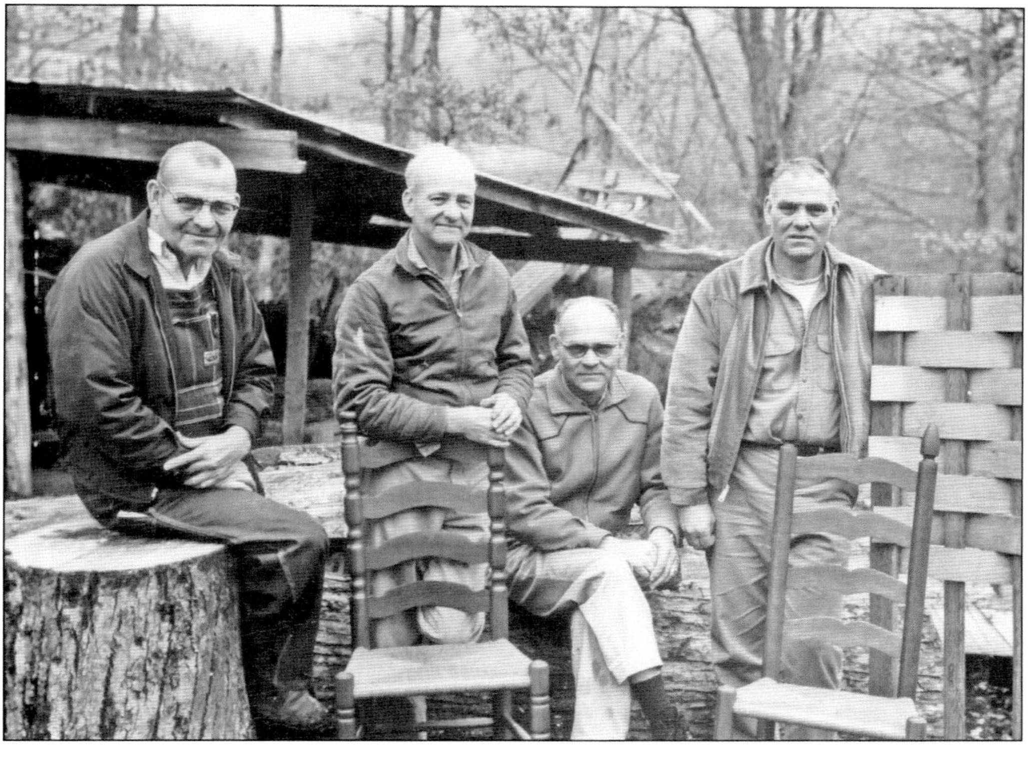

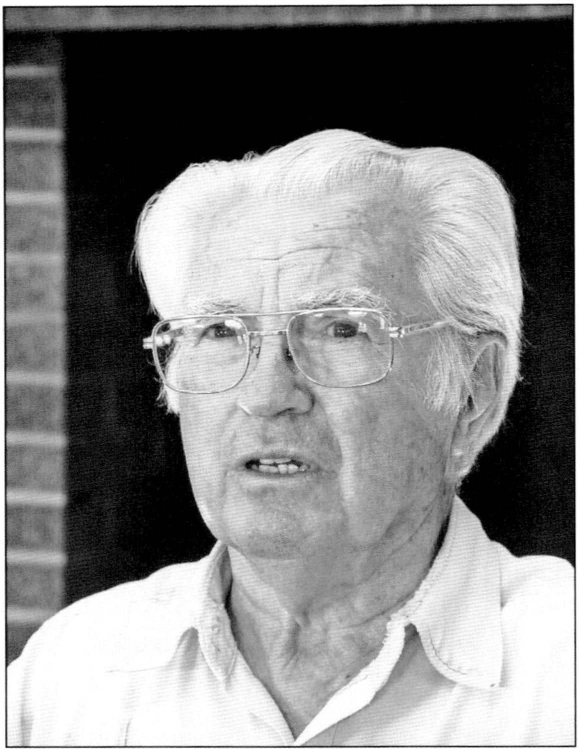

Bea Hensley began his blacksmithing career under the tutelage of Daniel Boone VI. Following World War II, he purchased Boone's forge and started his own ironwork trade. One of his first projects was to finish Boone's work on restoration at Williamsburg, Virginia. He received the 1993 North Carolina Heritage Award, and the National Endowment of the Arts presented him the National Heritage Fellowship Award in 1995. (Courtesy of David Biddix.)

Three generations of clockmakers in the Stroup family are pictured below. Rev. H. M. Stroup (center) began the business in 1949 when he retired from the ministry. His son Bob (left) took over the reins after he retired, and his son Luther (right) started working with the business in 1972 and continues it today. They have delivered more than 2,500 clocks to 48 states, Canada, and Mexico. (Courtesy of Luther Stroup.)

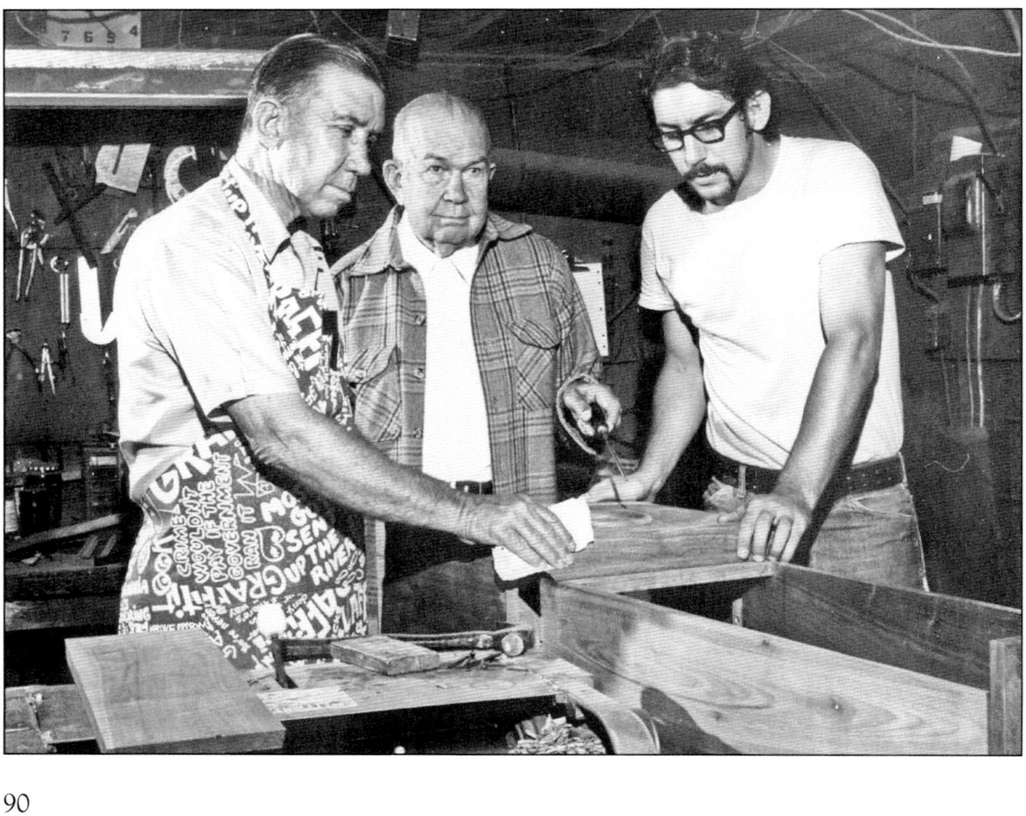

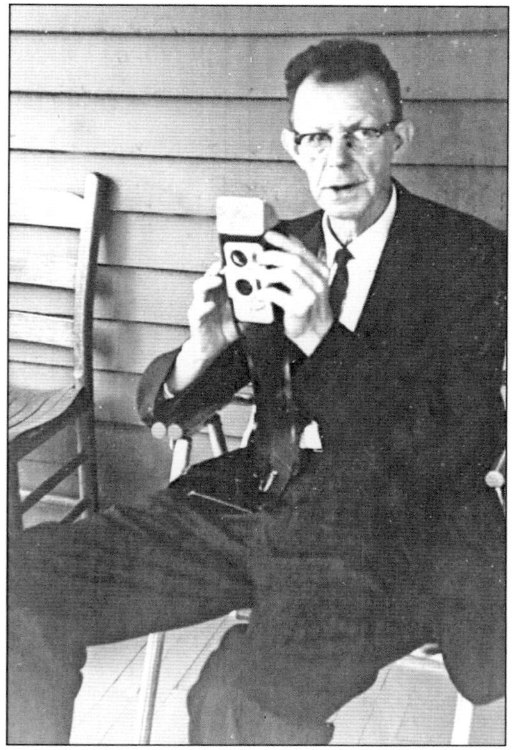

Documenting the people and events of a region is an important task, and these two men left records of their times that are beneficial today. On the right is Jim Jones. He was an accountant for the Phillips and Coulter Oil Company for many years, and he took up photography as a business after he retired. During the 1940s, Jones recorded everyday life in town, from the train to taxicabs and good food. Craig Jenkins (below) moved to Spruce Pine in 1969 after a career in television in Miami, Florida, and began a photography business. He made portraits and group shots along with documenting events, people, and places in the 1970s, 1980s, and early 1990s. Several photographs in this book were taken by these men. (Right, courtesy of Daniel Barron; below, courtesy of Kerry Jenkins.)

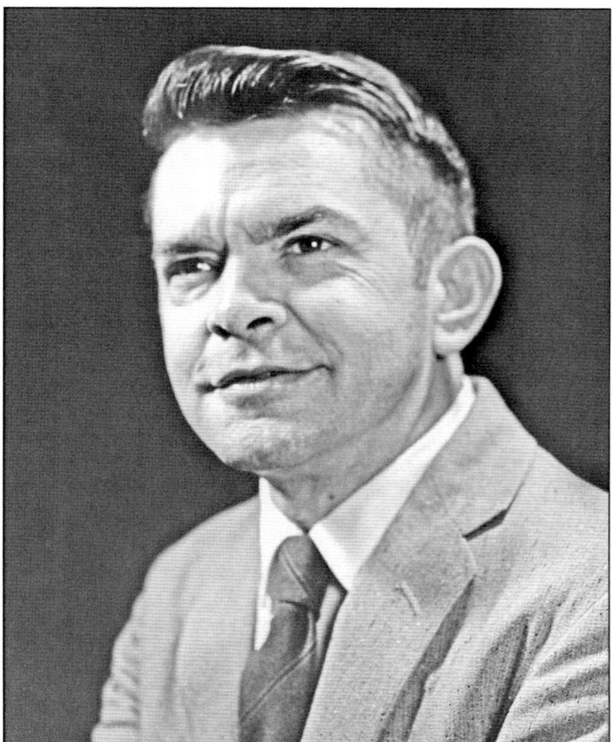

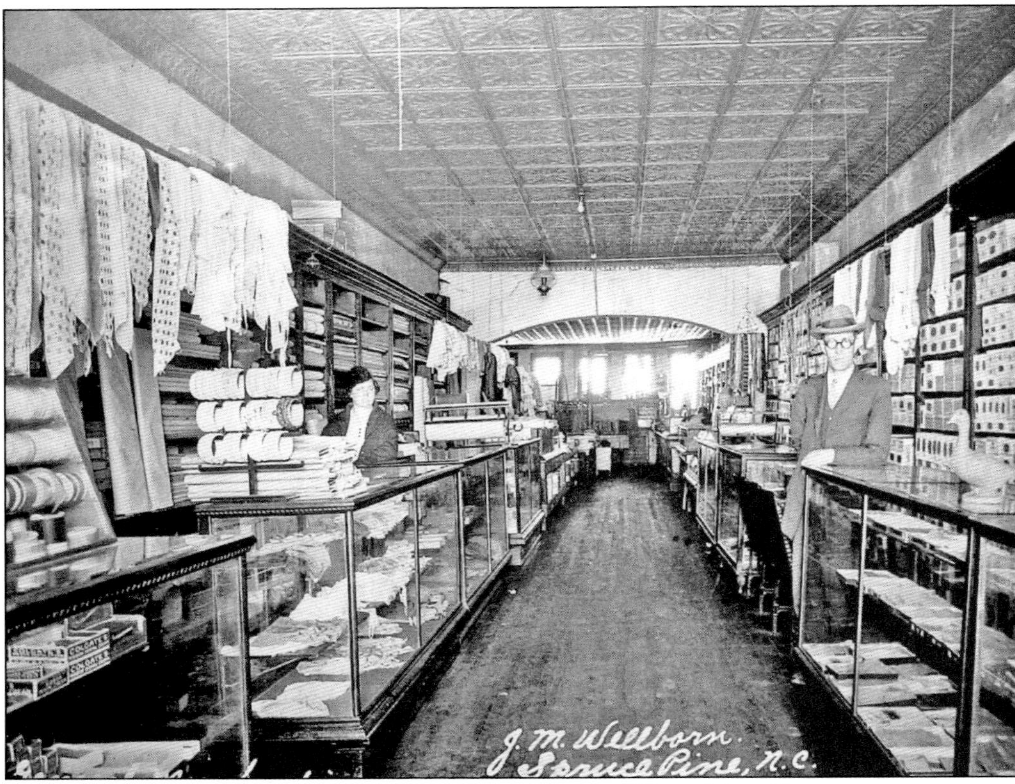


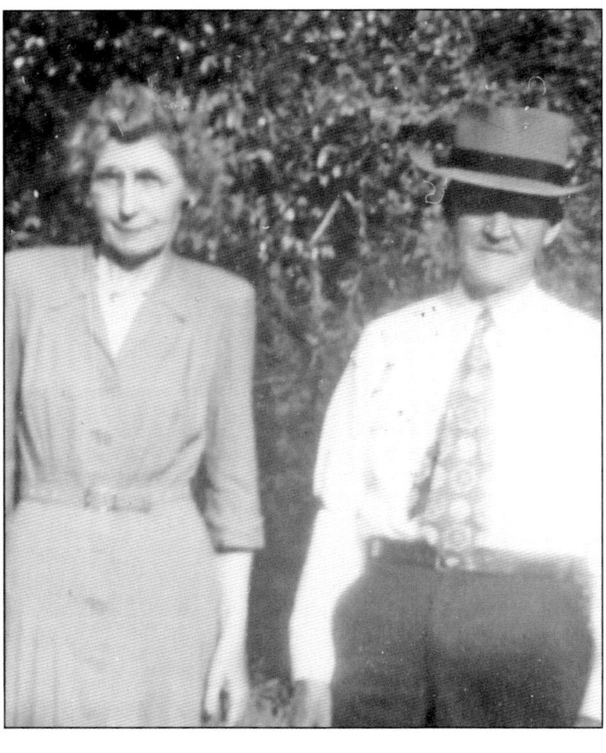

Two of the oldest stores in town share an intertwined history during their existence. Robert Shell (R. S.) McCall (pictured at left with his wife, Annie) opened his first store in 1914, moving to several locations before settling downtown in the Peterson building. In 1928, Joseph Marion (J. M.) Wellborn came to Spruce Pine and bought McCall's store, prompting him to move down the street and open again. Wellborn's moved twice, ending at its final location next to McCall's in 1938. The two stores continued separately until 1988, when Shell McCall, son of R. S., retired and once again sold the McCall's store to a Wellborn, this time John, son of J. M. He operated them separately until his retirement in 2007, when they were closed. (Above, courtesy of John Wellborn; left, courtesy of Forrest McCall.)

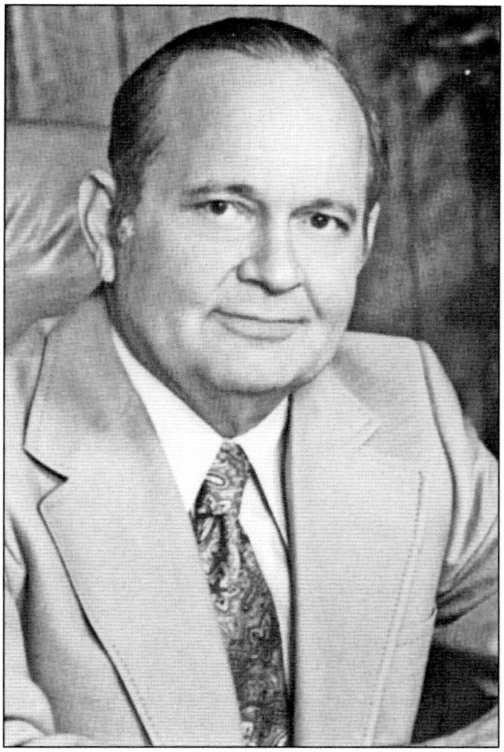

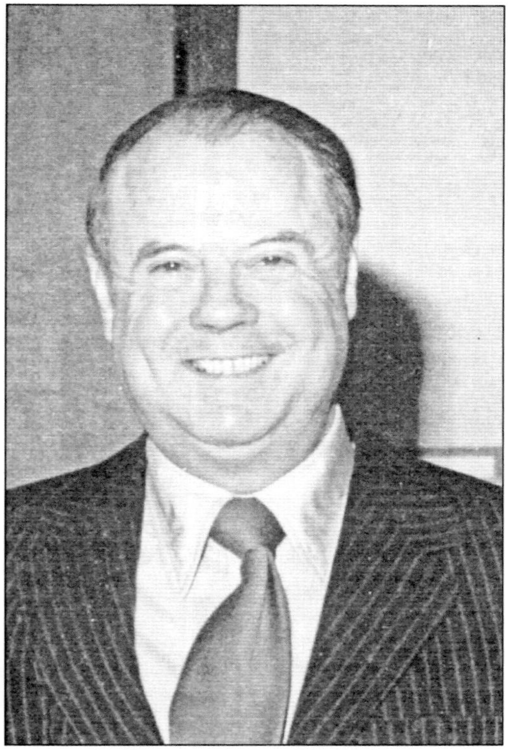

These three businessmen led growth in Spruce Pine for decades. Brad Ragan (above left) opened a store on Upper Street in the 1940s. He expanded and formed the Carolina Tire Company and its parent, Brad Ragan, Incorporated (BRI), headquartered in Spruce Pine. BRI became Goodyear Tire's largest retailer, with worldwide operations. Ragan was civic-minded, donating to community causes, and he led efforts to create a recreation park. On December 21, 1979, he was killed in an airplane crash near Provo, Utah. Sam Phillips (above right) was instrumental in establishing mica as a strategic mineral, which led to a boom in local mica businesses. Ray Howell (at right) was a merchant and real estate developer who worked to promote the region for both tourists and residents. (Above left, courtesy of Mildred Harris; above right, courtesy of Gina Phillips; right, courtesy of Bill and Brenda Sparks.)

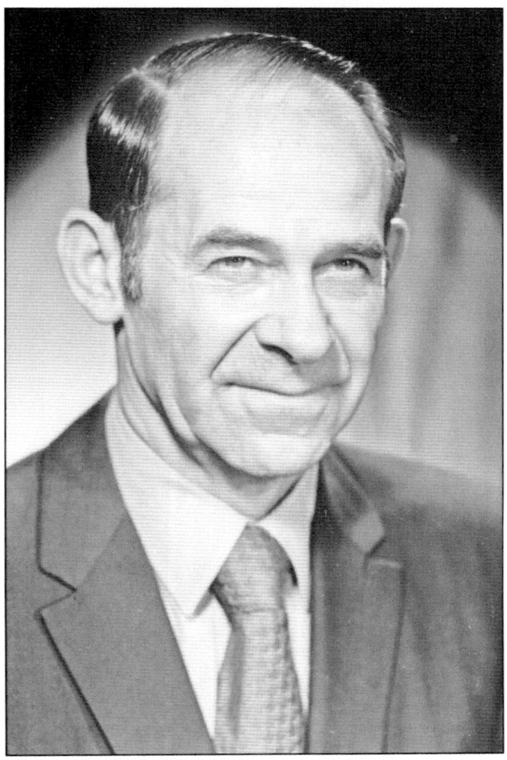

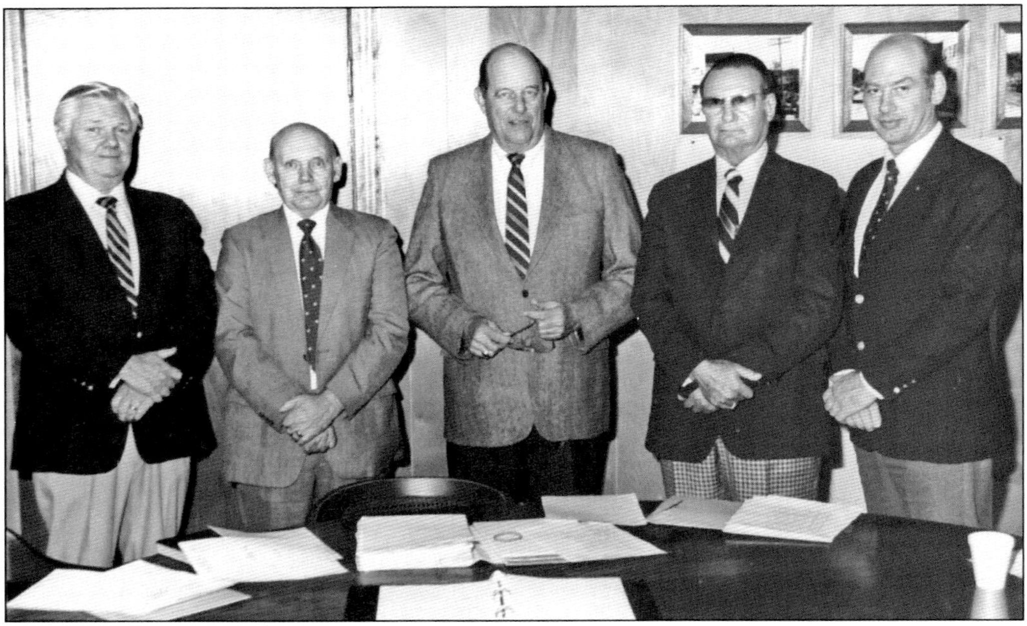

The above photograph, taken by noted photographer Craig Jenkins, shows the Spruce Pine Town Board in 1987. From left to right are magistrate Bob Thompson, alderman Carroll Canipe, Mayor David Blevins, and aldermen Brown Norman and Phillip Frye. Over the years, these men served in a variety of functions in Spruce Pine's town government and oversaw tremendous change. (Courtesy of Phillip Frye.)

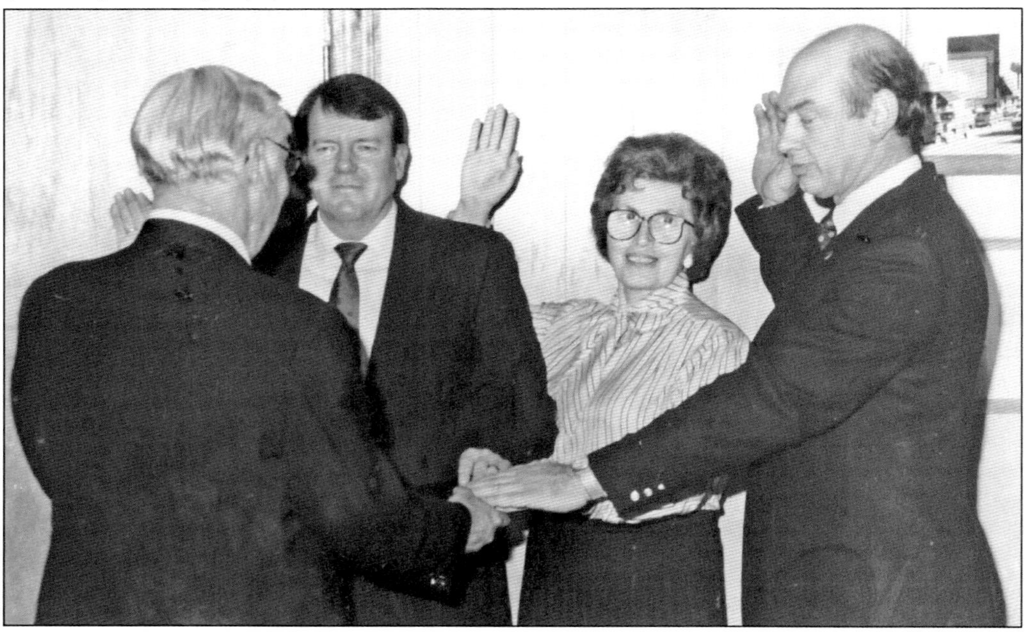

Doris Thompson (center) takes the oath of office with Danny Burleson (left) and Phillip Frye (right) as aldermen for the Town of Spruce Pine. Thompson was the first woman elected to the town board. She was elected in 1990. Since then, Brenda Pittman has been elected to the board. (Courtesy of Doris Thompson.)

# *Seven*

# Our Town
## A Moment in Time

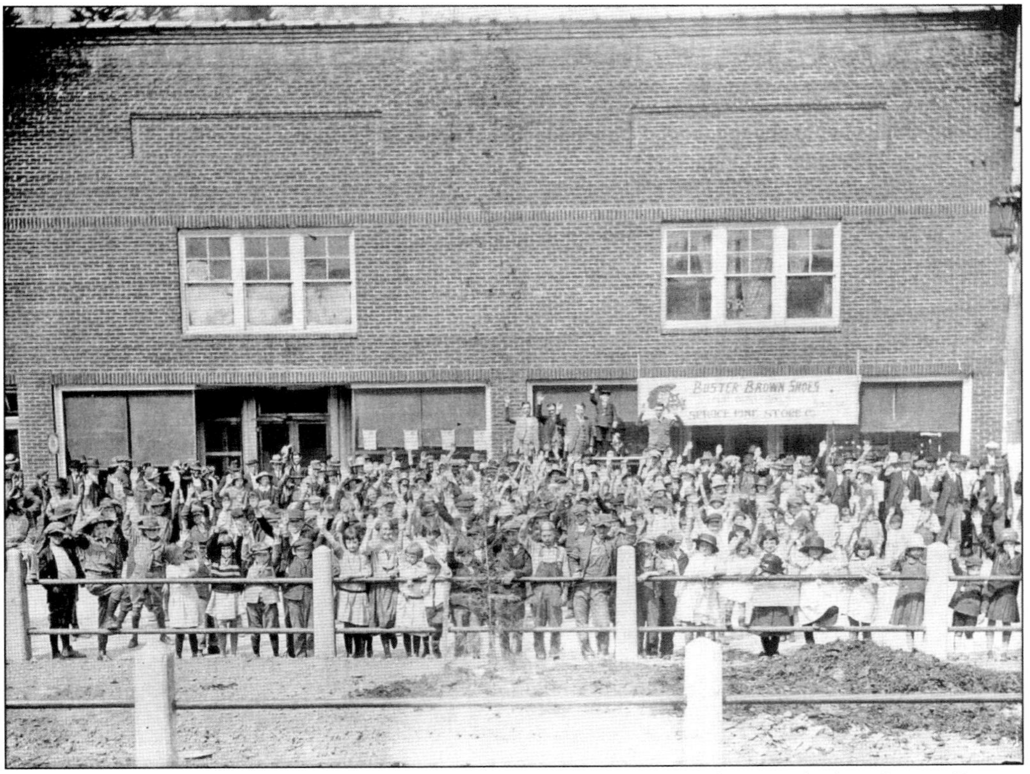


Turning out when a celebrity visits town has always been commonplace, and when Buster Brown and his dog Tige stop by the new Spruce Pine Store building in the 1920s, the whole town turned out to say hello. The store, owned by the Harris Mining Company, offered general merchandise and moved to this location in the early 1920s. (Courtesy of Guss McKinney.)

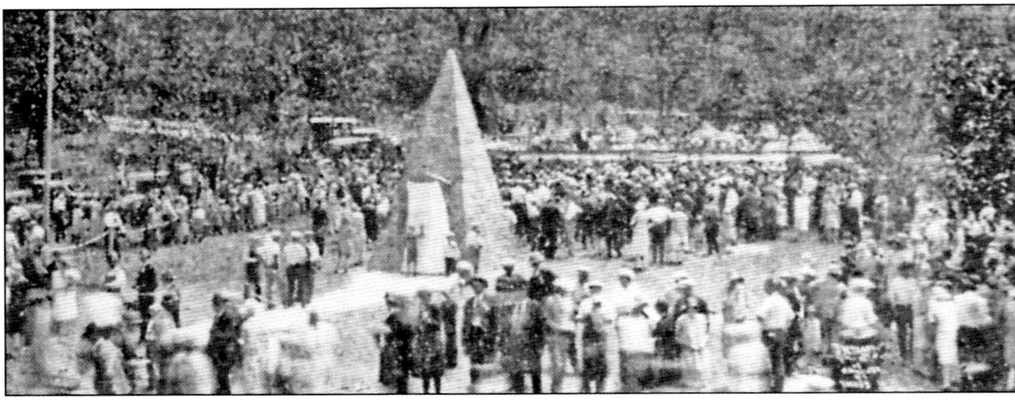

July 4, 1927, was a special day at Gillespie Gap, south of town. The North Carolina Historical Commission dedicated a monument to the Overmountain Men and to Francis Marion. The Overmountain Men crossed the Blue Ridge near the spot on their way to fight the British at Kings Mountain. A portion of a trading path, Gillespie Gap was known as Etchoe Pass by the Cherokee and may have also been the scene of a battle between Francis Marion and Cherokee forces. The community turned out for the ceremony, which included a performance by the Spruce Pine Band, pictured below. (Above, courtesy of the *Mitchell News-Journal*; below, courtesy of Chris Hollifield.)

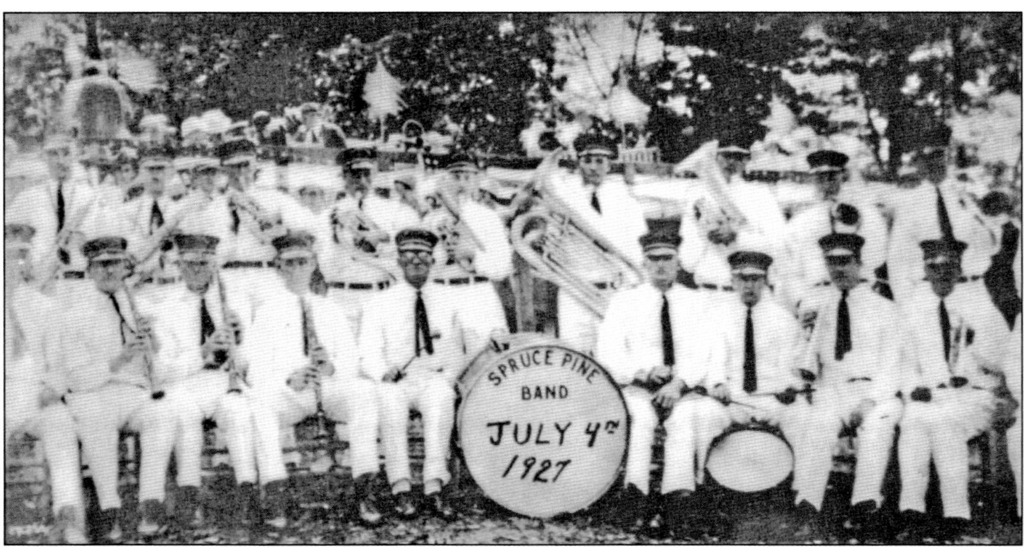

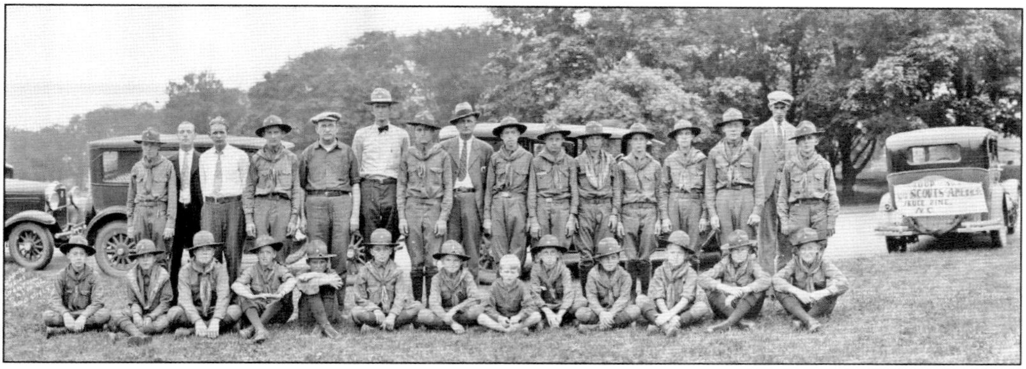

The Boy Scout troop from Spruce Pine traveled to Washington, D.C., on August 8, 1929, posing for this photograph. From left to right are (first row) William Zeb Buchanan Jr., Brown Hughes Burleson, James Phillip Young, John Dallas Swann, Albert Lee Canipe, James Carter Phillips, Frank Marvin Whitlock, Billy Smith, Jurians Haywood Goforth, James Hendrix Lyons, William Yarbor Brown, Daniel Oscar Blevins Jr., and John William Greene; (second row) Frank Alexander Swift Jr., Guy Wiseman, Harold Berry, Robert Johnson Gilbert, J. W. Gilbert, William R. Smith (scoutmaster), Ernest Lee Murphy, Reid Berry, William Sydney Kester, John Lewis McNeil, Charles Dorman Berry, Earl McBee, James Clifford Mayberry, Howard Britton Lyons, B.B. "Mutt" Burleson, and Sam B. Cannon Jr. (Courtesy of Tess Burleson Coulter.)

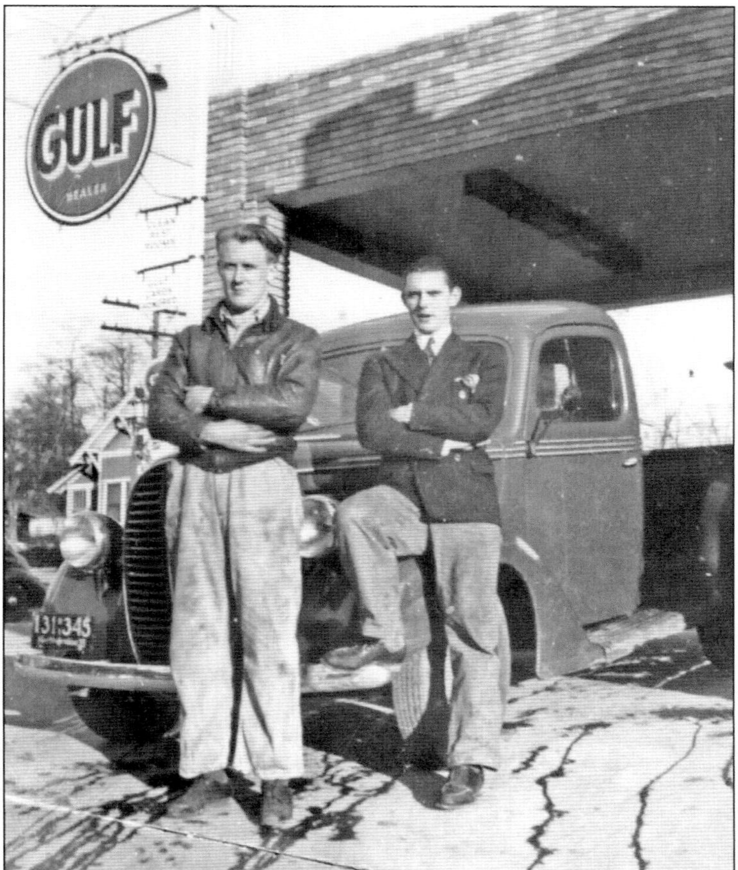


A dashing, dapper Albert Canipe (right) poses with John Phillips at the Gulf station on Oak Avenue. Canipe went on to serve as Spruce Pine's mayor, in the North Carolina State Senate, and as a member of the North Carolina Low-Level Nuclear Compact Commission. John Phillips was part owner of the Phillips and Coulter Oil Company and a prominent businessman. (Courtesy of Emma Lee Wilson.)

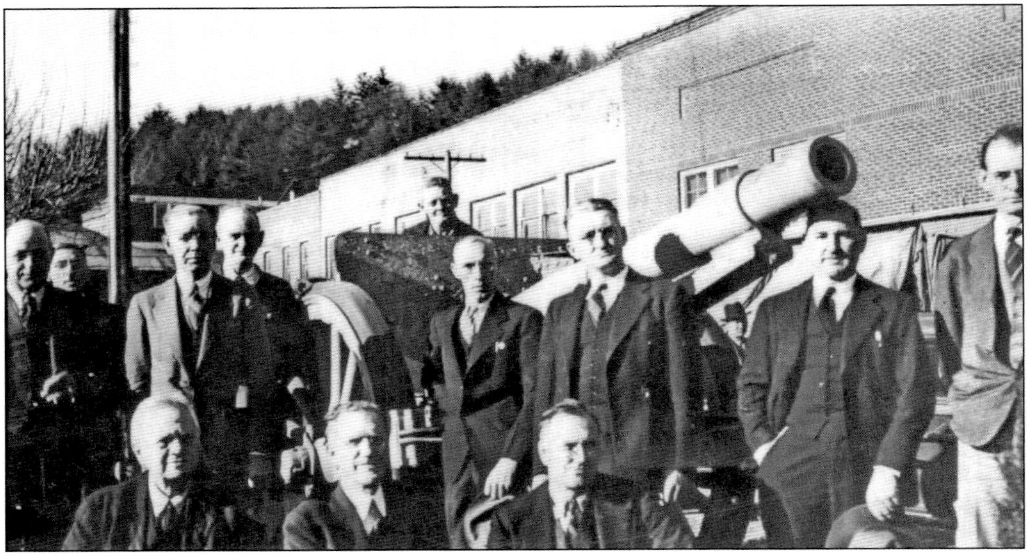

The American Legion dedicated this cannon in honor of World War I veterans at the depot on Lower Street. Pictured from left to right are (first row) John McBee, A. N. Fuller, and Rep. Charles Jonas; (second row) Ed Scott, a Mr. McLure, J. H. Duncan, a Mr. Loven, unidentified, Cliff Gibbs, Arnold Phillips, A. R. "Guss" Craig, and unidentified. The cannon was later cut up for scrap metal. (Courtesy of Chris Hollifield.)

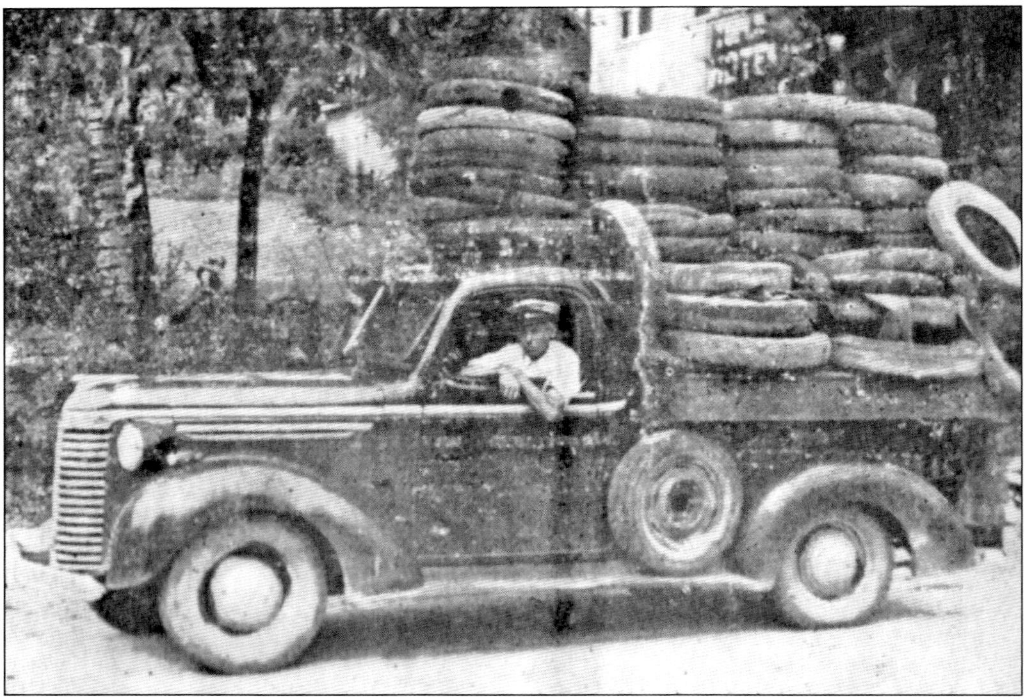

Rationing was a part of life during World War II. Victory gardens were common, and certain items, such as aluminum, were collected for the war effort. The supply of rubber tires was severely restricted, and they were recycled. W. F. Smith hauls 2,285 pounds of tires to be loaded onto a train and transported in this image. (Courtesy of the *Mitchell News-Journal.*)

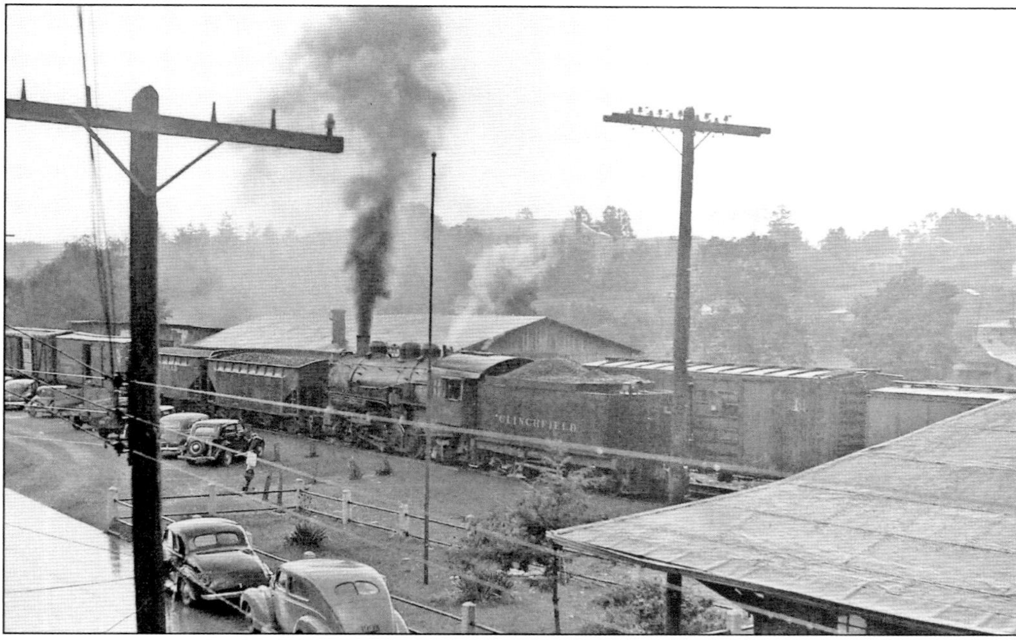

A common sight on Lower Street was the arrival of the train. Jim Jones captured this image of a coal-fired behemoth during a rainy day in the 1940s. (Courtesy of Daniel Barron.)

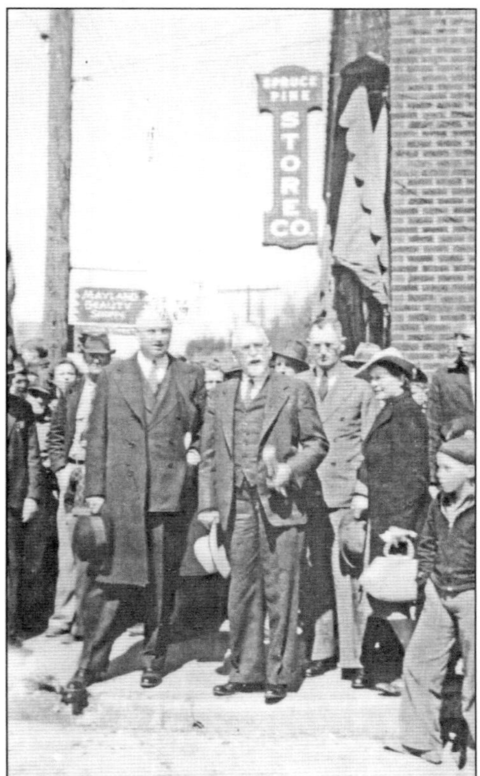


Postmaster General Jim Farley visited Spruce Pine in April 1940, and the town turned out to welcome him. Pictured here, from left to right, are Herbert Hickey, Jim Farley, E. Frank Watson, A. N. Fuller, and Zula Fuller. (Courtesy of Leo Riddle.)

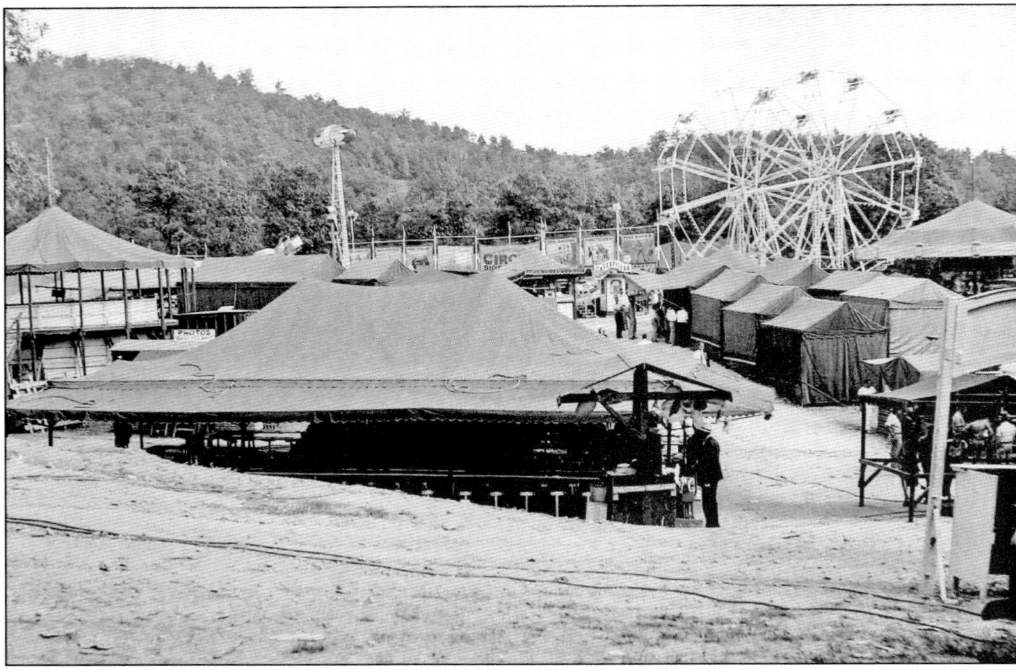

The Mayland Fair began in 1914 as the Toe River Fair. Held on the fairgrounds located above town on Walnut Avenue, it featured a midway, music shows, and traditional fair competitions. Photographer Jim Jones captured the midway around opening time and a cattle judging event, shown below. The fair was discontinued in the late 1940s by town fathers who felt it was having a detrimental effect on the youth. (Both, courtesy of Daniel Barron.)

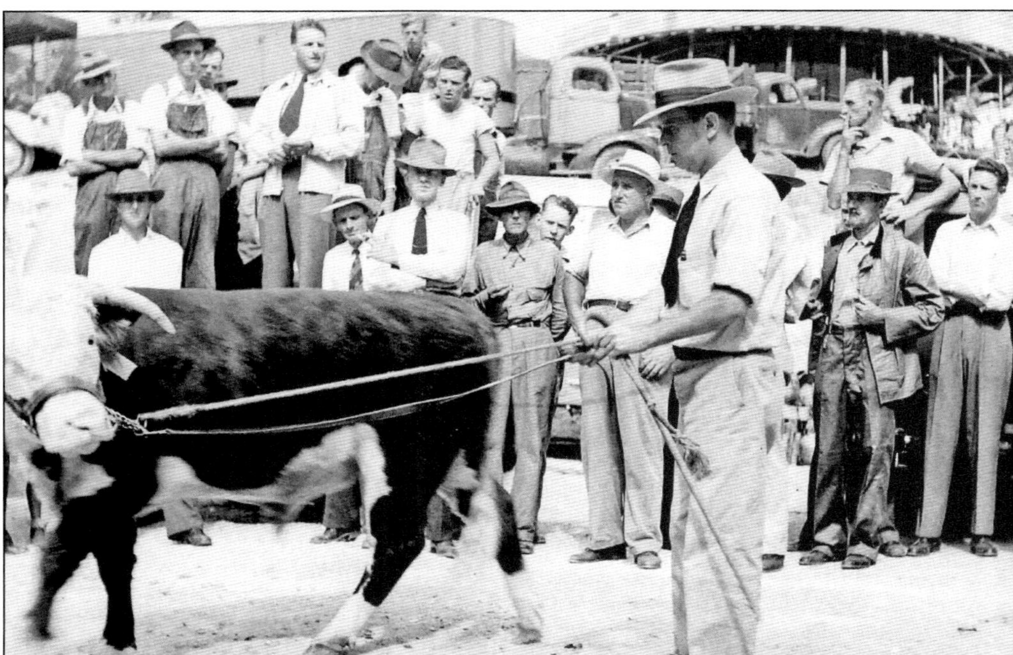

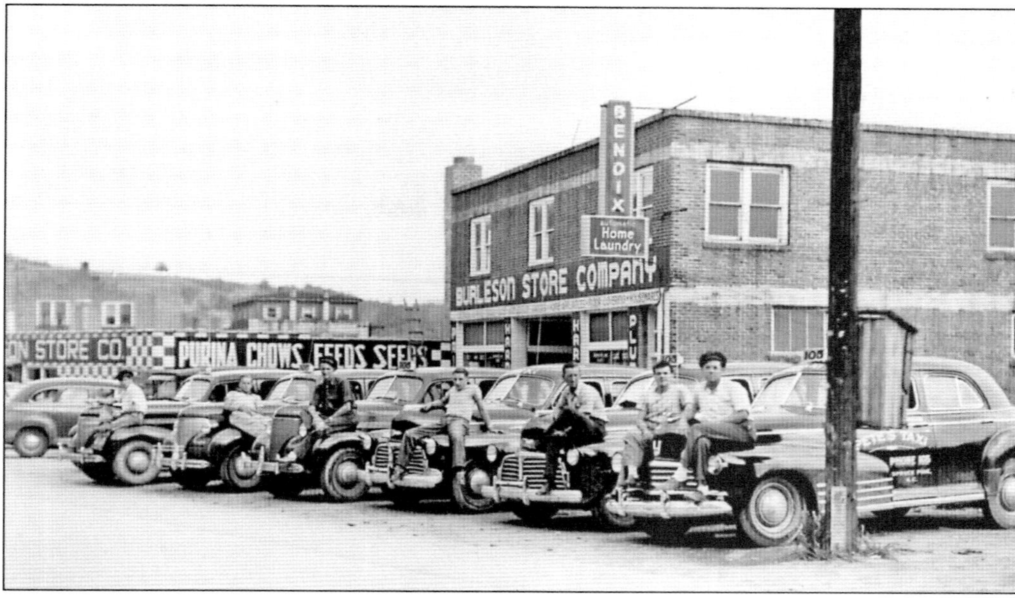


Getting around town in the 1940s was made easier by a fleet of taxis that served Spruce Pine. Their lineups on Upper Street are a poignant view of an earlier time. Pictured above, from left to right, are Pete Ellis, Plug Pittman, Ernest King, Lawrence Smith, Mutt Burleson, Howard Hise, and an unidentified man in front Burleson Store. Note the telephone box on the pole beside the cars. This was their office. Below, unidentified drivers await customers beside Wava's Lunch, a popular cafe on Upper Street. (Both, courtesy of Daniel Barron.)

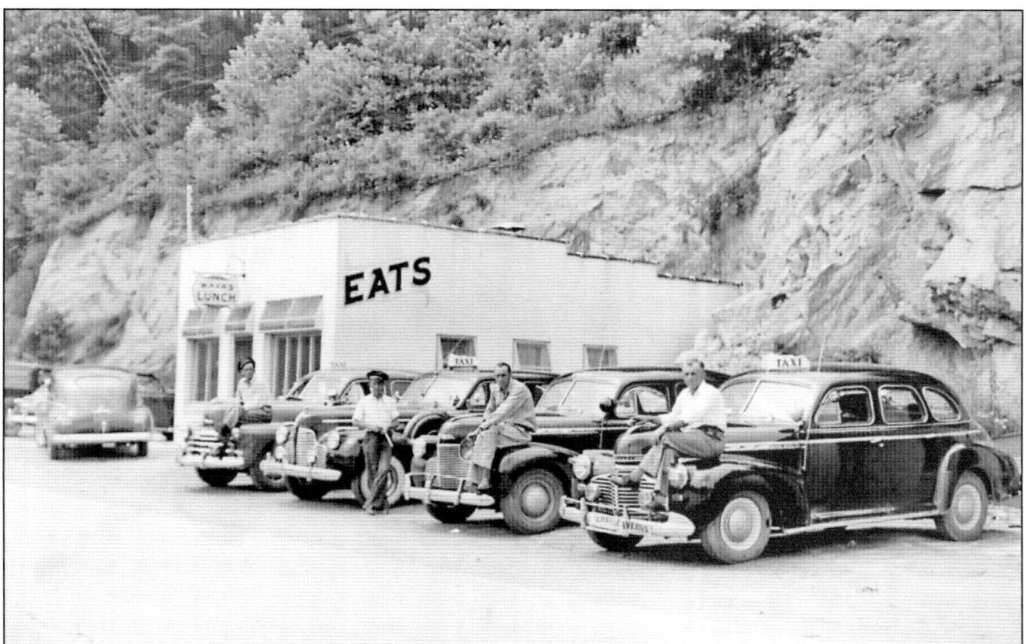

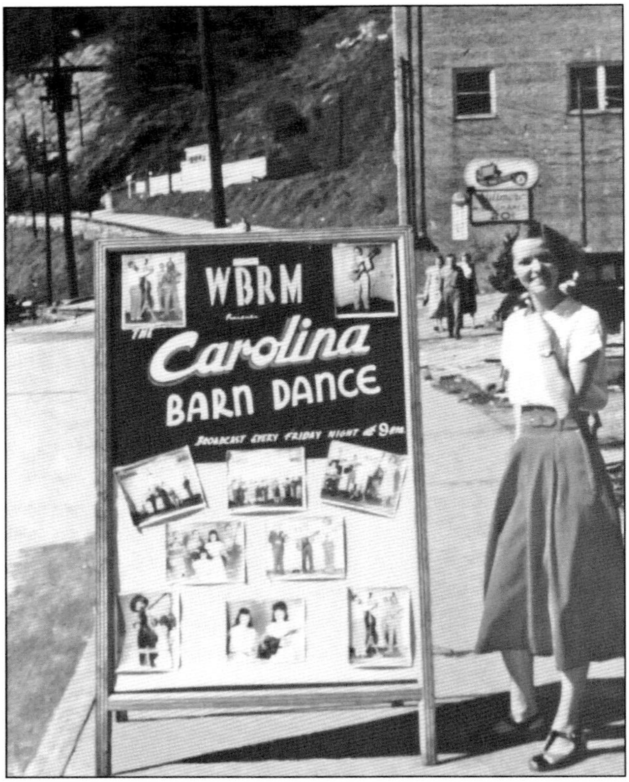


From September 1949 to November 1954, the Carolina Barn Dance was broadcast from coast to coast on the Liberty Broadcasting System. The program originated at the Carolina Theatre on Lower Street and was sent to the network's Texas studios over a telephone line on Friday evenings. It was taped and rebroadcast from 8:00 p.m. to 9:00 p.m. on Saturday nights. WBRM in Marion carried the show on Saturday mornings. It was the brainchild of O. D. "Cal" Calhoun and J. Myron Houston, who were looking for a moneymaker for the theater and decided to start a talent night. At left is a signboard advertising the show outside the theater. Patsy Harris Evans, who worked in a newsstand next door, is on the right. (Both, courtesy of O. D. and Mary Calhoun.)

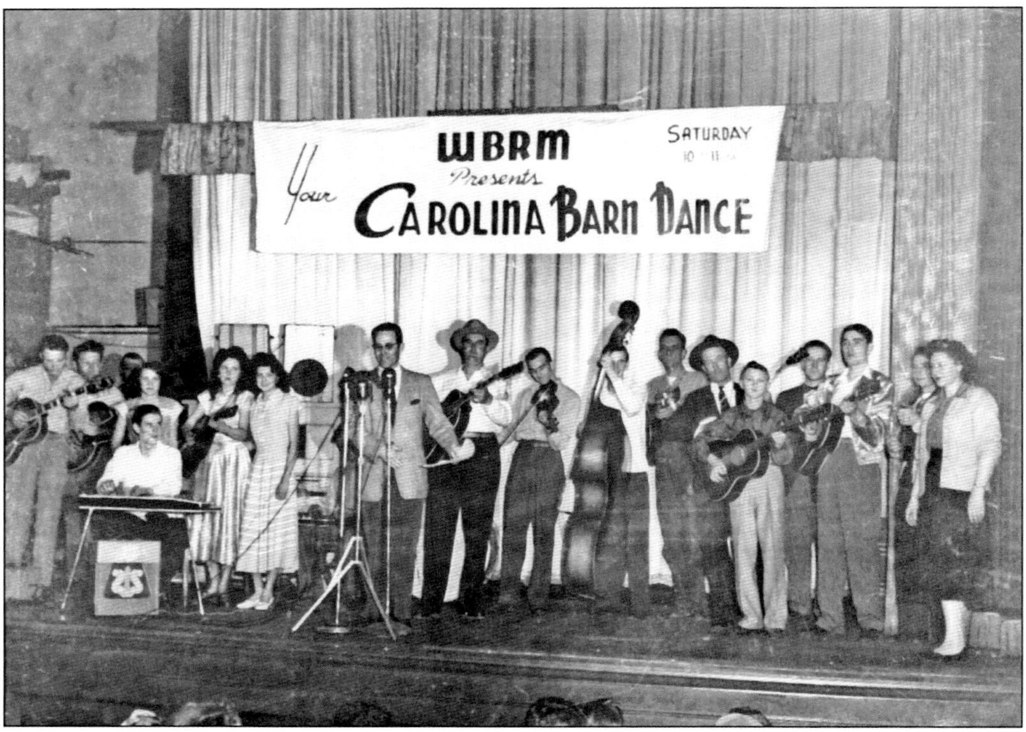

Calhoun's showmanship both on and off the air promoted the broadcast, attracting both locally and nationally known talent. Pictured at right with Cal are Lulu Belle and Scotty Wiseman, who, at the time, were one of the most-beloved acts in country music. Below is the Chestnut Grove Quartet, a local act that appeared regularly on the broadcast, singing gospel favorites. Calhoun and Houston ran a clean, family-oriented show each week. National acts that appeared included Chet Atkins, Eddy Arnold, Patsy Cline, "Tennessee" Ernie Ford, Sonny James, Bill Monroe, and Kitty Wells. The show ended when the Liberty Network folded in 1954. (Both, courtesy of O. D. and Mary Calhoun.)

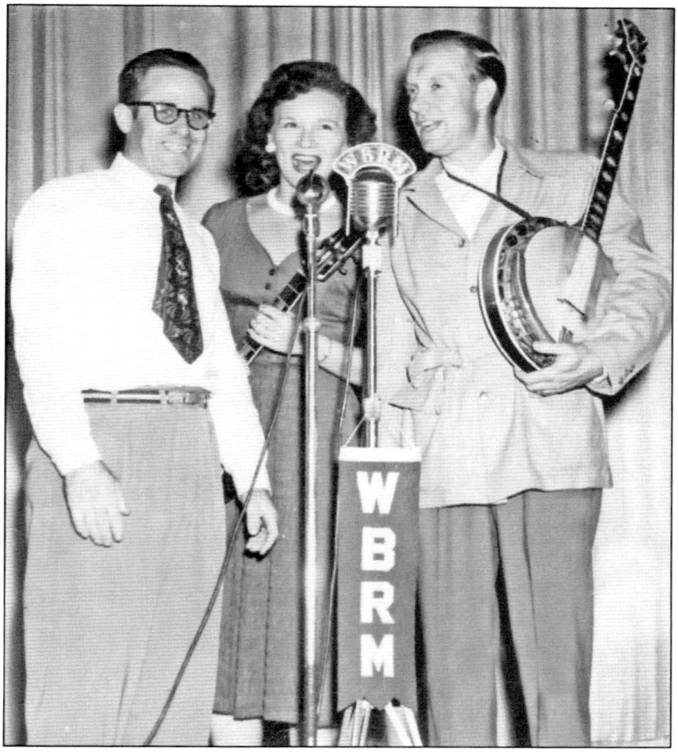


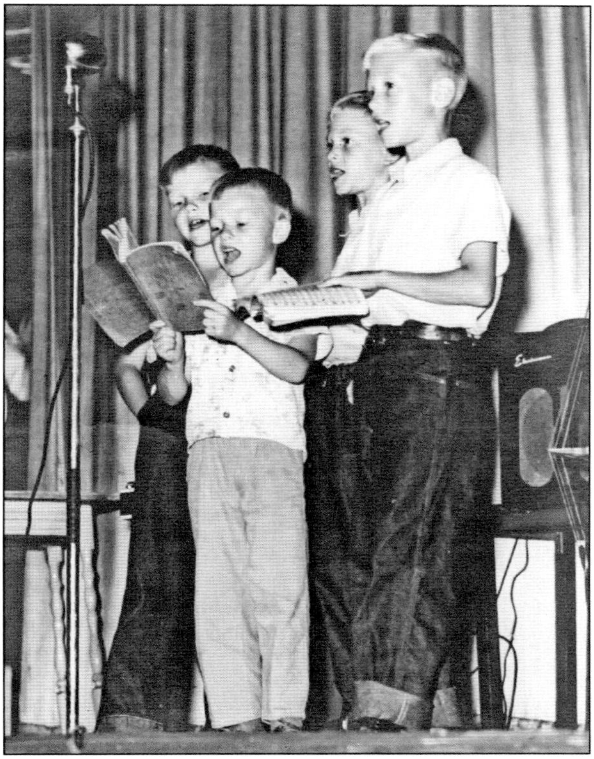

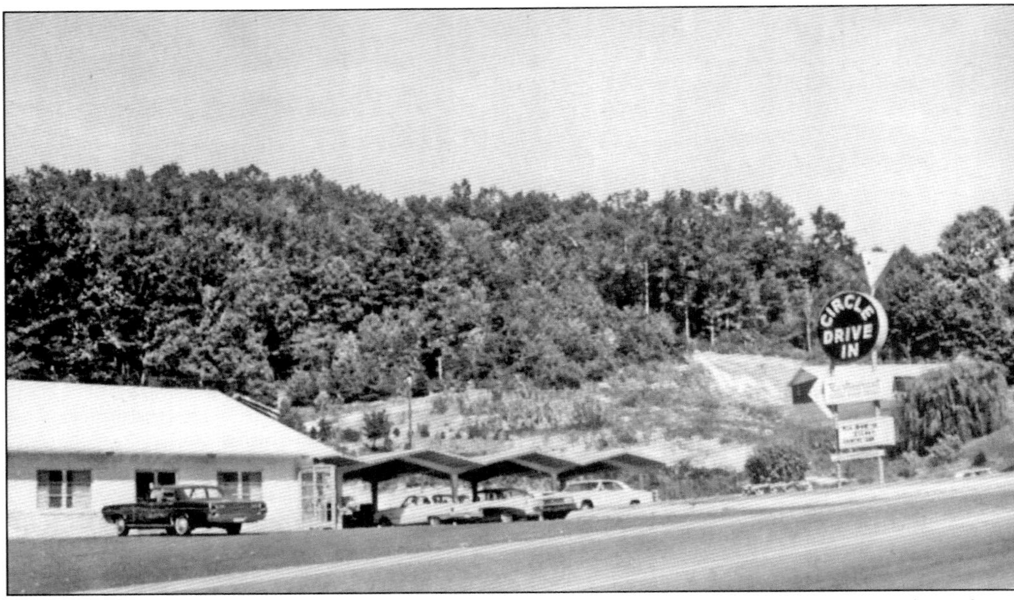


The Circle Drive-In, located on Chalk Mountain, was a popular hangout for Harris High students. It was operated by Ed and Mae Huskins, and it closed in the 1970s. (Courtesy of David Biddix.)

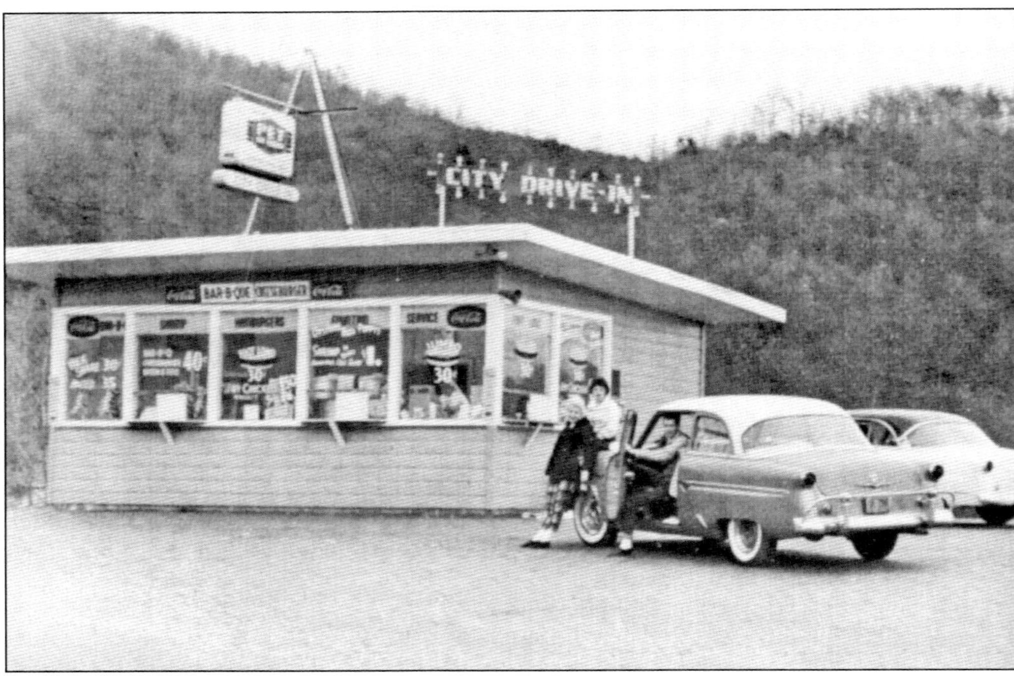


The City Drive-In, located on Oak Avenue, was operated by Donald Hobson and was well known for its city burgers. It has been open for about 50 years and was another popular hangout for teens. (Courtesy of Chris Hollifield.)

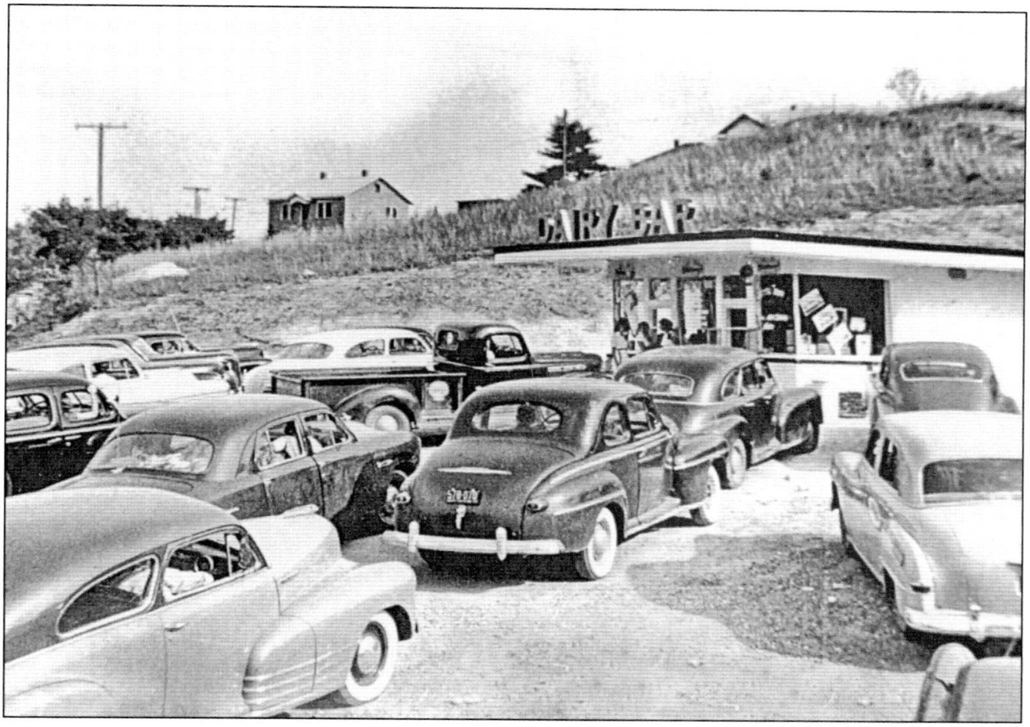


Don's Dairy Bar, located on Summit Avenue across from the First Baptist Church, was where residents turned for relief from the heat with a cool ice cream cone or milk shake. Operated by Don and Gloria Pendley, and later by their son Donnie, it was a Spruce Pine institution for many years. (Courtesy of Guss McKinney.)

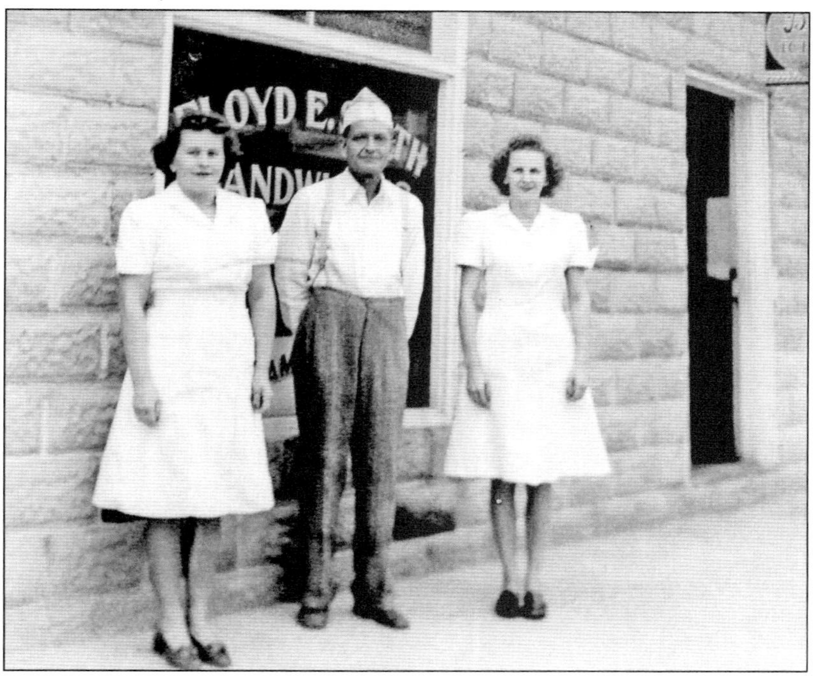

Floyd Smith fried hamburgers in the early morning to feed hungry customers for lunch at his sandwich shop at the corner of Link and Upper Streets. He is pictured with sisters and waitresses Lillie Pendley (left) and Arla Woody outside the shop. (Courtesy of Daniel Barron.)

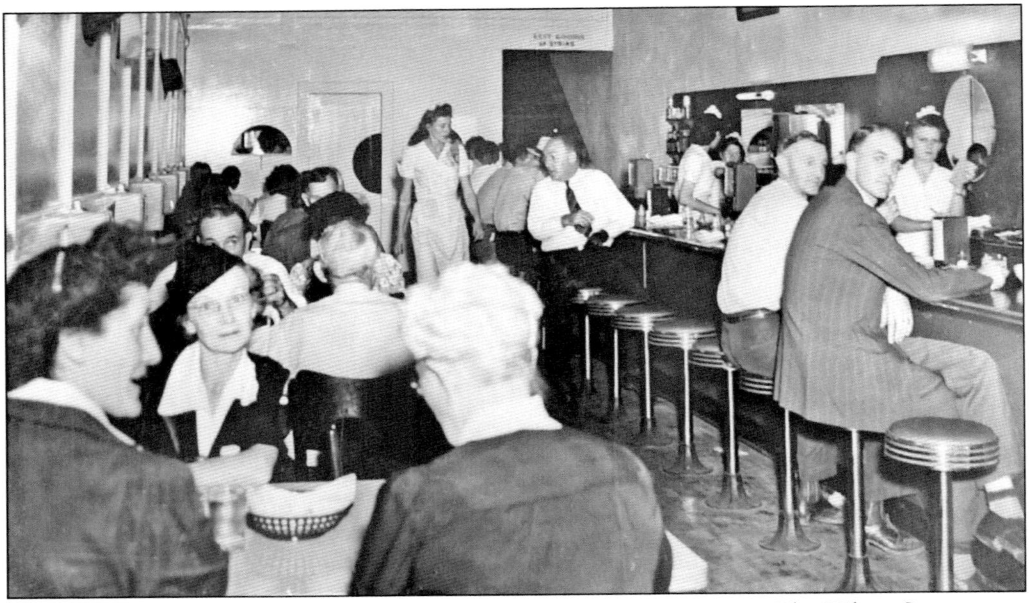

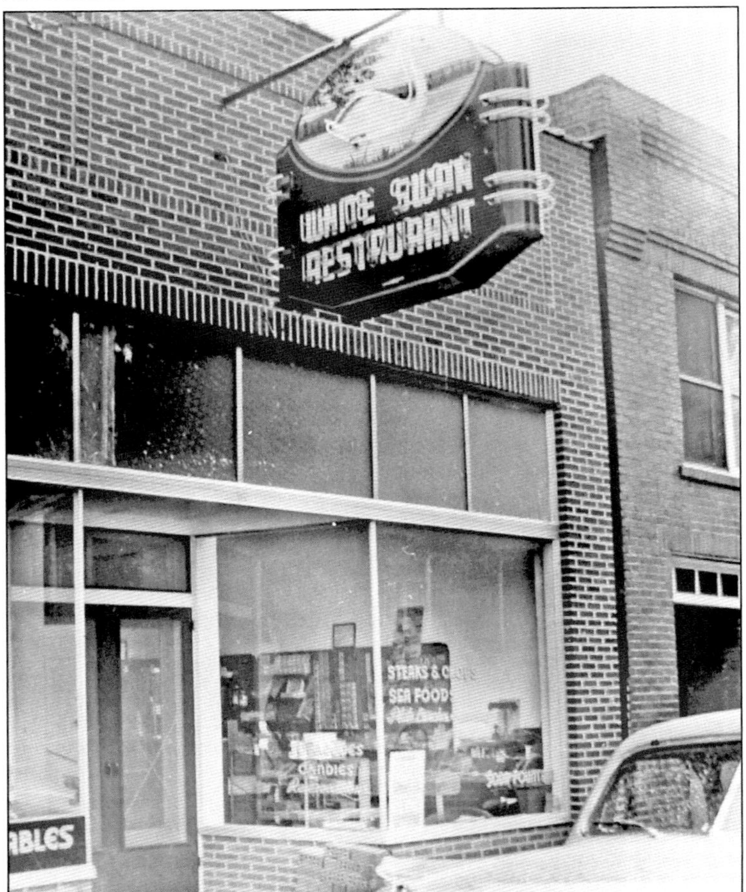


The White Swan Restaurant on Upper Street was the center of the town's business life at lunch. Operated by Floyd and Lou Baker, along with several other owners, it served a variety of dishes and was open late at night for a quick bite or cup of coffee. (Both, courtesy of Daniel Barron.)

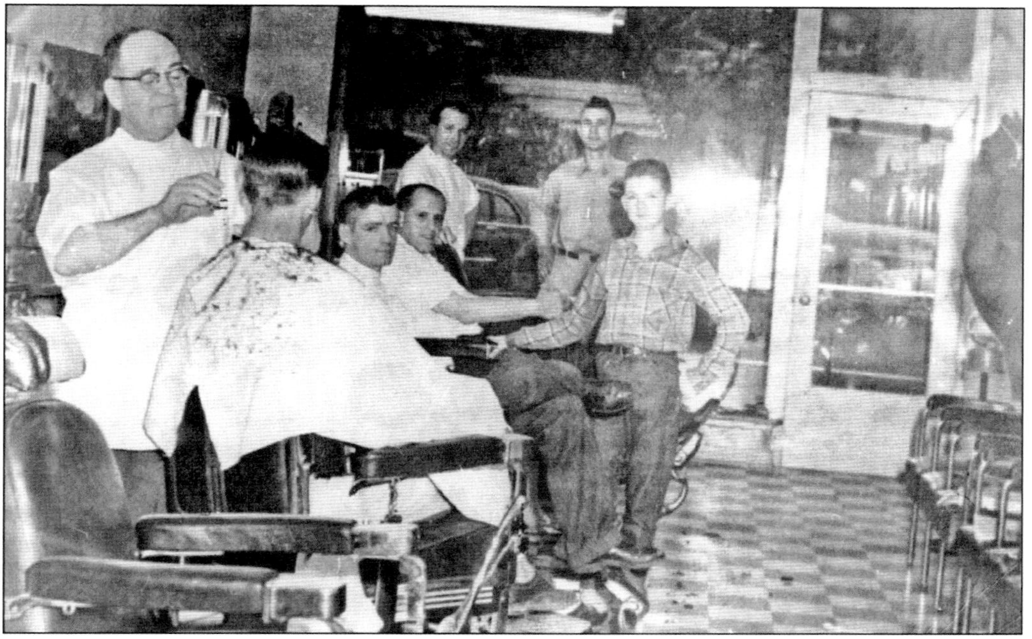

Getting your ears lowered in Spruce Pine often involved a trip to City Barber Shop on Lower Street. Pictured from left to right are Pill Greene, unidentified, Edgar Edwards, Howard Isaacs, Howard England, Fred Howell, and Emerson Barksdale. The shop is still in operation today. (Courtesy of Terry Buchanan.)

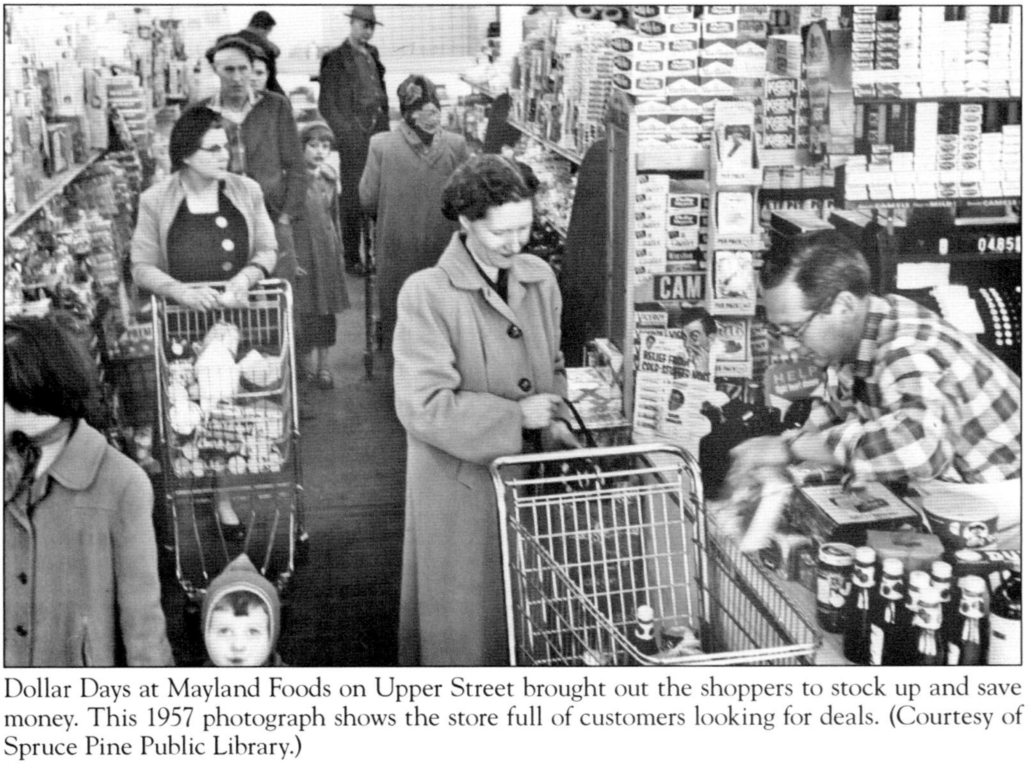

Dollar Days at Mayland Foods on Upper Street brought out the shoppers to stock up and save money. This 1957 photograph shows the store full of customers looking for deals. (Courtesy of Spruce Pine Public Library.)

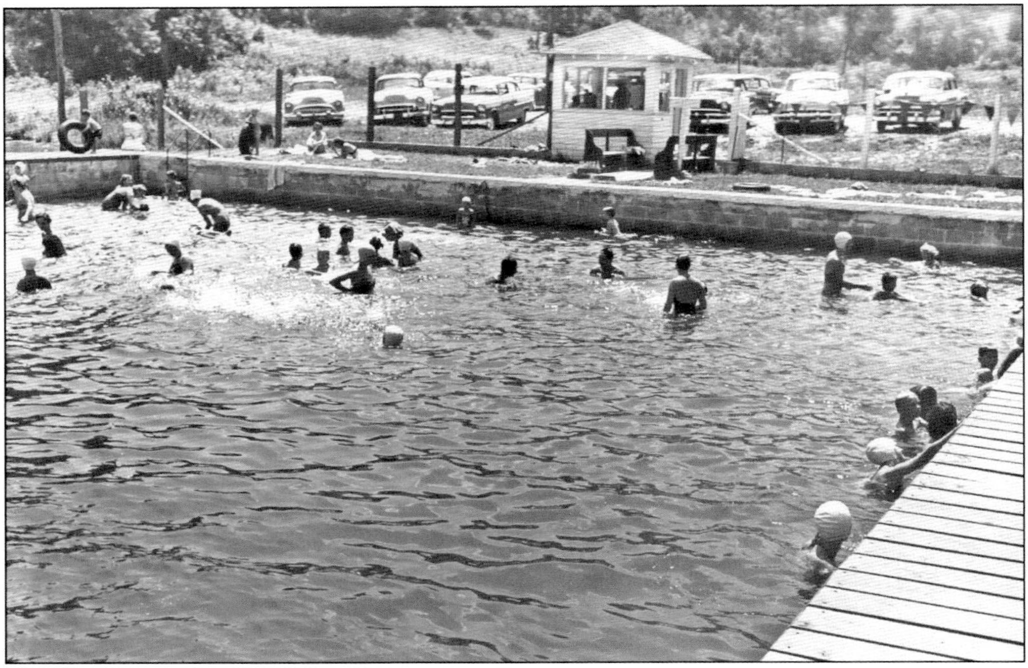

Cooling off in the summertime meant a trip to Emerald Lake, located west of Spruce Pine in the Estatoe community. This photograph, taken after 1955, shows swimmers enjoying a dip on a sunny afternoon. (Courtesy of Spruce Pine Public Library.)

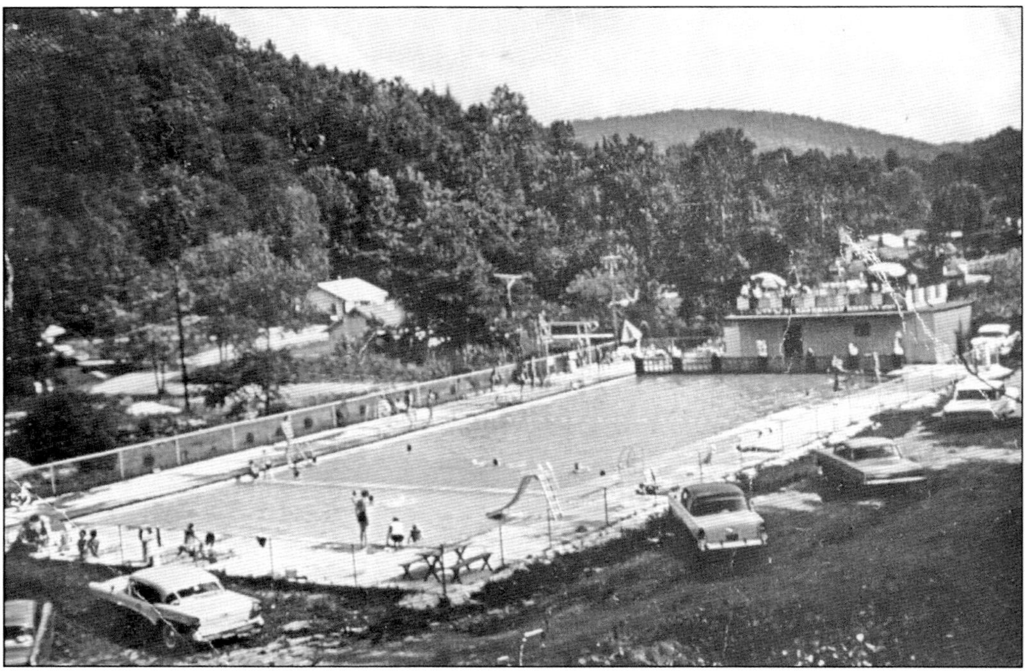

The Blue Marlin Swimming Pool, located in the Beaver Creek community, was another popular summertime hangout. Many a child froze in the early summer mornings taking swimming lessons at the Blue Marlin. (Courtesy of Deborah Owings.)

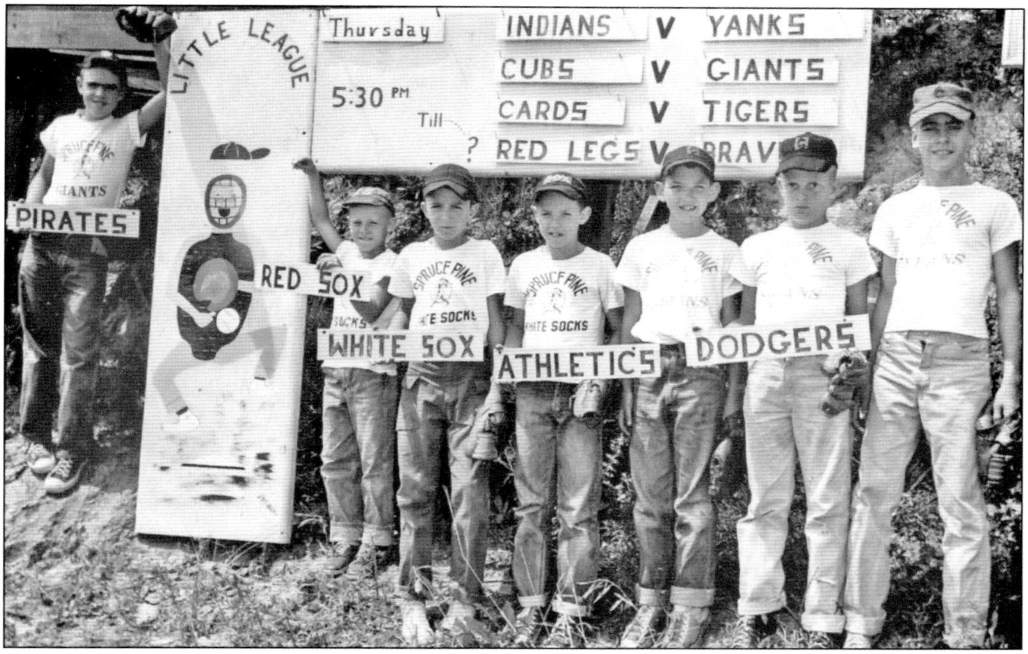


Little League baseball was played on the old Deyton Field, now Riverside Park. Pictured from left to right are Johnny Pendley, unidentified, Jerry Young, Dennis McAlister, David McAlister, Brad Ragan Jr., and Jeff Phillips. Many of Spruce Pine's boys learned the grand old game in the shade of the tall pines lining the field. (Courtesy of Spruce Pine Public Library.)

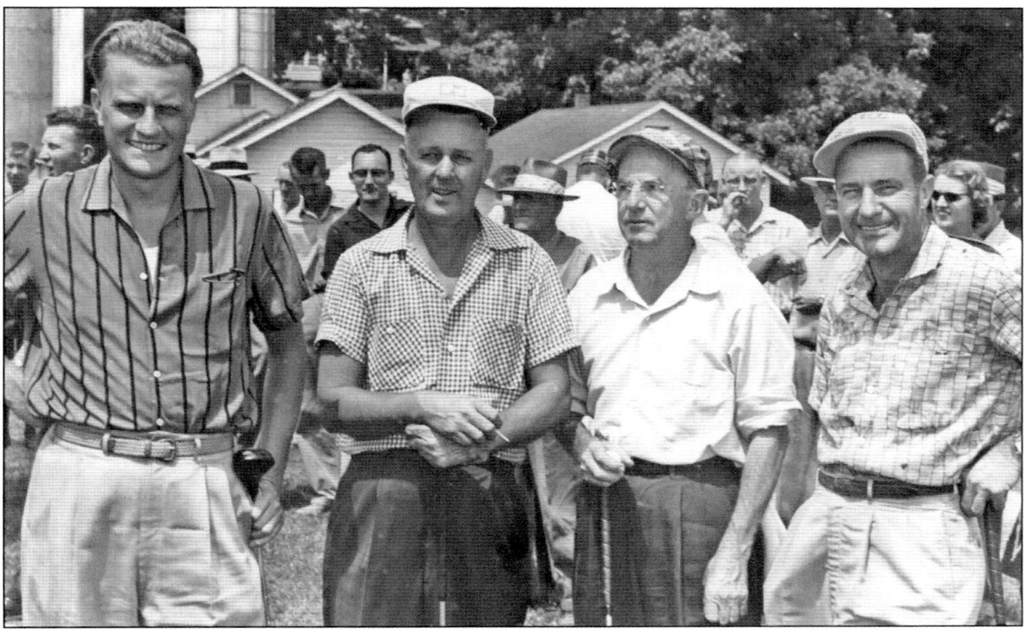

The Spruce Pine Golf Club (now the Grassy Creek Golf and Country Club) opened on August 15, 1956, on the S. T. Henry farm south of Spruce Pine. Pictured from left to right are Billy Graham and Black Mountain golf pro Ross Taylor, along with two unidentified golfers. The course eventually became an 18-hole, par 72 challenge for golfers. (Courtesy of Bruce Leverette.)

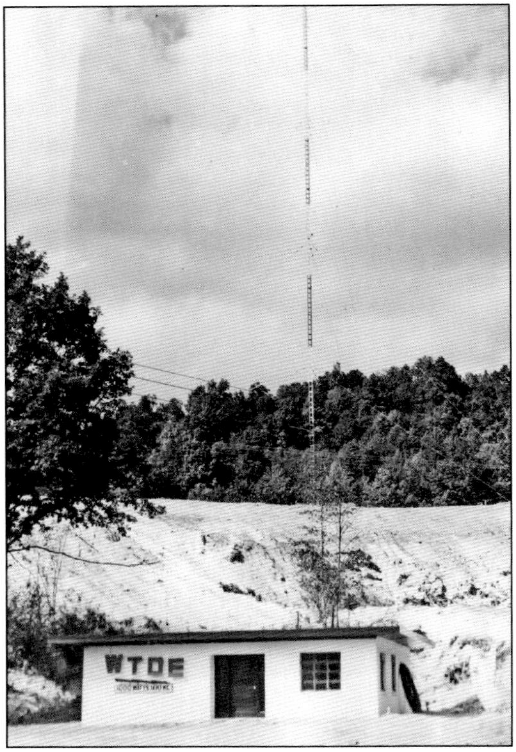


WTOE began broadcasting on 1470 Khz on December 24, 1955. The first voice heard was Jack King as he signed the station on the air. It was owned by the Toe River Broadcasting Company, whose principals included O. D. Calhoun, Baxter Johnson, and Tom Cooper. Several famous radio personalities, including Hugh Silvis (see the People chapter), made the station a stop on their career ladder. In 1981, the station increased power to 5,000 watts, and in 1987, it began nighttime broadcasts. Today the station is on the air 24 hours a day. Sundays were a time for live broadcasts from area churches and quartets. Below, J. C. Burleson of WTOE hosts the Skyland Quartet, from left to right, Charles Dover, Avery Carpenter, Joyce Burleson, Pete Huffman, and Buster Dover. (Left, courtesy of Spruce Pine Public Library; below, courtesy of Richard and Peggy Riddle.)

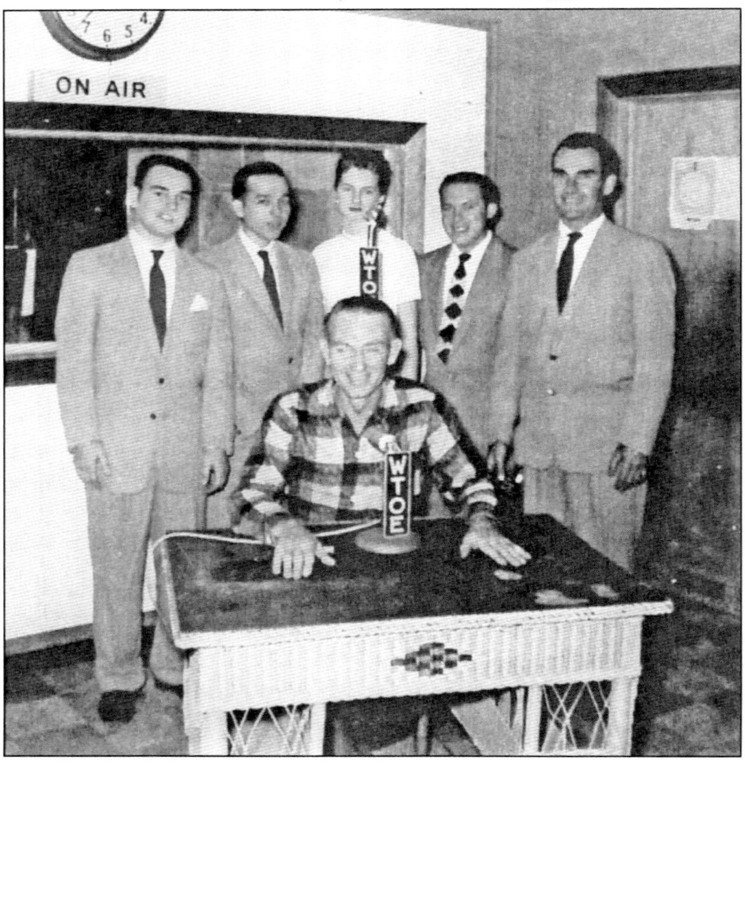

"How we love the Little Rascals," WBTV television personality Fred Kirby and singer Bobbie Staff sign autographs at Sullins Music on Lower Street. Kirby's Sunday afternoon television show on Channel 3 drew legions of kids with his music, "Uncle Jim" Mahaffey, and of course, the Little Rascals shorts that were aired. (Courtesy of Dempsey Sullins.)

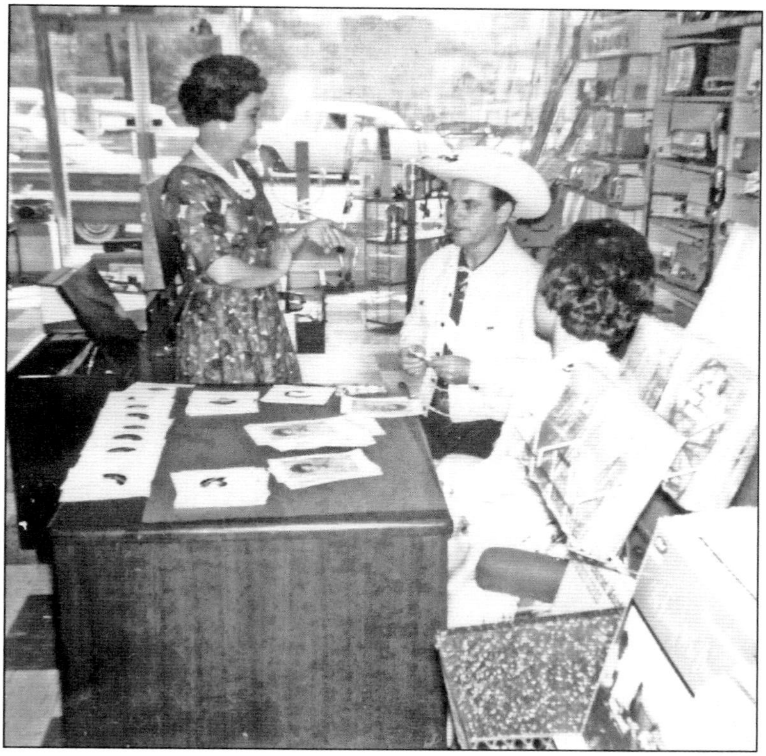

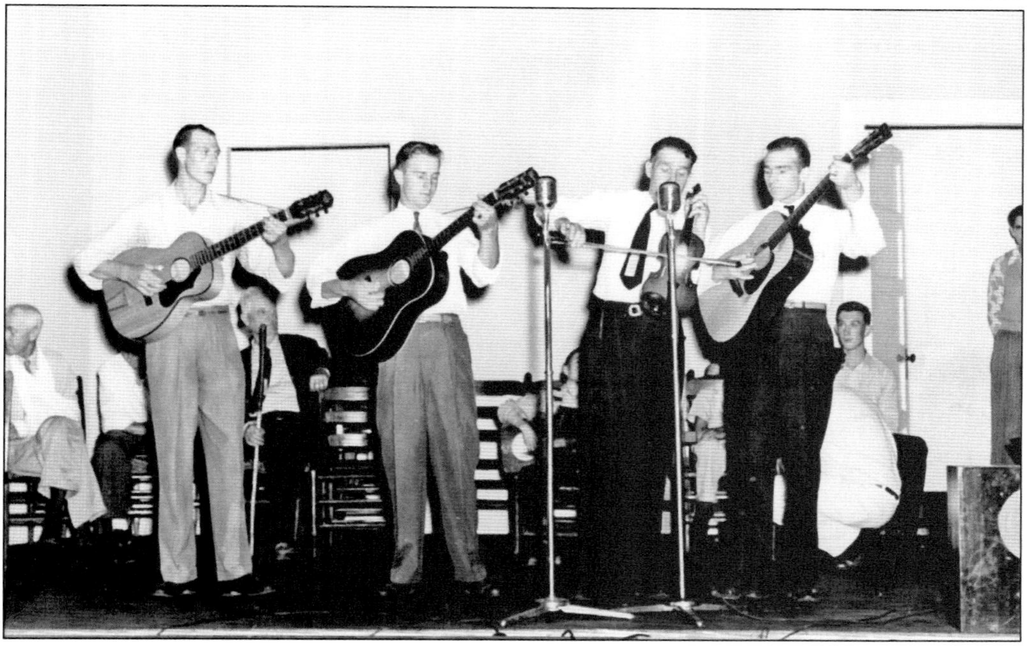

Many local musicians went on to fame and fortune playing mountain music. This performance features, from left to right, Millard Ward, Wayne Ledford, Steve Ledford, and Oscar "Red" Wilson at Harris High School. The Leford brothers toured the Midwest, and Wilson received the 2003 North Carolina Heritage Award after a long career. (Courtesy of Wayne Ledford.)

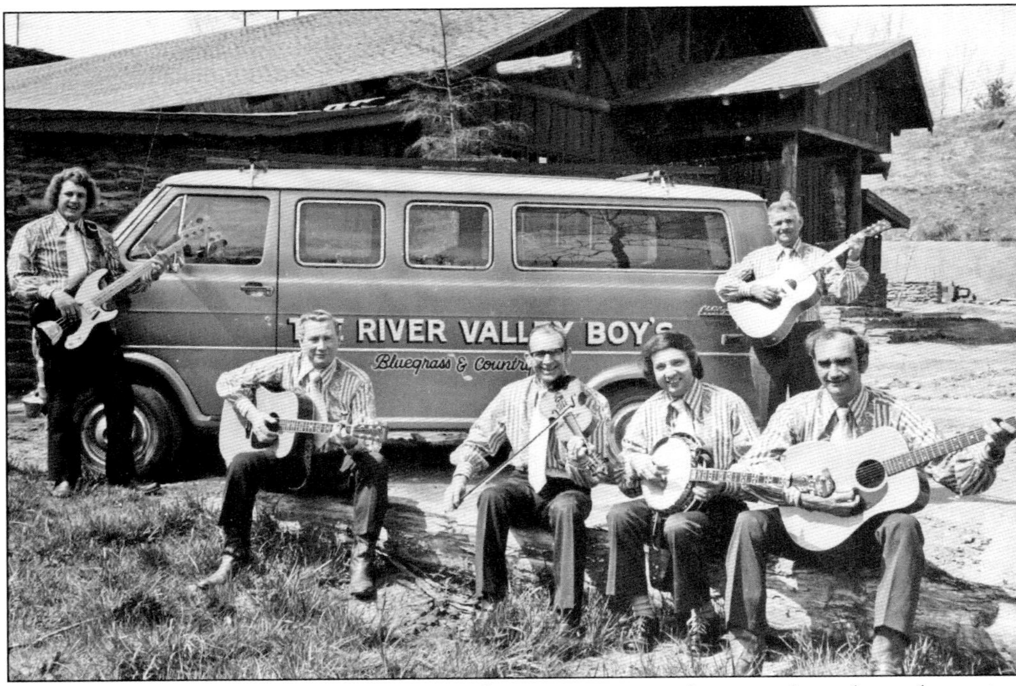

The Toe River Valley Boys spent 20 years playing concerts and events throughout the region. Pictured from left to right are Dempsey Sullins, R. B. Laws, Oscar "Red" Wilson, E. C. Miller, Gus Washburn, and Charles Renfro. (Courtesy of Dempsey Sullins.)

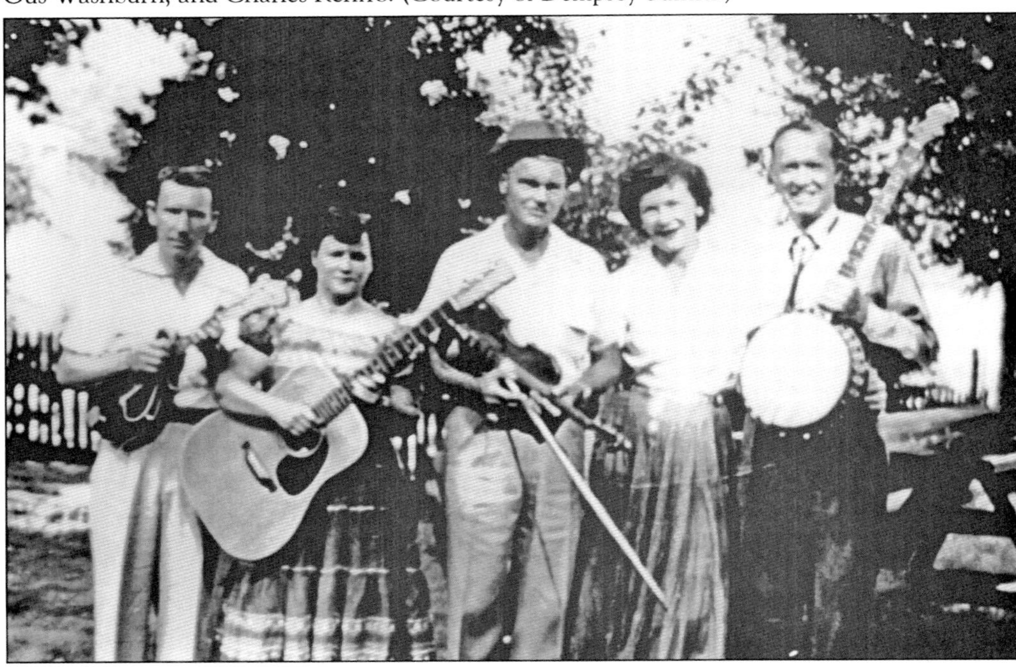

Despite a booming national career, Scotty and Lulu Belle Wiseman still made it back home and found the time to play with local musicians. Pictured here, from left to right, are Charlie and Mildred Hensley, Calhoun McKinney, Lulu Belle, and Scotty. (Courtesy of Guss McKinney.)

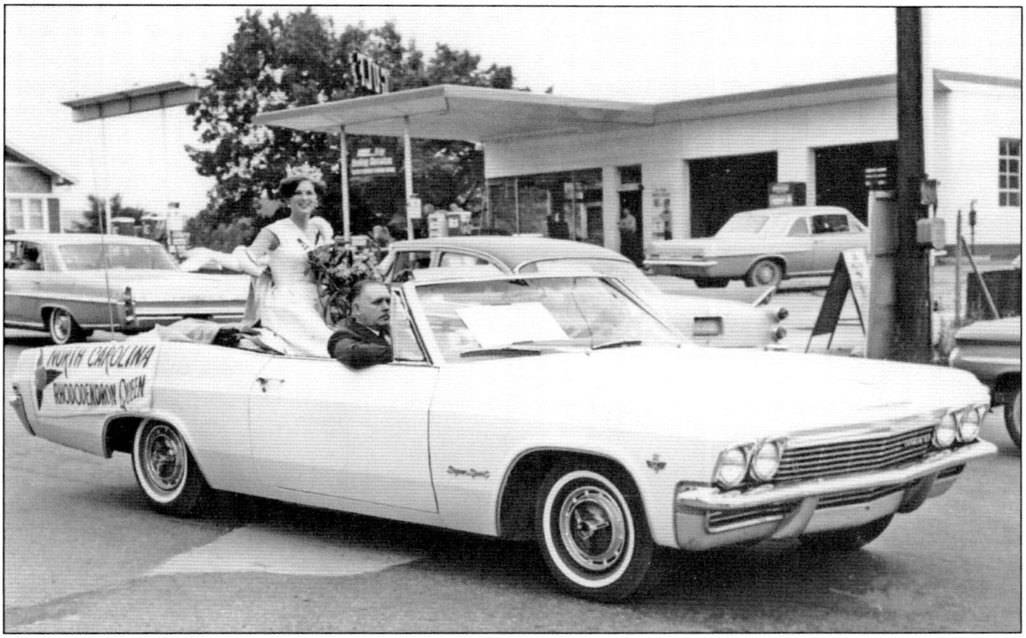


Parades have always been a big part of town life. Here is Jeane Rhodes of Matthews, North Carolina, the 1966 North Carolina rhododendron queen in a parade on Upper Street. Rhodes traveled the United States promoting the region. Spruce Pine mayor Albert Canipe accompanies Rhodes in the parade. (Courtesy of Spruce Pine Public Library.)

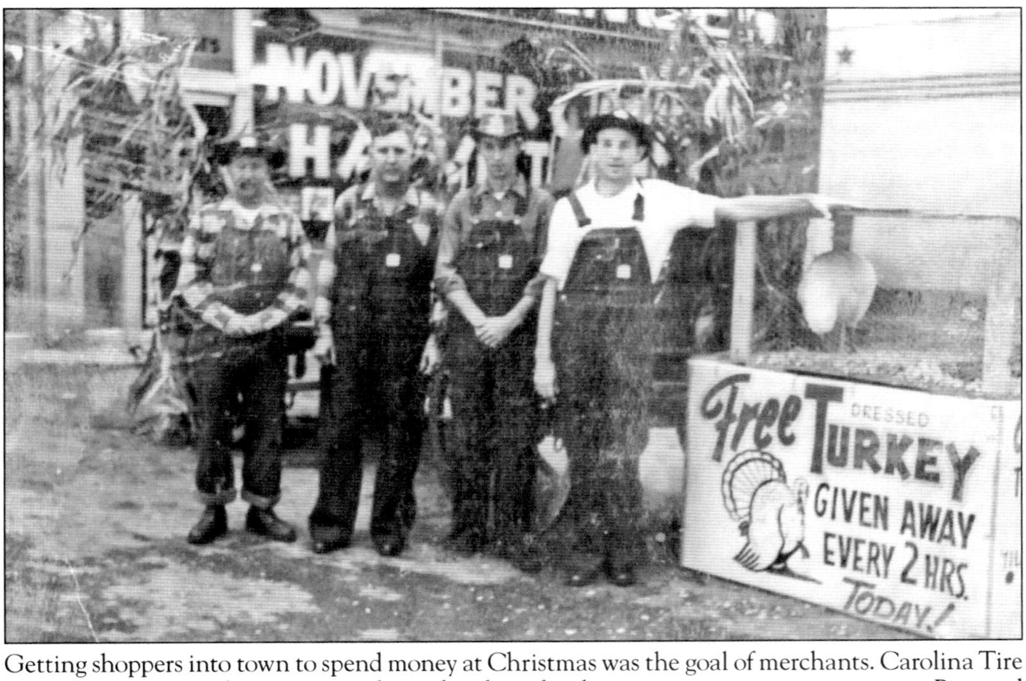


Getting shoppers into town to spend money at Christmas was the goal of merchants. Carolina Tire on Oak Avenue tried giving away dressed turkeys for the occasion to entice customers. Pictured from left to right are salesmen Bobby Greene, Ernest "Mutt" Biddix, Jim Edwards, and Ernest Buchanan posing with the live prize outside the store. (Courtesy of Richard and Peggy Riddle.)

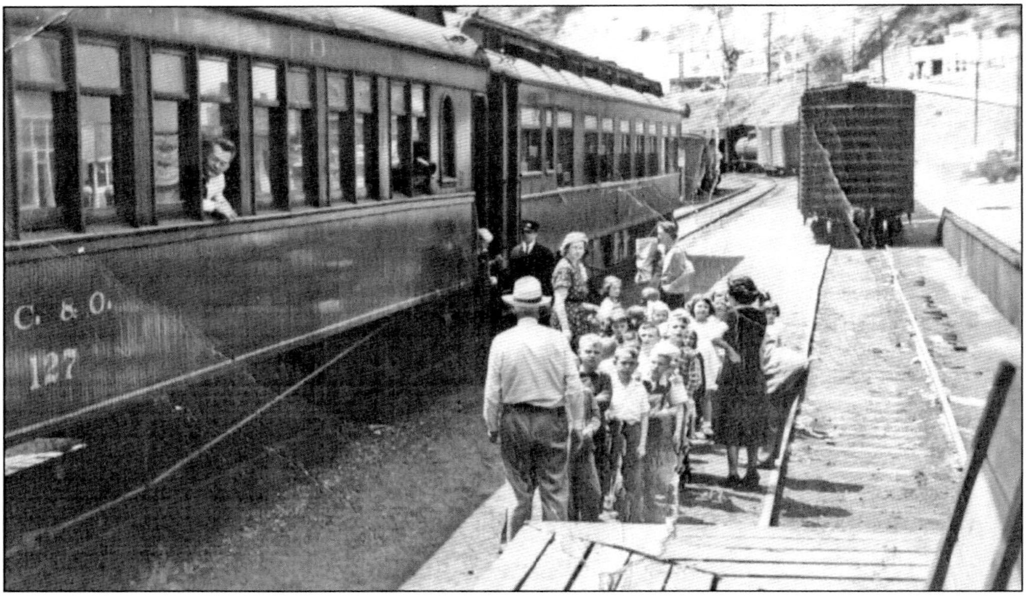


The 1950 first grade class of Maude Bennett disembarks from a field trip, a ride on the train from Toecane to Spruce Pine. The children were enjoying a vanishing service, as the Clinchfield Railroad discontinued passenger service in 1952. (Courtesy of Angela McKinney.)

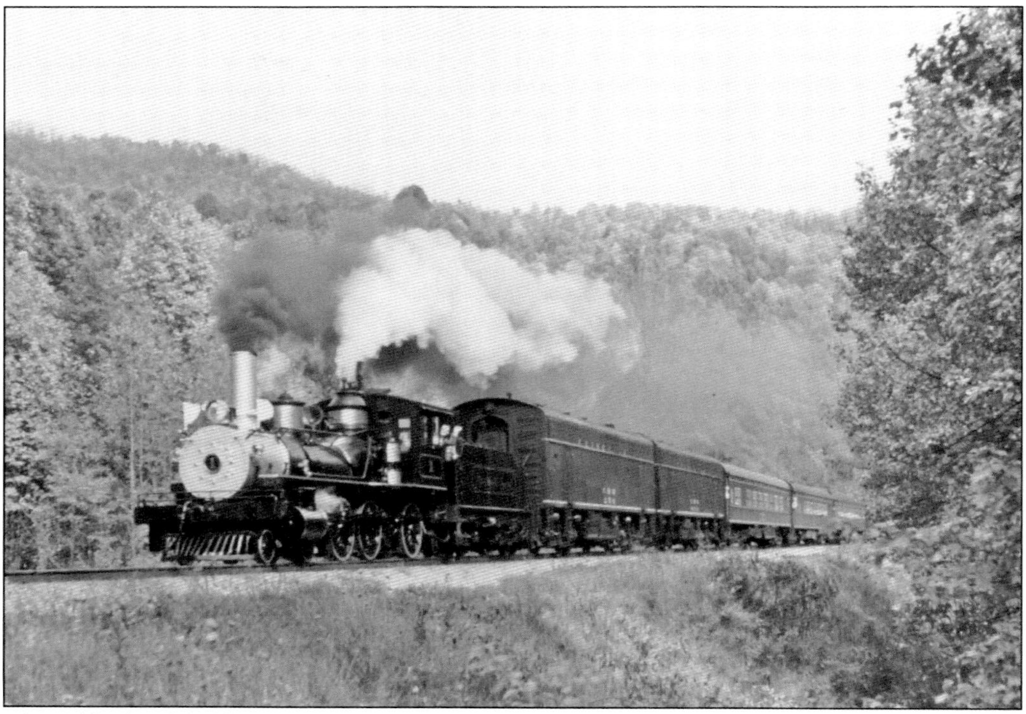

The Old Clinchfield No. 1 approaches Spruce Pine with a fall leaf looker's excursion in the 1970s. These special visits of the old train brought back memories of a bygone era. In 1979, Old No. 1 retired to Baltimore, Maryland, where it is on display at the Baltimore and Ohio Museum. (Courtesy of the Toe River Model Railroad Club.)

Spruce Pine has played host to two U.S. presidents. In 1958, then vice-president Richard Nixon and his wife, Pat, visited the Mineral City as part of a swing that included a stop at the Rhododendron Festival in Bakersville. He delivered a speech on Upper Street while receiving a key to the city. On March 22, 1976, Pres. Gerald Ford braved a pouring rainstorm to speak to a crowd at the Avery County Airport near Spruce Pine. He was scheduled to fly in aboard Marine One but was on a motorcade from Asheville due to the weather. (Right, courtesy of Guss McKinney; below, courtesy of Gerald R. Ford Library.)

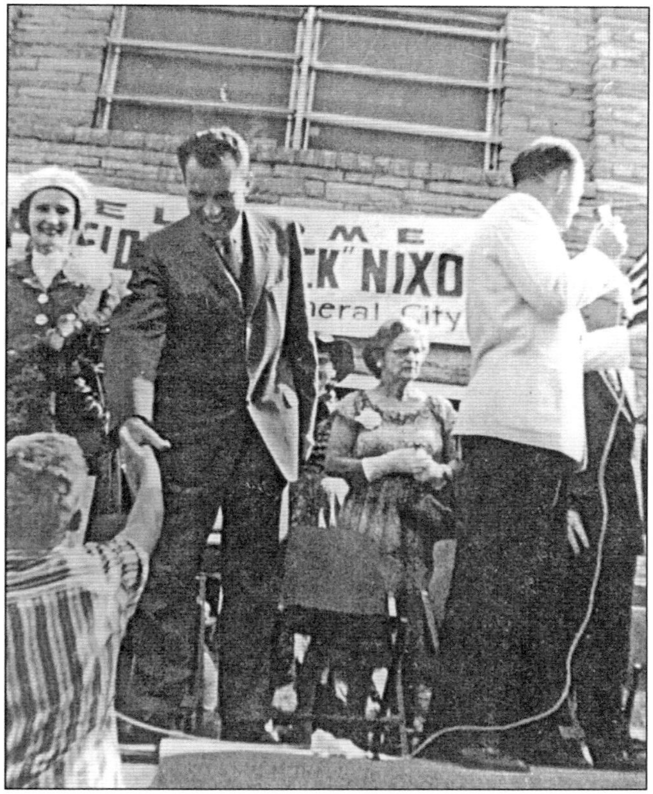

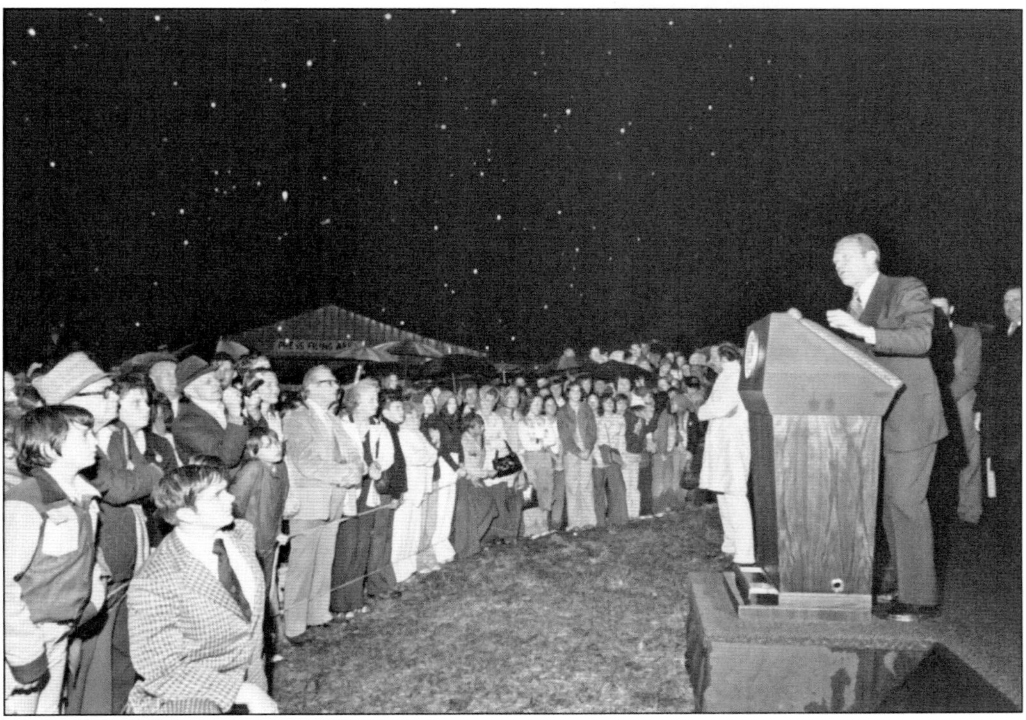

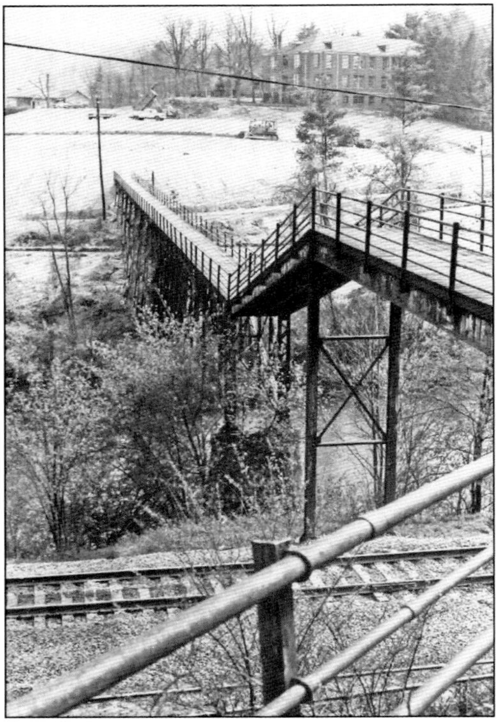

In 1982, Robert Bailey and Alvin Barrier, owners of the Buck Stove Corporation, embarked on a bold plan to redevelop the old Harris School property as an entertainment, shopping, dining, and lodging complex. They decided that the bridge between downtown Spruce Pine and the property would be a focal point, and they named it Pinebridge. It contained the largest ice-skating rink in the southeastern United States and other health club amenities, along with an inn and restaurant. The photograph at left shows construction beginning in 1982; the image below is of the complex today. The Pinebridge Complex hosts the North Carolina Mineral and Gem Festival each August along with other special events, and the inn has expanded to other buildings on the campus. (Left, courtesy of North Carolina Department of Cultural Resources; below, courtesy of Robert and Donna Bailey.)

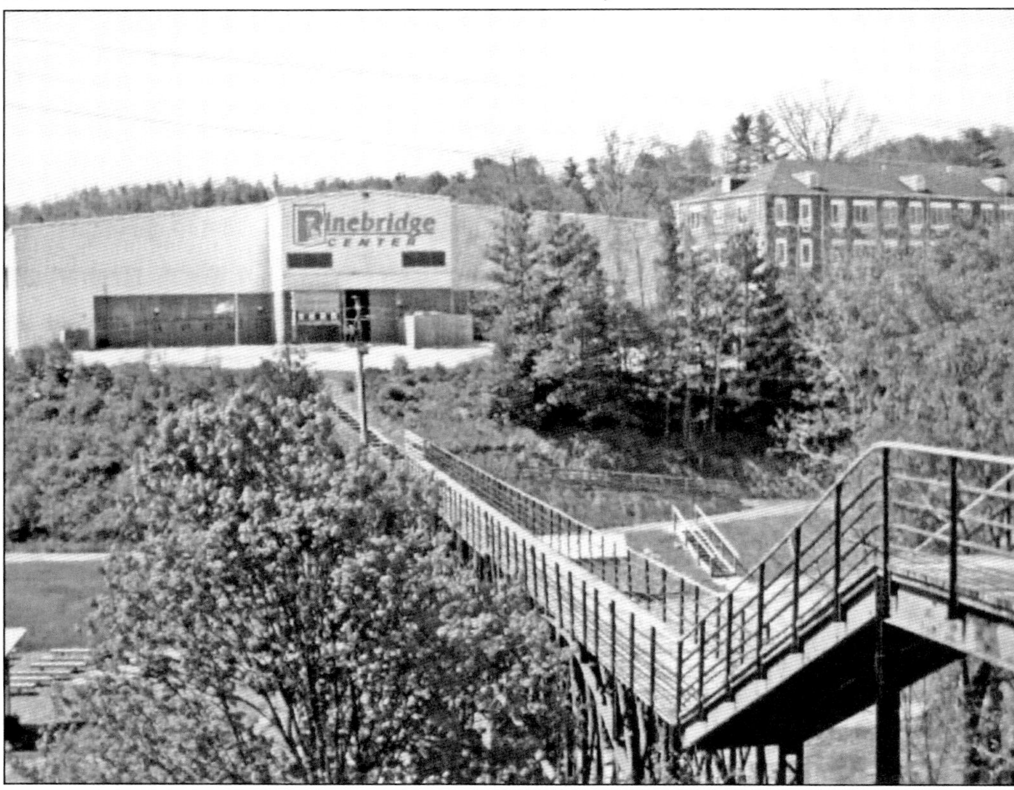

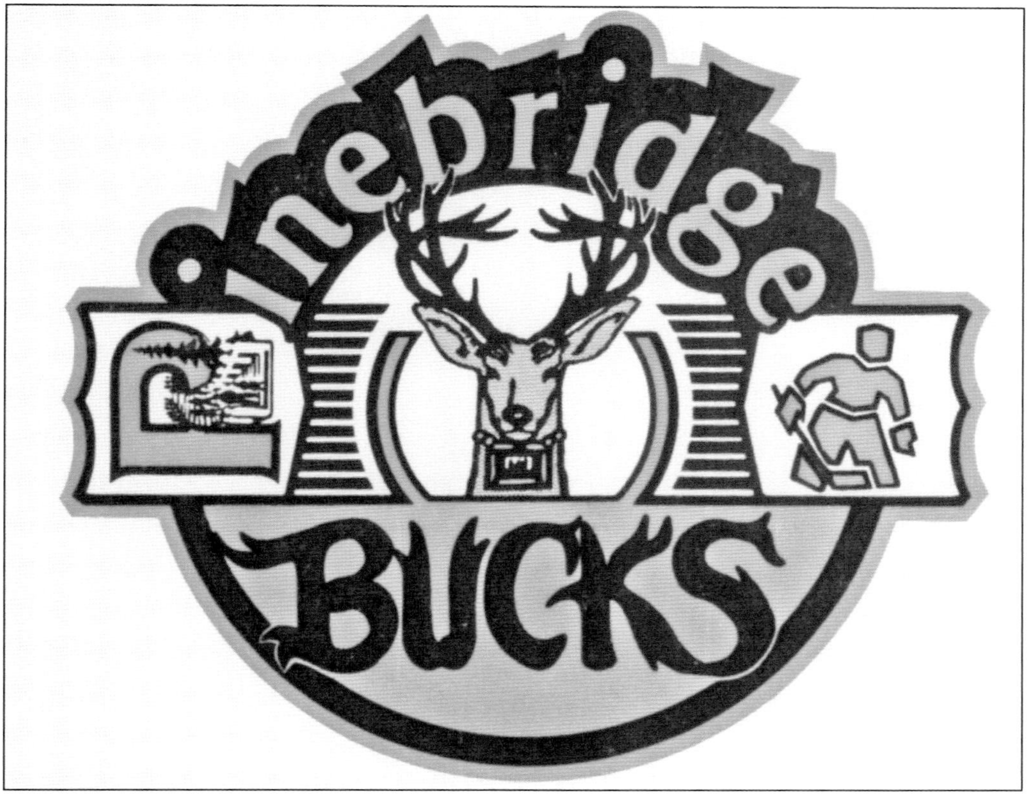


Spruce Pine became the smallest town to host a professional hockey team when the Pinebridge Bucks competed in the Atlantic Coast Hockey League from 1983 to 1985, compiling a 25-47-0 record (fifth place) in 1983–1984 and a 33-25-6 record (third place) in 1984–1985. The most famous Bucks player was goalie Ray LeBlanc, who goal tended for the 1992 U.S. Olympic hockey team. (Courtesy of David Biddix.)

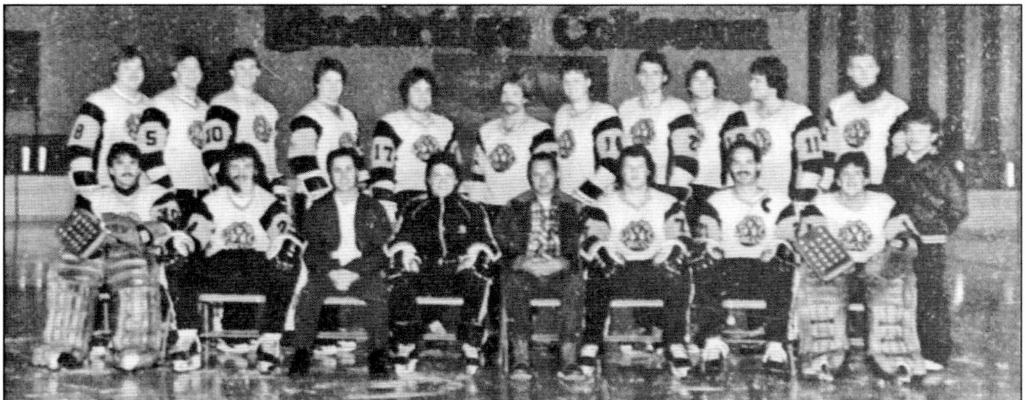

The 1984–1985 Pinebridge Bucks are pictured above. From left to right are (first row) Dave Jamieson, Tom Madson, Robert Bailey (owner), Frank Perkins (coach), Alvin Barrier (owner), Rick Harris, Kelly Rissling, and Steve Heittola; (second row) Mike Brisebois, Marc Pettegrove, Dave Burke, Larry Mollard, Bruce Aikens, Bill Smith, Todd Scott, Kim Collins, Dave Dziedzic, Ken Latta, Dan Burrows, and Frank Jury (trainer). (Courtesy of David Biddix.)

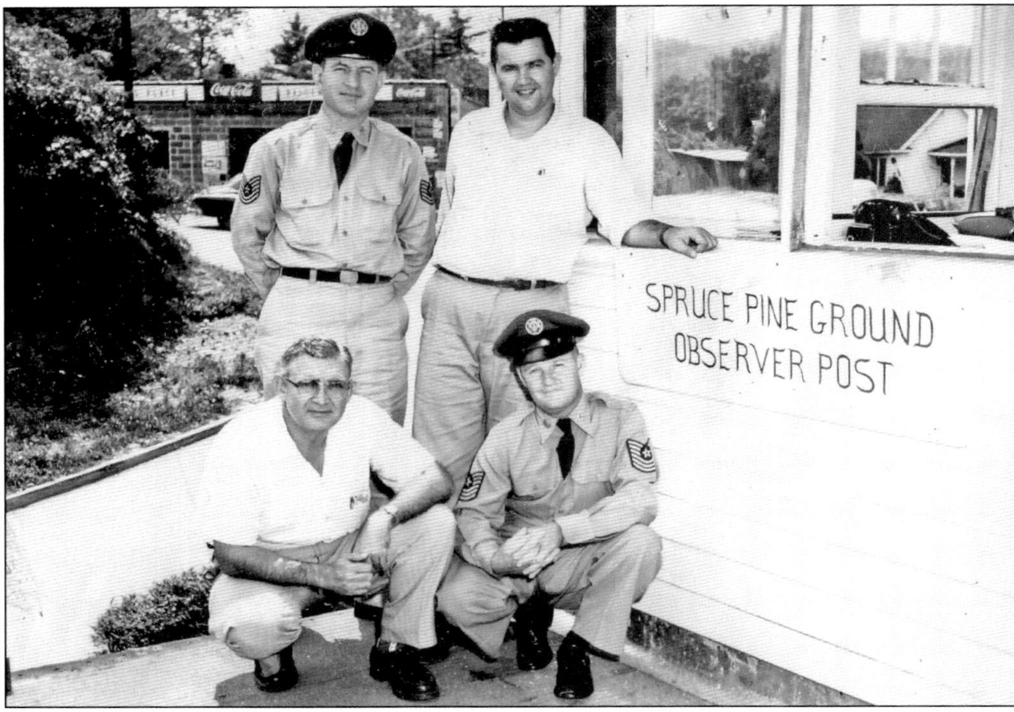


The cold war was raging in the 1950s, and residents of Spruce Pine were not immune to its effects. The Boy Scouts constructed a ground observer post atop town hall during that time and worked with the U.S. Air Force to watch the skies for suspicious activity. Scout leaders Dick Nichols (below, left) and Paul Willis Jr. (above, right) pose with air force officials at the post's completion. The post was short-lived; it had disappeared from the roof by the 1960s. (Both, courtesy of Spruce Pine Public Library.)

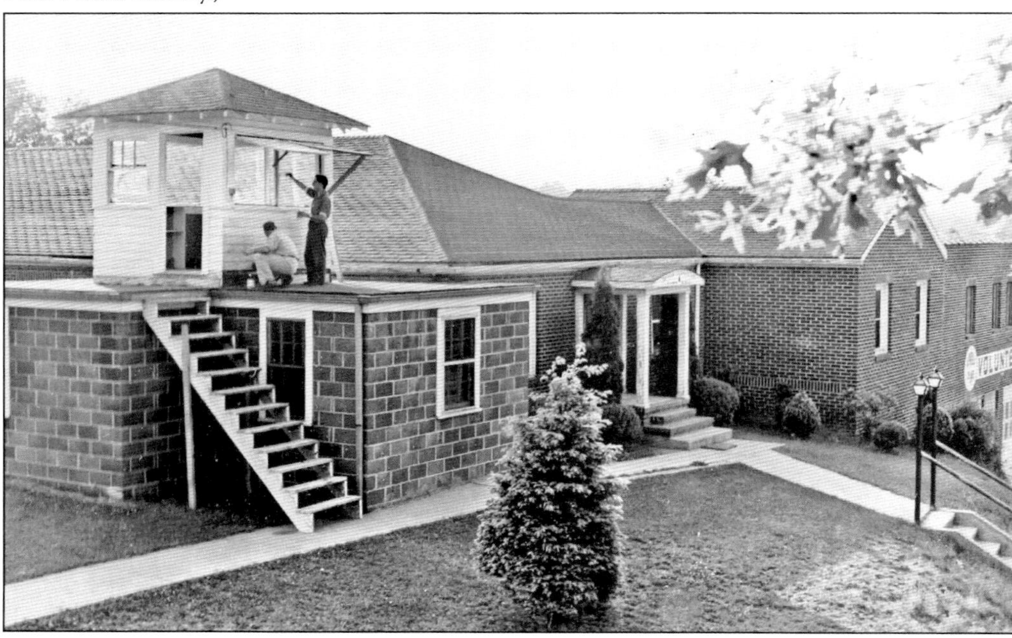

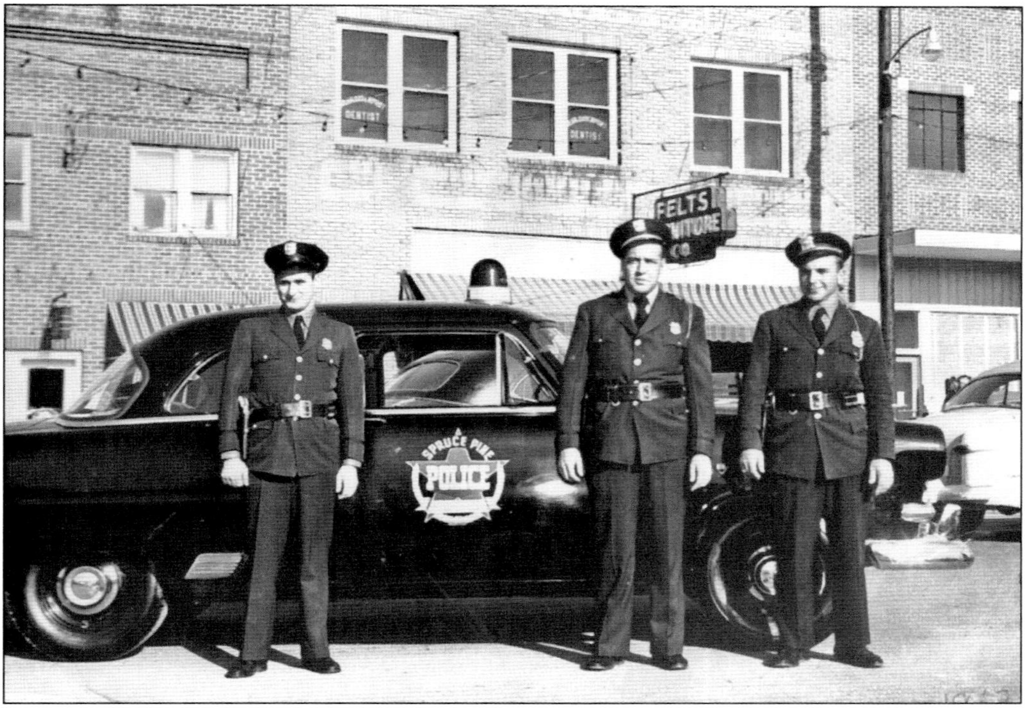


In Spruce Pine's finest pose with the town's first police car on Lower Street are, from left to right, Lane Buchanan, Arnold "Bear" Swann, and Chief Jack Young. The car was equipped with a two-way radio to communicate with other fire and police units. (Courtesy of Jack Young.)

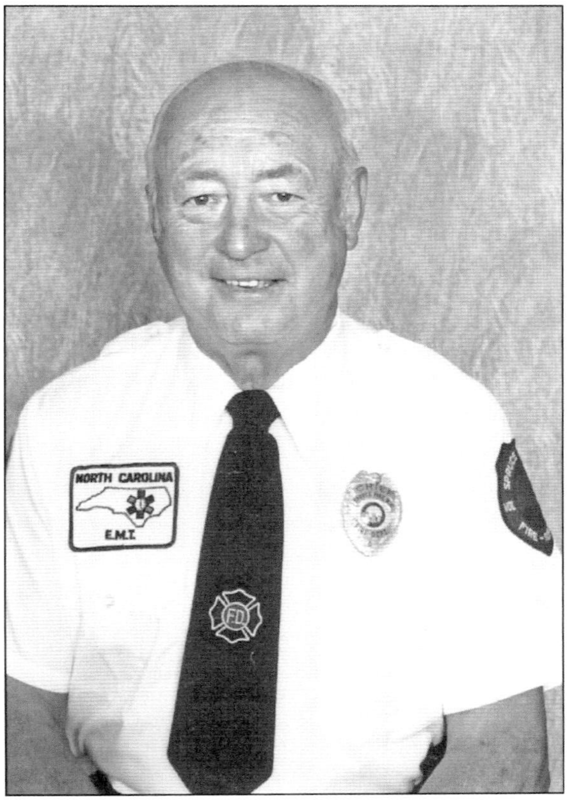


Charles Buchanan served Spruce Pine as mayor in the 1980s and as chief of the Spruce Pine Fire Department in the 1980s and 1990s. He owned People's Furniture and Alpine Motors, and he was a partner in Greene-Buchanan Chevrolet. A familiar face around town, he worked to make Spruce Pine a better place. (Courtesy of Keith Buchanan.)

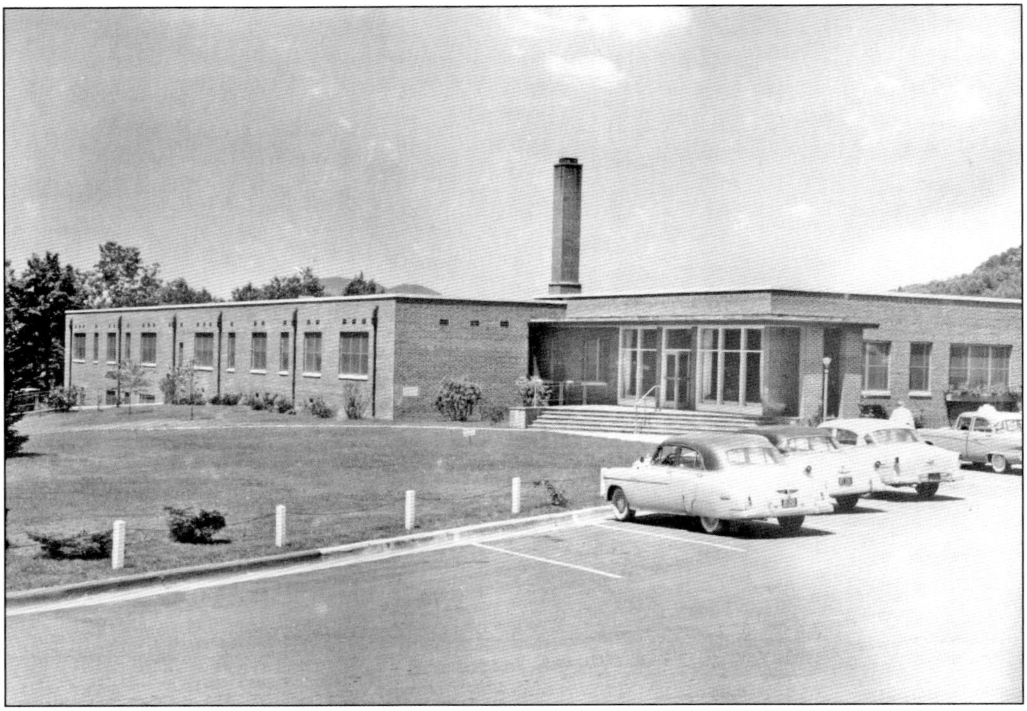

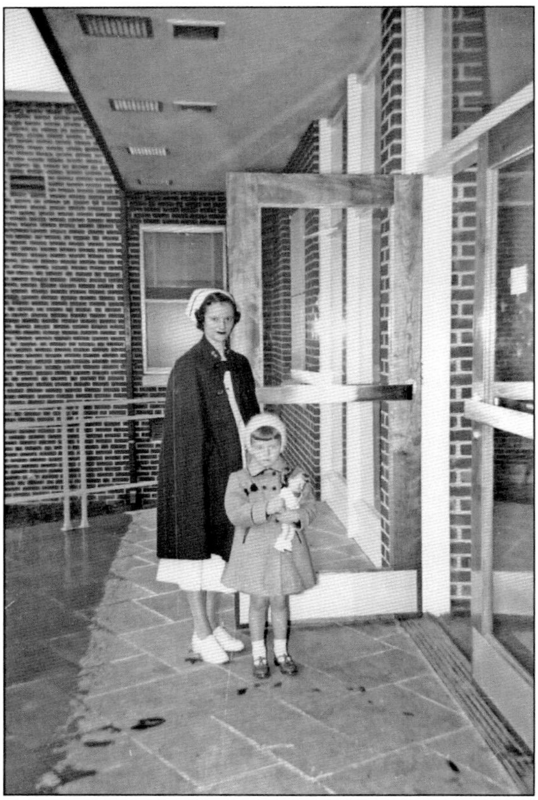

The Spruce Pine Community Hospital was the culmination of efforts to bring modern medical facilities to town, starting with work by Drs. Charles Peterson and Paul McBee to secure funding for a hospital in 1926. Completed in November 1955, the hospital was the result of approximately 2,500 people raising $102,000 to match funds from the North Carolina Medical Care Commission and the Duke endowment to construct the hospital. At left, the hospital's first patient enters the facility in 1955. The hospital expanded in 1974 and again in 2007, changing its name to the Blue Ridge Regional Hospital. (Both, courtesy of Blue Ridge Regional Hospital.)

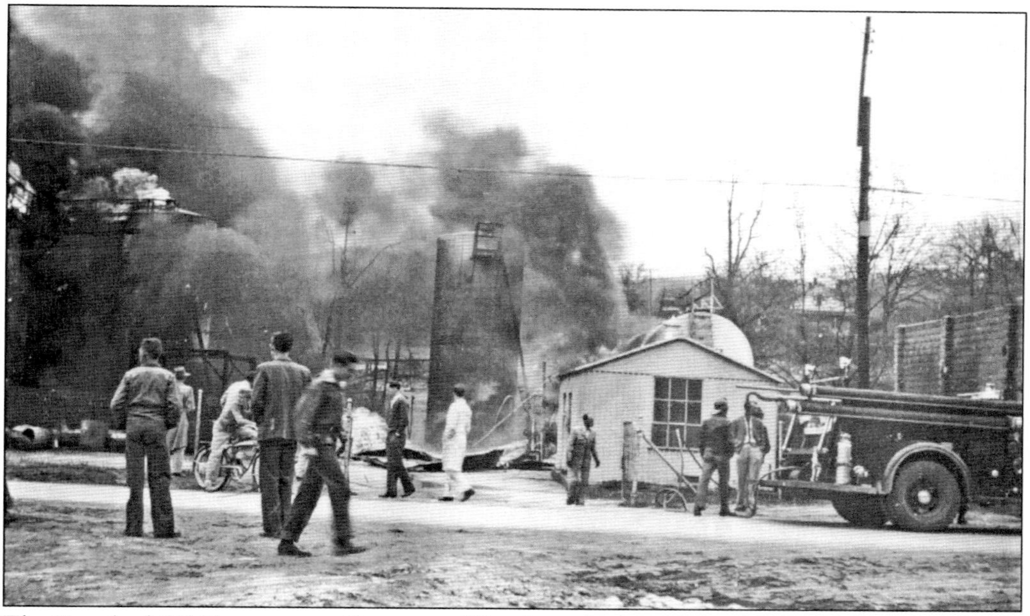

The Standard Oil Company on Greenwood Road caught fire on April 29, 1949, sending streams of burning oil into the Toe River. Residents watched in disbelief as the river burned while the oil floated on top of the water. Hard work by the Spruce Pine Fire Department kept the blaze contained, and Gouge Oil is still in the same location. (Courtesy of Buster Sparks.)

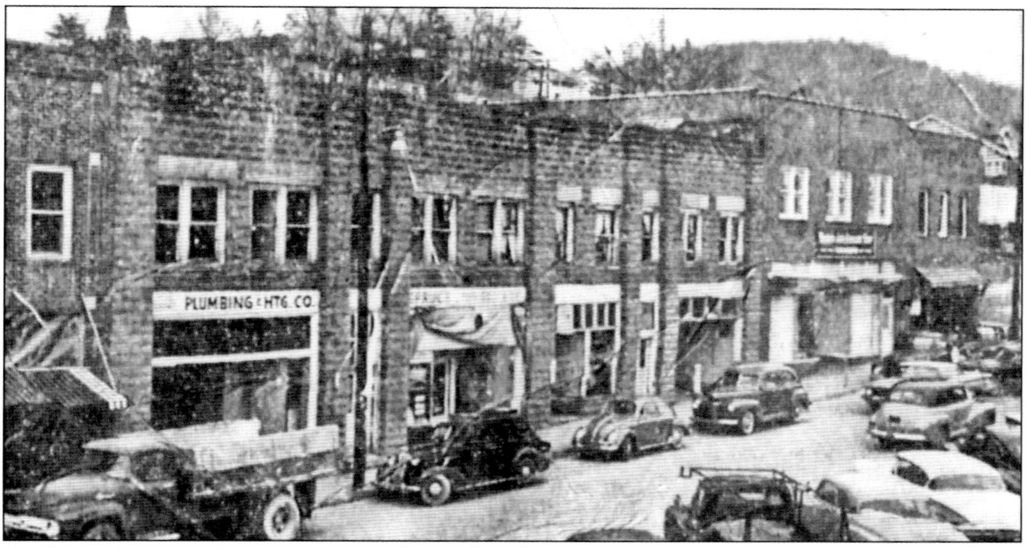


On December 31, 1959, Spruce Pine welcomed in the new year with a bang, as dynamite exploded in the Deyton Field opposite downtown. All but two windows in this string of buildings were knocked out by 99 sticks of dynamite. The explosion was heard 15 miles away. The pranksters bought the dynamite at a local hardware store to celebrate the occasion. (Courtesy of Chris Hollifield.)

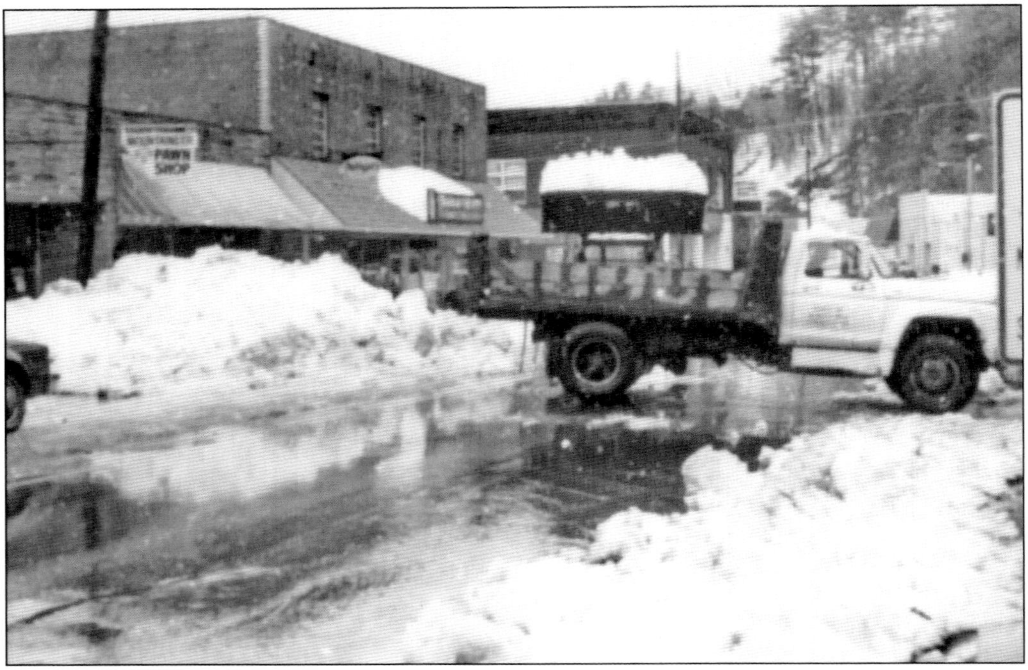

On March 12, 1993, snow began falling on a Friday afternoon. By Monday, March 15, the storm of the century had dumped upwards of three feet of snow on the region, paralyzing travel and causing widespread power outages, bringing to an end hopes for an early spring. Town maintenance crews are removing snow from Upper Street in the above photograph, while the image below illustrates the depth of the snowfall at the entrance to the Deyton Primary School. (Both, courtesy of the *Mitchell News-Journal*.)

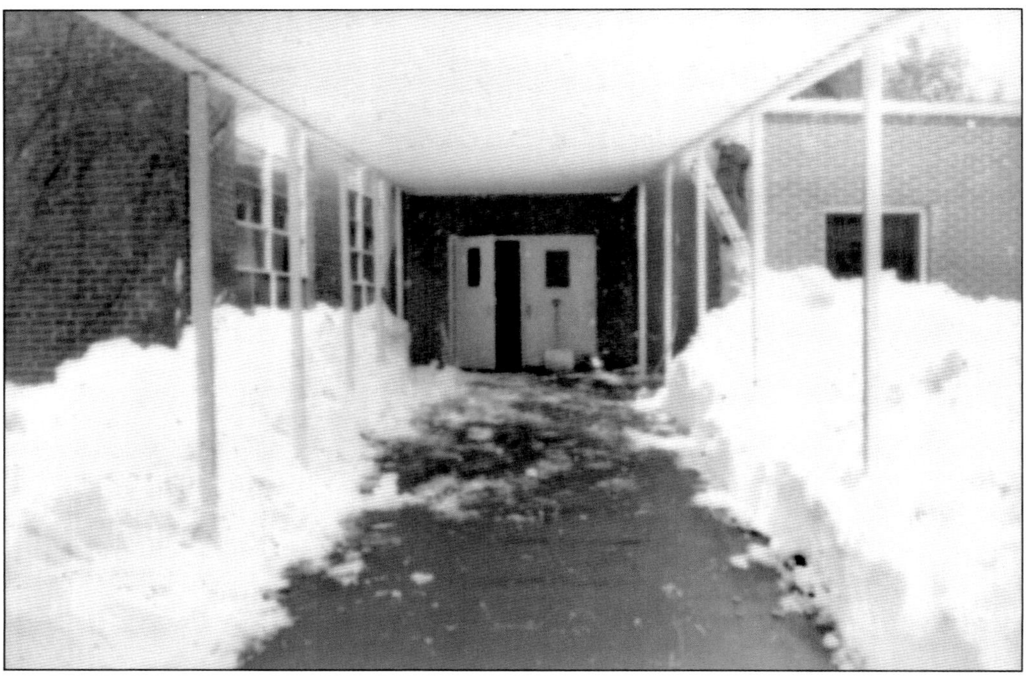

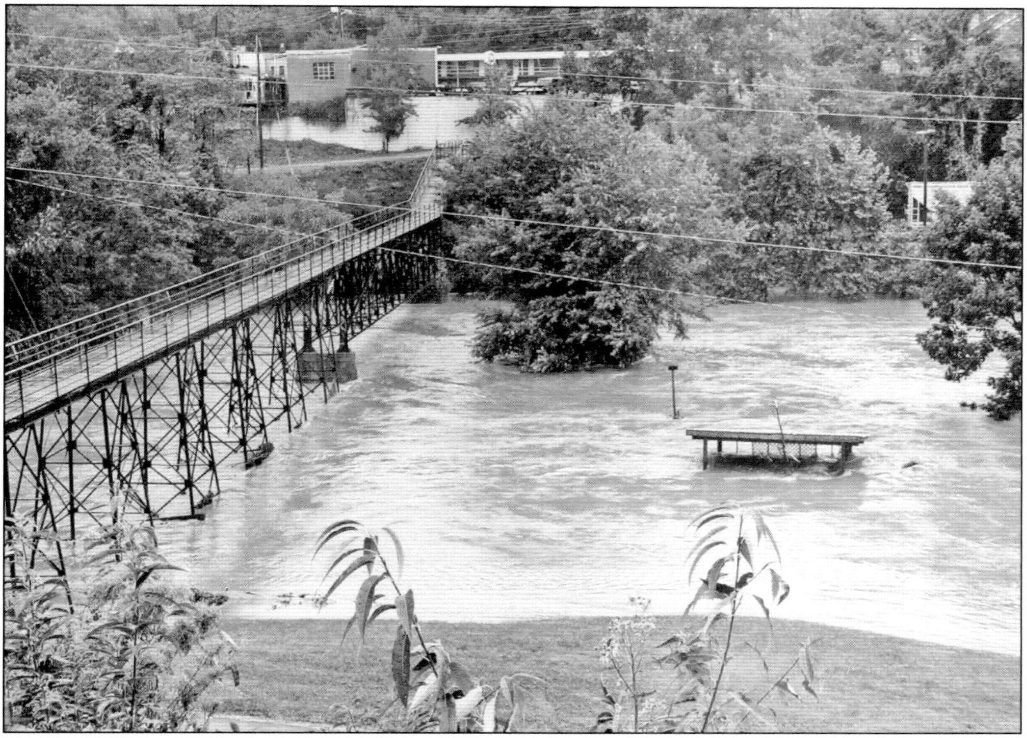

September 2004 was a memorable time because, just as in 1916, two major hurricanes struck the region in a short time. Hurricane Frances was first, dumping copious amounts of rainfall and sending streams out of their banks. A short time later, Hurricane Ivan inundated the region with rainfall and winds, leading to destruction. This photograph is of the Toe River flooding the Riverside Park during Hurricane Ivan. (Courtesy of David Biddix.)

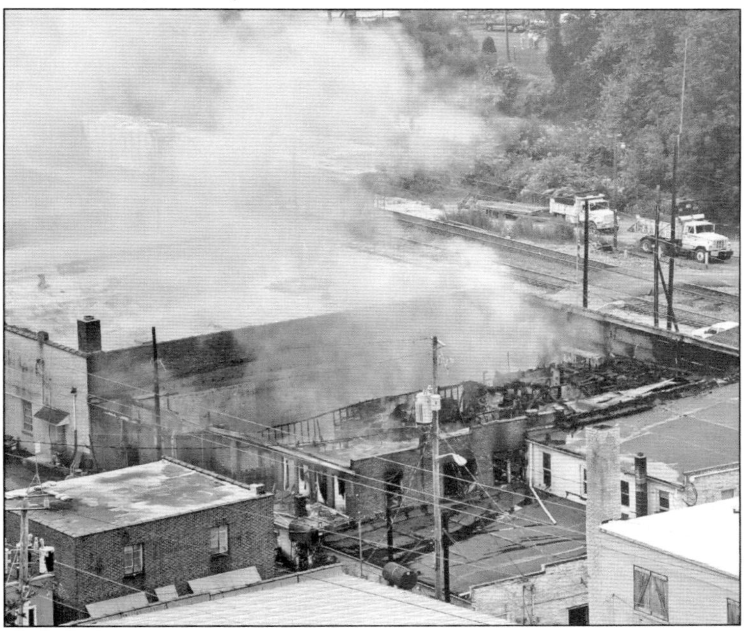

Beginning on August 4, 2007, an arsonist started several fires in Spruce Pine, succeeding in burning the Baker Restaurant building on Upper Street and then torching buildings housing Cheapskates Music and Loan and the old Spruce Pine Pharmacy on Lower Street. In December 2008, the man arrested for arson accepted a plea arrangement in connection with the blaze. (Courtesy of David Biddix.)

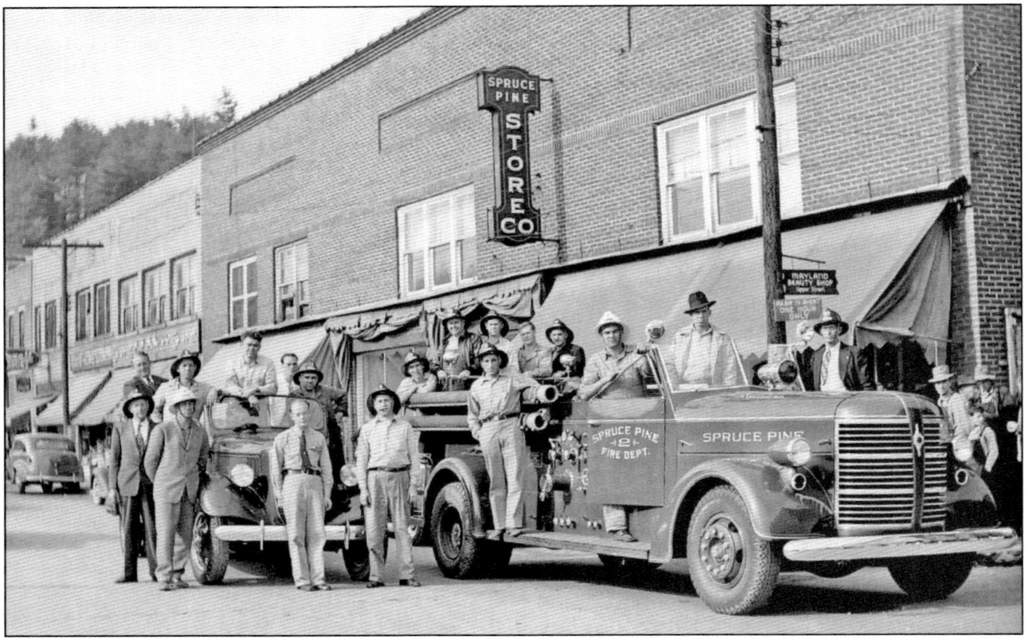


The Spruce Pine Fire Department has responded to big blazes over the years. In 1937, the Villas Mica Company burned in Beaver Creek. In 1940, Harris High burned down; on January 8, 1942, the upper end of Locust Avenue burned, destroying four businesses; on August 6, 1948, the Topliff Hotel on Upper Street burned; on April 29, 1949, the Standard Oil Company's storage tanks burned; on December 24, 2002, the old Brad Ragan, Incorporated, building burned; in August 2007, an arsonist set fires all over town; and in December 2008, Unimin's plant at Minpro was destroyed. These brave volunteers risk life and limb to protect others. Pictured above are the 1948 members shortly after the Topliff Hotel fire. They are, from left to right, Chief Jack Tappan, Assistant Chief George Bartlett, Wren Tolley, Carl Gunter Jr., Claude Young, Eray Burleson, Charles Buchanan, Floyd Duncan, Millard Duncan, Didy Wright, Fate Buchanan, C. E. Boone, Hoyle Gunter, T. E. Bell, Arnold Swann, Claude Riddle, and John Phillips. (Both, courtesy of Daniel Barron.)

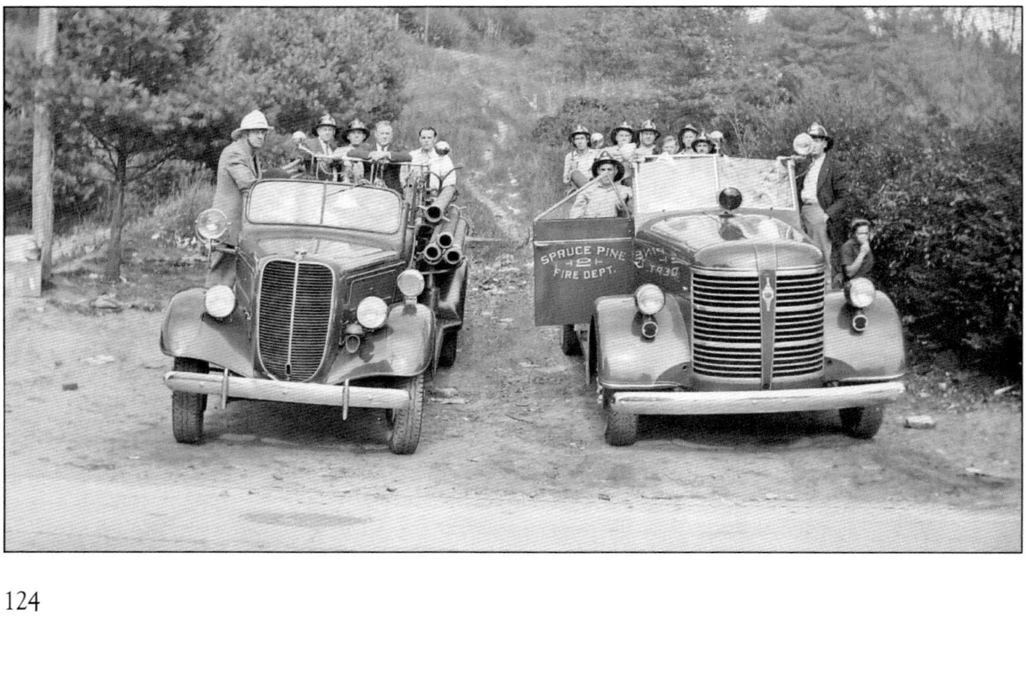

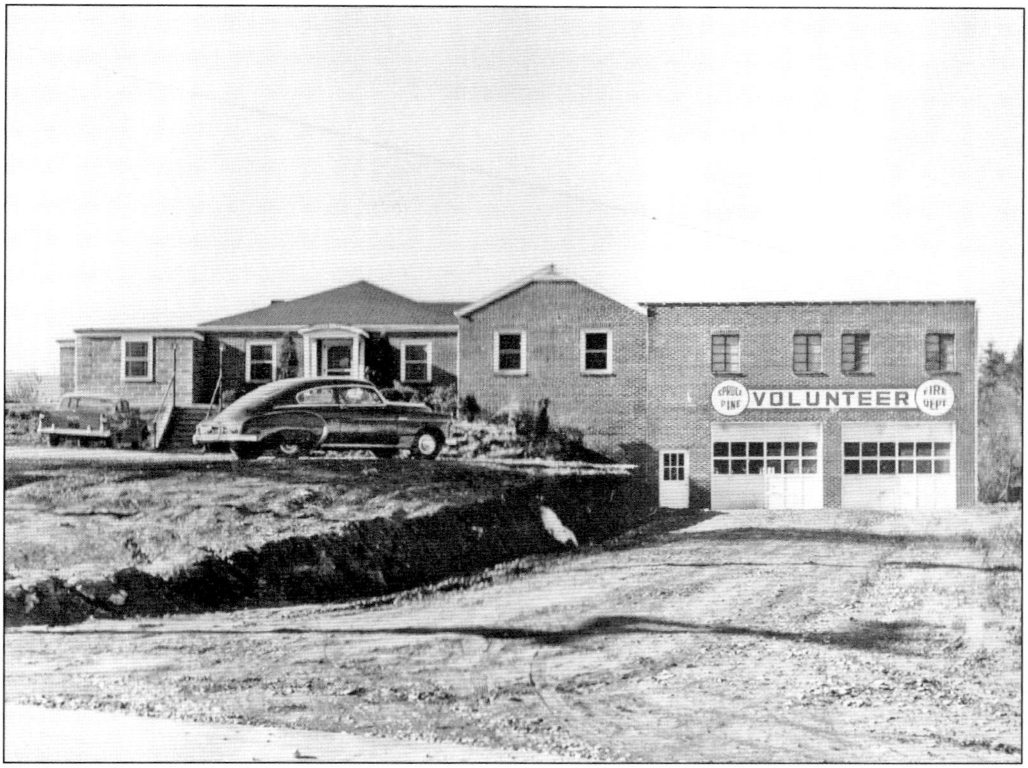


With modern-day firefighting equipment, space is at a premium, and in 2009, the Spruce Pine Fire Department opened a new stationhouse on Firefighter Way near the Spruce Pine Bypass (pictured below). The department was originally on Upper Street in the old town hall (now an art gallery). In the 1950s, it was moved into the new town hall (pictured above), which had been converted from the Williams' Clinic when the Spruce Pine Community Hospital opened. The department's modern facility will serve the community's needs for years. (Above, courtesy of Spruce Pine Public Library; below, courtesy of David Biddix.)

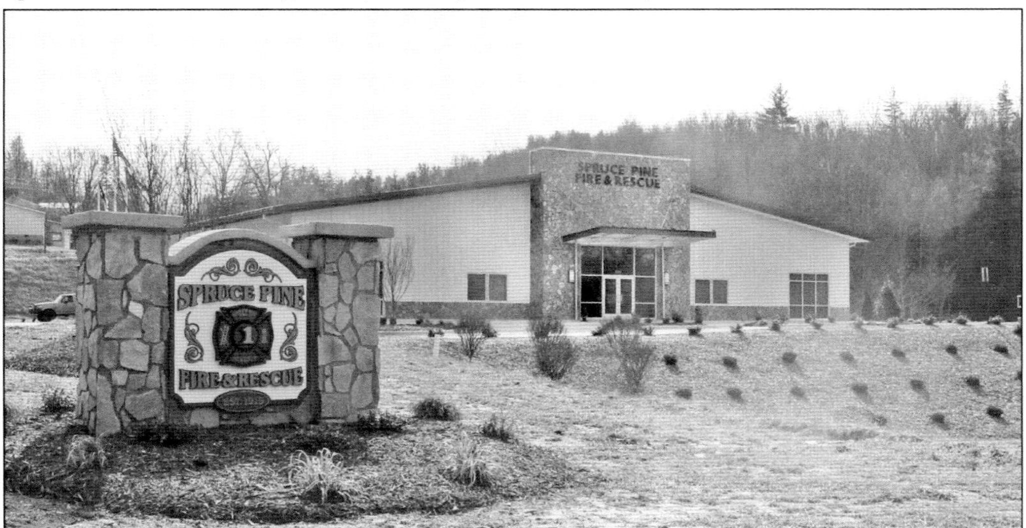

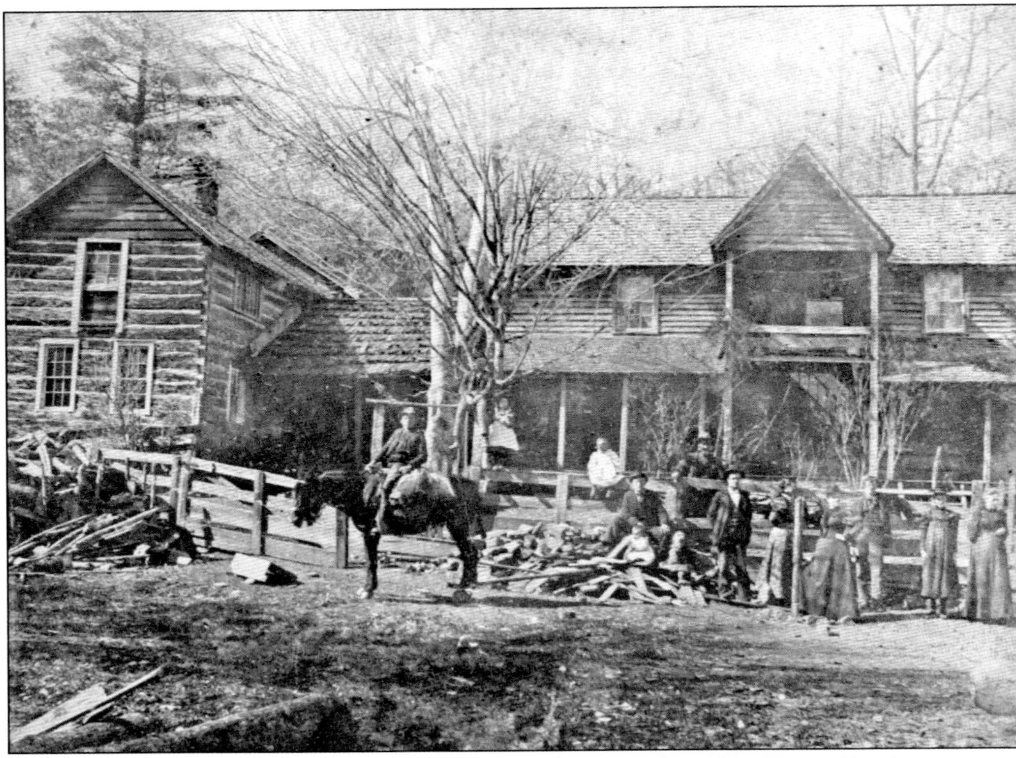

The Isaac English family poses in front of the English Inn in the 1880s. Spruce Pine's origins can be traced to the old inn, and it has seen many changes over the years, but it has been the one constant in the community. It still stands in the English Woods section of town and is a testament to the perseverance and character of the community. (Courtesy of Michael Hardy.)

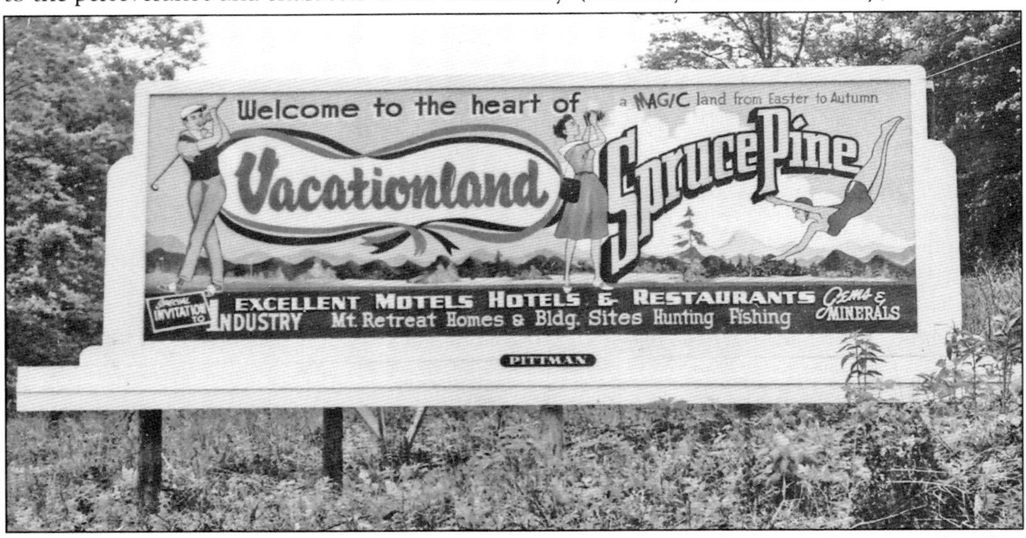


Tourism has long been a driving force in Spruce Pine's economy. In the 1950s, the junior chamber of commerce erected this billboard, welcoming visitors to the area. This was part of the Finer Carolina Community Improvement competition sponsored by the Carolina Power and Light Company. (Courtesy of Spruce Pine Public Library.)

# Bibliography

Bailey, Lloyd, ed. *Toe River Valley Heritage*. 7 vols. Durham, NC: L. R. Bailey, 2008.
Deyton, Jason Basil. "The Tow River Valley to 1865." *The North Carolina Historical Review*. Raleigh, NC: State Department of Archives and History, Vol. XXIV, October 1947.
Earley-Sheppard, Muriel. *Cabins in the Laurel*. Chapel Hill, NC: University of North Carolina Press, 1991.
Goforth, James A. *Building the Clinchfield*. Erwin, TN: Gem Publisher, 1989.
Presnell, Lowell. *Mines, Miners, and Minerals of Western North Carolina*. Boone, NC: Parkway Publishers, Inc., 2005.